SPECIAL ED

M.OM
survival guide

ALSO BY BONNIE LANDAU

Grounded for Life,
52 Exercises for Daily Grounding

Same Journey, Different Paths:
Stories of Auditory Processing Disorder
(co-author)

FOR MORE INFORMATION, PLEASE VISIT:

www.SpecialMomAdvocate.com

SPECIAL ED

MOM
survival guide

How to prevail in the special education process and
discover life-long strategies for you and your child.

Bonnie Landau, MS, PPS

special ed mom + educational consultant + advocate

Edited by: Miriam Landau, PhD
Cover Design: Bonnie Landau
Interior Design: Bonnie Landau
Publisher: Landau Digital Solutions

Library of Congress Catalog Number: 2017958296
ISBN-10: 0-9995316-0-3
ISBN-13: 978-0-9995316-0-0
1. Special Education 2. Parenting 3. Special Needs

First Edition
Printed in the USA

To My Mom, Miriam Landau

Thank you for raising me to believe that
I can do anything I set my mind to, and for
supporting my hunches when nobody else did.

I am the mom I am because of you.

Table of Contents

Section 3: Take Care of Your Child 113

Section 4:
Take Charge of the Special Ed Process 213

Section 5:
Understand the Special Ed Process....... 255

How to Use This Book

I am so thrilled you have picked up this book and I do hope it makes your special education journey easier. I wrote this book because I ran into so many obstacles during my process that in retrospect I wish I'd had a guide that could help me navigate all the challenges. This book can be read straight through, or you could skip to the chapters you feel you need most. It is meant to be a reference book once you have completed it. I have organized it into 5 sections.

Section 1: Create the Right Mindset

This section is meant to get you into the right frame of mind for managing this process. A lot of it deals with the emotional upheaval of being a Special Ed Mom, while several of the chapters help you find a positive frame of mind so you can focus forward. While you are strong and courageous, and I know you have the ability to get through this, there may be times when it feels overwhelming. I wrote this section to help you find some calm in the midst of that storm.

Section 2: Take Care of Yourself

We hear it over and over, but how often do we put ourselves first? Well, I'm here to say it again, and I hope you will take it to heart. In this section I tell you how and why you need to focus on yourself so you don't burn out. Sometimes taking care of yourself means asking for help, and I share how you can do that. I also share some of the strategies I have used to maintain a grasp on hope.

Section 3: Take Care of Your Child

With special education we think about dealing with the school, but it is important to consciously pay attention to how you care for your child. I share some of the ins and outs of parenting that made a big difference for me, and how you can employ them to help your child flourish. I also share about other family members, like convincing Dad there is a problem and how to help your neurotypical children comprehend this journey.

Section 4:
Take Charge of the Special Ed Process

This section provides ideas for how to work with the school and manage your special education journey. It speaks to the need for you to take charge and lead when possible, and how to work with the school to maintain a positive relationship. I also point out some specific things you should pay attention to so you have an understanding of the school dynamics at play that affect the special education program. The key here is to take the bull by the horns and make sure you stay in the game and ahead of others if possible. Knowing how your school operates is key to maintaining a positive focus.

Section 5:
Understand the Special Ed Process

This section gives an overview of the special education process. It is not meant to be a comprehensive description of every step involved since there are already many excellent in-depth resources that can help you learn about special education. I just want you to have a clear overview of what is involved, and these chapters highlight some of the more critical pieces you need to pay attention to. While it includes information about both 504 plans and IEPs, many of the chapters only apply to IEPs. IEP and 504 plans are governed by different federal laws, so some of the features of IEPs are not available in a 504 plan.

NOTE:

I use the pronouns he/she or him/her alternately in the chapters of the book. Whether I use male or female pronouns, I am referring to both unless I am telling a story about a particular person. It makes the book read easier this way, so please know I include all children, even if it seems I am referring to only one gender.

All names and some details in vignettes have been changed to protect the privacy of the parents and the children.

Prologue

"Start by doing what's necessary; then do what's possible;
and suddenly you are doing the impossible."
~ Francis of Assisi

"Your son's brain function is severely abnormal. I recommend you begin saving
for his group home care as an adult."

My mind was numb. I tried to absorb the words. I didn't want to look at my husband sitting on the couch beside me. I did not want to lose it here in the neuropsychologist's office; look at him and I would cry. I tried to hold it together. I pushed back the tears that began to seep. Did she really say that? He would never be normal?

We had come to this doctor, a UCLA-trained neuropsychologist, in hopes she could shed some light on our son's unusual cognitive function. He had a strange array of symptoms, and he didn't seem to fit into any diagnostic box. As she spoke those words, I realized I had had an entirely different expectation for the outcome of this meeting. I thought she would say that he was a bright child who just had a different way of thinking. He definitely had some cognitive challenges, but I was certain she would recommend some ways those could be fixed. I could not take in the thought of saving for group home care.

I listened anxiously while she gave her justification for diagnosing him PDD-NOS. She explained in detail that he did not fit the symptoms for autism. Based on his testing, he did not have all the criteria for that diagnosis. At least that I agreed with. She just didn't know where else to put him, so she put him into the catch bucket of Pervasive Developmental Disorder, Not Otherwise Specified. At a minimum, she recommended a 1-on-1 aide in a general education class. At best he should be placed in a special school for severely delayed children. She was certain he would never be able to function at normal level, and we should not have an expectation that he would improve. She basically left us with this thought, "Your son is severely impaired, and nothing can be done to help him."

I left her office feeling like I'd been punched in the stomach. I had a son whose brain did not function properly. It was not what I had dreamed of, and I had no idea how I was going to cope with this. I had had many dramas in my life, but nothing else felt like my heart had been ripped out and stomped on.

I went to pick the kids up at Nadia's house, our long-time babysitter/daycare lady. She asked me how the appointment went. I tried to tell her. The words would not come. I fell into the nearest chair and the tears flooded forwards. I sobbed from the deepest recesses of my heart. I sobbed as she stood, worried for me as much as for my son. When I finally choked out the words, "She said he would never be normal." Nadia shook her head in disagreement. "Bonnie, I have worked with kids for decades. He is normal. Do not listen to her."

I tried to smile and muster some agreement, but instead resumed the agonizing sobs. Nadia had told me for years how bright he was and that he would grow up just fine. But in this moment I struggled to believe. My boy walked over and put his head on my shoulder, as he always did when he saw me crying. I looked at my angelic child and wondered what God had in store for him. Then I cried even more.

For three more days the river of tears fell. I felt as if I was in mourning. Nadia's words echoed in my mind, and I had to reach way deep down into my inner strength to find a thread of belief in them. When the biggest shock had worn off, I finally did find it. I decided to give up the tears and grab that thread of hope.

Nadia was not the first person to tell me he would be okay. I remember my dear friend Melody, a child development specialist, who explained that our son was smart, yet different. He would find his rhythm, and one day I would see just how fine he is. There was also Christina, a preschool teacher who babysat him 5 days a week for a couple years, and always reinforced how clever he is, despite his struggle to communicate. I remembered his occupational therapist, Silke, who always reminded me that he would be okay. We just needed to continue with therapies that brought improvement. And I could never forget David Garcia, a learning specialist, who said over and over that everything our son was challenged with was fixable. Most of all it was my mom who encouraged me to seek the answers and find solutions, no matter what anybody said. She made me believe I could help him even when other specialists were reluctant to give me hope.

My intuition agreed with all of them, even though for a moment that neuropsychologist had caused me to lose faith. In my heart I knew that some day my son would be okay. This book is everything I learned while proving we were all right.

Section 1

Creating the
Right Mindset

*Getting into the right frame of mind
for managing this process.*

1

Believe In Yourself:
You DO Have the Ability
to Help Your Child!

"If we all did the things we are capable of doing,
we would literally astound ourselves."
~ Thomas Alva Edison

Imagine you are sitting and talking to a friend, and she says, "Do you have what it takes to help your child?" What thoughts or feelings come to your mind? Do you feel confident and strong? Perhaps you think, 'well I'm not sure,' or 'I don't know', or 'I don't even know what I should know to help my child.' Are there feelings of strength and empowerment? Are the feelings coming up colored by a sense of worry, fear or lack of confidence?

You are your child's best hope of having a successful educational experience. I know there's a big team at school that claims it knows best how to help your child. The truth of the matter is, YOU are the consistent thread from that early preschool experience on up through high school and beyond. Hopefully you will always be there for your child making sure that he gets exactly what he needs.

There is no alternative: you MUST be your child's support system. Try and accept that, otherwise you are short-changing your child; because if not you, who will take the lead and run with it? Your child needs you to have confidence in your ability to take charge. You need to have confidence in your leadership ability so as to counteract the many, many naysayers that you will encounter along the way.

Many people will tell you that you can't do it, you shouldn't do it, or you don't know what you're doing. You have to be strong enough to follow your own intuition, to follow your own gut reactions, to trust your research, and to know that you will find the right path. You must BELIEVE with every ounce of your being that you are the expert who knows your child best. Even if you do not have the formal education, you know better than anybody how to help your child succeed. Not only are you intimately familiar with the nuances of his capabilities, but because you profoundly and unequivocally care about his success more than anybody else. In other words, it is because you love him and his success impacts your life.

Manage the Sense of Overwhelm

I know it can feel very overwhelming. I know that there's a lot to learn; that there will be many challenging people. There are family members who disagree with you. Some will say, "You know it's the school's job, not yours." Others will say you don't know what you're talking about or you should let the experts tell you what you should do.

I know because I've been there. Scared for my child. Unsure and confused about what I could do about it. I have been there when the deepest part of my gut knew I was on the right track for helping my child, and the professionals and some family members told me that I did not know what I was doing. Some had a degree or credential or ex-perience, and therefore I should not dare to question their verdict and express my thoughts or knowledge. Formal education or not, **I knew on the deepest level I was right because I was his mother.**

I remember the exact moment when I took charge of my son's ed-ucation. He was transitioned from special ed preschool into general ed kindergarten with zero support. It was a total disaster. Beyond disaster — it was positively horrific. The district's solution was to write on his assessment for his November IEP that he had come up very high on the

Connor's scale for ADHD. The school psychologist told us to see the pediatrician and get medication for attention problems. She *actually* told me that, and now I know that's illegal. At the time I didn't know that. So I began researching how to help a child with ADHD (attention deficit hyperactivity disorder). That is when everything changed.

I found an article that compared symptoms of ADHD and auditory processing disorder (APD). And when I read the symptoms of APD, I knew without a doubt that is what he had. My mother's intuition kicked in, and I took charge. I began researching. Auditory processing disorder is like dyslexia of the ears. The person's hearing is fine, but their brain misinterprets the signals sent from the inner ear. Words are perceived differently than what is actually said. For example, "I want you to go to your room and get your shoes," the child may hear, "I want you to go to your broom and get your twos." What is heard does not usually make sense, so responses are inappropriate. The child is confused, and as a result, he often does not respond at all.

Throughout that process, so many people told me to just stop what I was doing because it was nothing but a stab in the dark. They insisted he did not have APD, and I did not have the credentials to prove that he did. I remember one time the speech therapist telling me that she had a Masters and a PhD. Since I had none of those degrees, she said I was definitely wrong. To make matters worse, even the UCLA trained neuropsychologist told us that his auditory processing was normal, and that I was wrong to think that was the problem. My husband said I was grasping at straws because I was desperate for an answer. It had been four months since I first read that article about ADHD versus APD, and all these people, except for my mother, were telling me I was wrong. She's a psychologist. She'd always taught me to be persistent and not to give up, and this was no different. She believed in my mother's intuition, and she encouraged me to follow it wherever it took me.

When I first took charge of my son's situation in kindergarten, she was the only person who said I was on the right track. She knew I was following my intuition, and she supported my efforts, even though I had no experience helping a child in special education. I shared my research on auditory processing disorder with her. She found a continuing education course on APD, which we attended so I could understand what it was, what caused it, and how we could help it. Every time we talked she asked about progress and new research I had discovered. I called her one day to share a hunch I had about a class on primary reflex integration, but lamented it was in Seattle and I could not afford the trip. She trusted my intuition and she made the trip happen. She trusted my instincts and research, and she supported me in discovering ways to help, even if it seemed like I was walking blindly.

So I kept on trying to find solutions. I didn't listen to the school personnel, the school psychologist, the school speech therapist or the UCLA neuropsychologist who were all telling me I was wrong. I persisted and finally started meeting people who agreed with me. Like David Garcia, the first person who screened our son for auditory processing disorder using the SCAN-C and TAPS. David found severe deficits in auditory processing. David asked us to take our son to a private audiologist to rule out any hearing problems. The audiologist was not an expert in APD, but she did say he had all the symptoms and she agreed with my hunch. After the screenings and audiology report, the school district finally agreed to have a district audiologist screen him. Of course he failed the test. It showed he had significant auditory processing deficits. Even then, the school refused to do a full APD assessment. Finally, seven months after I first read that article, he was assessed for APD by a private audiologist who specialized in APD. He was finally diagnosed with severe auditory processing disorder.

Think about it. Before he got to the diagnosis of severe auditory processing disorder:

1. On my own I found an article about comparing ADHD and APD. This prompted me to research and educated myself about APD.

2. There were three meetings with the school that resulted in no help.

3. I was told by 'professionals' that I was wrong and I didn't know anything.

4. We paid privately for screenings and assessments to get an accurate diagnosis for the problem.

5. The school *finally* did a screening that proved my point, but still refused help.

6. We paid privately for a full APD assessment and got the diagnosis.

I was forced to run through a maze before I finally got the diagnosis that was obvious to me from the start!

How do you think this story would have ended had I not had faith in my ability and determination to help my child? What if I had listened to all those people around me telling me that I was wrong? What if I had bought into their script that I didn't know what I was talking about, and I didn't have the credentials or the education to discover my son's proper diagnosis? I had to have confidence in my ability to know what was best for him.

This is why I start this book by telling you this: **YOU must believe in your ability to help your child.** The universe has entrusted you with the care of this child, and you DO have everything it takes to help this child succeed!

The entire first section of this book is dedicated to helping you get into the right frame of mind for this journey. It is really critical that you get out of your own way; that you don't allow your feelings of being untrained or inadequate to interfere with your capacity and determination to pursue what you know are the right choices in this situation. I have confidence in your ability to find solutions to help your child. Now let me share what I have learned so you will have more resources to achieve that.

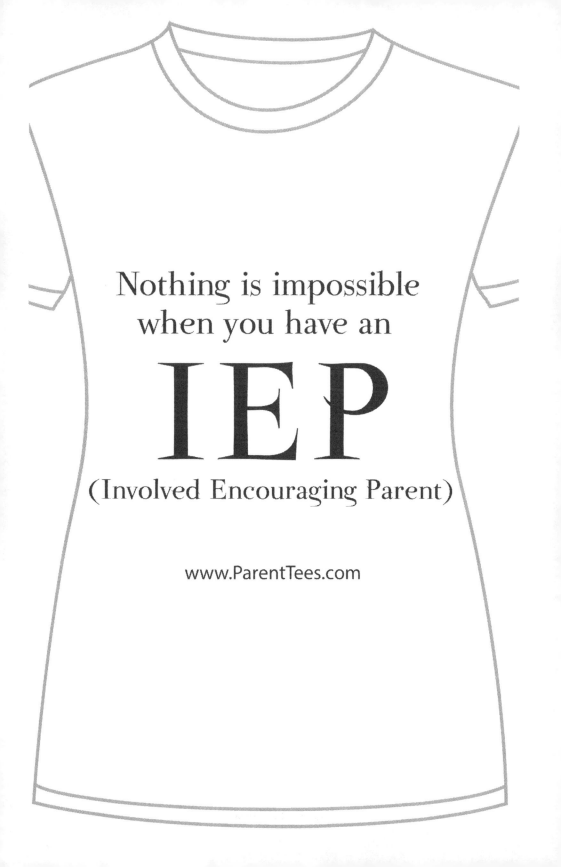

Accept That This is Hard

"We must rediscover the distinction between hope and expectation."
~ Ivan Illich

One of the most difficult things about being a Special Ed Mom is coming to terms with the fact that this is just hard. Plain and simple, it's a very difficult and long process — especially if your child's challenges involve behavior problems.

When he was 4, I can remember my trepidation when I took my son to birthday parties. If they had a bouncer, I would be flooded with horrible anxiety the entire time. I knew if he started jumping, he would get over-stimulated. Then he would start pushing kids, resulting in both kids and parents getting very upset. Then when I tried to get him out of the bouncer, he would have an absolute, total, and complete meltdown. Everybody would be staring (of course nobody helping), while he shrieked and thrashed and had an absolute fit.

I only wanted him to have regular childhood experiences, but it was hard, and I hated it! Every time I went to a birthday party, there was a part of me that held my breath and hoped and prayed that this time would be different. Maybe this time he would just have fun and be just like all the other kids. But it never got better, and instead of accepting that it was a crappy situation that I should avoid, I braced myself and took him to the next party hoping that he would act typical.

Some days being a Special Ed Mom can be really gut-wrenching.

This is a fact that we must accept it. We can't escape it. We have to be honest about the challenging experiences instead of always hoping they will magically get better. By facing this, and adjusting our expectations, we will not be disappointed all the time. The problem is always there, and there is very little relief. This leads to a sense of inadequacy and defeat. Sometimes we give up trying because there appears to be minimal change and no hope that things will get better.

If you're spending the whole time at a birthday party hoping and wishing your child would behave differently, you're throwing away the opportunity to experience your child where he is. Our kids do find joy at birthday parties, even if it ends in a meltdown. If you are focused on the impending meltdown, you miss the opportunity to see the happiness because you're not in the moment. You miss it because you are in a fantasy world wishing that things would change. The impending dread of the meltdown effects how you interact with your child. This impacts your relationship because you are focused on the problem aspects of your child's behavior rather than the joyful experiences.

It is important to manage expectations.

Managing expectations is crucial to accepting that you are on a difficult path. This is a very key skill for any life situation, but especially when you hold on to a hope for a unlikely outcome. When you expect things to turn out a certain way, and they don't, you are very disappointed. Often, the emotional fallout from a life experience is not from the experience itself, but rather from the disappointment that we didn't get the outcome we wanted. It is really important for you to be 100% honest about what you expect to happen versus what will probably happen. If you realize you are hoping for a specific outcome, you need to let go of it.

After realizing this, I was able to manage not only my expectations but also my son's expectations. I recognized that staying too long at a birthday party would result in a meltdown. Accepting this, I limited birthday parties to 90 minutes. I would tell my son ahead of time we would be leaving early. In this way I was managing his expectations in order to reduce the impact of the 'I don't want to leave!' meltdown. I gave him a fifteen-minute warning before we started to leave so he was not surprised. With my new birthday party rules, I was able to attend parties and enjoy them. My son was able to enjoy them and avoid leaving in an overwrought state. It worked well for both of us.

Face the problem and find ways to minimize it.

When you are faced with an anxiety-producing situation, look at it straight on beforehand. Determine what outcome you want. For example, say you have a child with a speech issue and she has to get up and give a presentation in front of the class. You know that this is going to be difficult for her, but you want so much for her to be able to do this because all the other kids her age can do it. You hope and pray that your child will be able to do it just fine, even though you know full well it's a very, very tall order for your child. Instead of worrying about it, look at the situation and ask yourself, "What can we really expect from our child at this point in time?" And then increase your expectation one or two notches.

You might say to your child: "I just want you to stand up in front of the class and tell them the name and the author of your book. If you can do that much, I think that would be huge for you!" If this is what she accomplishes, compliment her. Say something like, "Wow, look at that, you achieved your goal!" If she does more than that, of course you are going to tell her, "Wow, you really outdid yourself!" This way you're helping her know that she's not expected to be doing something that's extremely difficult for her. You will be happy if your child achieves a reasonable goal. It might be a bit of a stretch, but not so much of a stretch that you put her out of her league. Then the next time a book report comes up, she'll stretch a little bit more, and you basically work through it as a process over a long period of time.

Manage expectations for yourself too!

Managing expectations is a skill that will help you too. For example, if your child often has meltdowns after school, you might find yourself wishing and hoping that the afternoon would go smoothly and calmly. Looking at your family patterns, you know afternoons are difficult. If you accept that, then you're not so upset when it happens, and you can deal with a meltdown much more calmly. When you are blessed with a calm afternoon and no meltdowns, it will feel so good because of the unexpected relief — a very positive experience.

As a mom who is overwhelmed with many responsibilities, I know you often expect too much of yourself. Modifying these self-inflicted expectations is critical to surviving. It's part of accepting that you're only human. The hardest thing for me is being okay with the house-work not getting done. I love my house really clean. It doesn't happen often, unless I pay somebody to do it. For many years I really struggled with that and wished it would be different. Learning to let it go was very freeing for me. Not that my house is a disaster, but it's not spic and span all the time. I'm the queen of expecting too much of myself, so this was huge.

You are somebody who juggles many plates. It's crucial you have realistic expectations of what you can actually get done in a day, a week, or a month, The added pressure of unrealistic expectations aggravates the intensity of the whole situation.

Some people might ask, "How can you say that? Try to have a pos-itive attitude!" I agree, we don't want to be negative about the whole thing by thinking, "Oh my God, look at me. It's SO hard!"

Adjusting expectations is not about wearing the victim badge. Nor is it about being pessimistic. It is about recognizing that things are not al-ways going to turn out the way you wish. You are setting yourself up for a fall if you dream your child will act exactly like other children, and it doesn't happen (right now). However, if you dream of your child acting like neurotypical children *some day*, then please, go ahead and visualize that! It absolutely could happen!

If you expect a specific outcome, and it consistently doesn't hap-pen, you are going to be disappointed over and over. This injects more emotional infusions into an already stressful situation. By setting real-istic expectations, you experience less emotional upheaval when things are difficult. You also give yourself a break when measuring how much you got done. This is a hard process, and some days are going to be challenging. Accept that and you will have a much easier time working through it.

POINTS to PONDER

- What expectations (hopes) do you have for your child?
- Have any of these things ever happened before?
- Are they hopes or wishes, or actual realities right now?
- Write about a situation where you realize you had hoped for a specific outcome.
- Write down what you really expect to happen.
- Adjust your expectations for the outcome of the experience, or the event.

Troubles are tools by
which God fashions us
for better things.

www.ParentTees.com

You Did Not Cause
Your Child's Difficulties

"Forgive yourself for not knowing what you didn't know before you learned it."
~ Doe Zantamata

When I first figured out our son had auditory processing disorder (APD), I figured it had to come from my husband's side. I never had problems with speech, reading or writing. My husband's side had speech problems, so I figured it must have come from that side of the family.

It was kind of presumptuous on my part because I'm adopted, and at that time I knew nothing anything about my genetics. Several years later I did find the paternal side of my biological family, and discovered APD is prevalent in those genes. It was not the APD itself that was genetic, it was the predisposition to have ear infections. Our son had many of those, and unfortunately excessive ear infections can cause APD (Borges, Paschoa, Collela-Santos, 2013).

When I discovered this, I felt horrible. My genes had caused my son's challenges. Then I reconsidered. A genetic profile comes with positive and negative traits. After all, my son inherited my creativity and mechanical abilities. He builds complex structures that boggle my mind. Blaming myself doesn't help my child, and it certainly won't change things. All it does is make me feel worse. I realized I had to stop thinking that way.

Recognize your belief tapes.

There are many ways we blame ourselves for our child's disabilities and struggles. They become part of our belief system. The (False) Belief that:

- we caused it (through some contribution of genetics, environment or life choices)
- we waited too long to get help
- we should have known how to help our child
- we should have tried harder to help our child
- we should have known to try a different doctor or therapist
- we had the power to end our child's suffering

Think about this carefully: If you had known better, of course you would have acted differently!

Let that sink in for a moment. If you had KNOWN how to help your child, you would have done it, right? That is the full truth here. Your not doing something is definitely not because you were 'neglectful,' it's because you didn't know how, why, where or what to do.

It is sometimes very difficult to let go of these beliefs. After all we pass our genetics down to our child, or we pass our habits down to our child. We are the ones who raise our child and make decisions that affected his life and his body and his brain. Of course it's really hard to not blame ourselves for our child's struggles.

This is particularly hard if your child has the same challenges as you do, and you believe it's because of your genes. You might think: "Gosh, I know how he's struggling. I feel so bad because I know first hand how hard it is for him." You must realize that things happen in life that you could not and cannot control. It's absurd to blame yourself because your child inherited certain genes or it's absurd to blame yourself for unfortunate events that occurred. You really aren't that powerful that you can control genetic makeup or life experiences. The merging of a man and woman's genes *both* impact the outcome. There are many components that go into the development of a child, including genetics, environment and experience. So thinking that you alone caused the difficulties is pointless.

Let go of the blame game.

It's really important that you stop thinking this way. Constantly telling yourself, "It's my fault," will make it all the more difficult to find energy to help your child. Find alternative messages that you can say to yourself when these blaming thoughts enter your mind.

For example, you might say: "Genetically speaking everybody passes down different traits. My kid got this predisposition that may have led to his developmental challenges, but along with this trait he also inherited some good traits as well. My kid got above average visual spatial abilities from me." Reframe your perception, so you can come to accept the complexity of genetic predisposition. It is not your fault any more than the genetic makeup you inherited is your parent's fault. It's just the way the genetics were distributed.

Part of my belief is that we choose to live our lives in order to learn lessons so we can evolve as spiritual beings. This comes from the teachings of spiritual psychology in which I was trained. These challenges of genetics happen to be part of those lessons. This thought helps me because I accept that my child's soul has chosen this journey; and that he has chosen me as his mom to support him through this journey.

I am not sharing this with you because I believe it is the only way to look at the situation. We all have different spiritual paths and beliefs. I am merely explaining what helps me handle my own guilt hoping it will help you find your way to alleviate your guilt.

It's particularly important if your child's problem was due to a choice you made. For example, if your child had a bad reaction to the vaccination you consented to. I know the big controversy surrounding vaccines. However there are reported cases of children with genetic mutations that prevent them from properly processing the ingredients in the vaccines. I personally know people whose children have gone from totally typical to completely regressed when they were vaccinated.

Some parents blame themselves for choosing the vaccine. They might regret not having investigated more and believe it is their fault their child was hurt. The majority of kids have no problems with the vaccines, so how would you even begin to know your child would be different? Especially since the media is intent on claiming vaccines are safe? It is difficult to withstand the pressure to force people to vaccinate. Like the law that passed in California that requires your child to be vaccinated in order to attend school. It is very difficult for you to get a medical excuse to avoid the vaccinations. How could you know that you shouldn't have vaccinated your child? And even if you knew, how would you muster up the strength to withstand the pressure of being denied an education for your child?

Another common source of blame and guilt is if your child was in an accident, particularly if you felt at fault somehow. That's what happened to us. We sent our son to summer camp. We thought the camp was safe. We never dreamed in a million years that he would end up with a head injury. The camp he went to was for special needs kids. Every single child had a one-on-one counselor. His counselor was standing there watching him climb the jungle gym. There was no way the counselor could have prevented him from falling. He was a four-year-old child. He was having a good time. He slipped. Things like this happen.

Self forgiveness is the key to letting the guilt go.

I would highly, highly recommend that you forgive yourself. Get rid of these blaming thoughts. Often our guilt feelings have a lot to do with anger towards ourselves. It's like an inner battle going on. Self-forgiveness can help minimize that guilt.

Many people think that when we forgive others we're excusing what they've done. Forgiveness is about releasing the emotions around the event so it no longer carries a charge for us. Forgiveness is really about ceasing to be in judgment of ourselves, others, or the situation.

We play the blame game when we judge. For example, I judged myself as a bad mom for sending my son to that summer camp. Sure my anger was directed at the camp, but deep down I was angry at myself for letting him go. I was judging myself. Forgiveness is about letting go of this judgment.

It was Rumi, a Persian poet, who said, "Holding on to anger is like grasping a hot coal with the intent of throwing it at someone else; you are the one who gets burned." Anger hurts us, especially under these circumstances. If you're angry with yourself for something you did or didn't do (like passing down genes), all you're doing is hurting yourself. As I said several pages ago, the more you are in this state of mind, the less you can be focused on helping your child.

One of my favorite books to help with letting go of judgment is *Forgiveness: 21 Days to Forgive Everyone for Everything* by Iyanla Vanzant. It has very simple exercises to follow. It really helps you to release the emotions around the guilt and anger.

Another book I recommend is *Journey of the Soul* by Ron and Mary Hulnick. They were my professors in my spiritual psychology program. Their book talks a lot about the soul journey that we are on in this lifetime. It also talks about the crucial importance of self-forgiveness.

> **You have to realize that it is absolutely impossible to go back and change anything that happened.**

Whatever you are angry at, it boils down to: I did not protect my child enough. No matter the circumstance, on some level, you blame yourself for what has happened to your child. That blame comes from the belief that you somehow could have done something to create a different outcome. Really think about the logic in that. Honestly, what could you have really done differently?

Maybe now you would research things instead of just thinking it's nothing. Maybe you would approach things differently. Back then, how could you possibly have known that situation would turn out this way? The truth is, if you had known better, you would have made a different choice. You made the best choice you could with the information that you had.

Fixating on the past, reviewing it over and over again, and beating yourself up for it is not going to help the present or the future. You have to let it go.

Despite your working very hard to help your child, if you keep blaming yourself, you will reach a point where your motivation and hope decreases. You will surrender to your anger, guilt and despair. Who then will be your child's warrior?

Believe it or not, as you go through this journey you will see that a lot of good can come from it. I know some days this can sound like a phony cliché. I guarantee you, I have talked to so many parents with special needs kids, and they all mention the blessings that have come out of this challenge. You'll get there, but not if you keep blaming yourself. There's nothing for you to blame yourself for. **You did not cause this.** You are not God. You are an ordinary mortal who must deal with a less than ideal set of cards dealt to you. You are blaming yourself for not having any super powers!

POINTS TO PONDER

1. If you could go back, what would you change in your child's life?

2. How do you feel about these situations?

3. Are you angry about your child's situation? To whom is your anger directed?

4. Do you feel guilty about your child's challenges? What could you have done differently?

5. What do you blame yourself for?

4

Don't Allow the Diagnosis to Handicap You

"The diagnosis is not a prognosis!"
~ Bonnie Landau

"Your son is so cognitively abnormal you should start saving for group home care when he is an adult." The words were a knife in my gut. A UCLA-trained neuropsychologist was telling us our son would never have a typical life. He would always struggle with academic learning. Worse yet, he would never be able to take care of himself. College was out of the question; a job was probably not in the cards. When I asked her what we could do to help him, she said, "Nothing. You need to accept him as he is."

I was heartbroken. We had been fighting with the school to get him more services, and we chose to pay thousands of dollars of our own money to get an assessment from this neuropsychologist. She diagnosed him with PDD-NOS (pervasive developmental disorder – not otherwise specified) because he didn't meet the criteria for an autism diagnosis. He did not display repetitive or stimming behaviors; he attempted to be social, even though his efforts were often erroneous. He did have severe speech delay, fine and gross motor difficulties, serious attention problems and was very hyperactive. He was also extremely sound sensitive.

She did recommend that he have a one-on-one aide in school (something we'd been fighting for). She said if the school would not provide that, he should be placed in a private school for children with severe special needs. She went on to add that his IQ testing was the most confounding; extremely high scores on visual tasks, but extremely low scores on non-visual tasks. His pattern recognition scored at the high school level (he was 6-1/2), but she attributed that to lucky guesses or an anomaly. Many years later I learned that a wide discrepancy in IQ subtest scores is a red flag for learning disabilities.

When I asked her if she had taken into account auditory processing difficulties, she said she had assessed his auditory processing and it came up within normal limits. As a result, she did not make any accommodations for auditory processing (4 months later an audiologist diagnosed him with severe auditory processing disorder).

Devastated and confused barely described the crushing emotions I felt. My intuition did not agree with what this neuropsychologist was saying. I saw my son exhibiting extremely bright abilities, despite his not being able to demonstrate them in a school setting. The neuropsychologist was telling us to give up; that we must just accept the fact that our son would never be a contributing member of society; that we would need to care for him his entire life.

I cried for three days after this meeting, and then I decided she was wrong. She could have 10 degrees for all I cared. I chose to follow my mother's intuition instead. In my heart I believed my son would grow up and have a typical life. I chose to focus on that. Thank God I threw out her 'diagnosis!'

The Diagnosis is Not The Brass Ring

Many parents fight long and hard to get the 'right' label for their child. After all, the label will then tell you what is 'wrong' so then you can help or fix it. Have you been fighting hard to figure out exactly what the problem is? I know I did, over many years, and never came up with one global diagnosis.

Diagnoses (particularly Autism, Dyslexia and ADHD) are arrived at from observations, skills tests and from the SUBJECTIVE INTERPRE-TATION OF THE ASSESSOR. Heck, even a pediatrician that is told a child is having attention problems in school will quickly label the child ADHD. Often he prescribes medication based on the parent's reporting, not by the pediatrician observing the child in the classroom. That means diagnosis is based on the doctor's interpretation of an anxious parent's description of what the teacher said is happening in class. Obviously it's not made based on a rigorous process of assessment and observation.

The real challenge with diagnosing learning disabilities is that there are no standards for diagnosing specific conditions. Each diagnostician will choose which assessment tools and observation methods they will follow to reach a diagnosis. There are hundreds if not thousands of assessment tools, so the process for reaching a diagnosis will vary. This is why one psychologist will diagnose autism but another will not. The same is true for dyslexia, ADHD, dysgraphia, sensory processing disorder, or any disability a child might have that impacts school.

For over a decade a team of audiologists have been attempting to create a standard diagnostic process for auditory processing disorder. In all this time they have not been able to reach a consensus on what tests should be used and what data limits should be set to determine a person has auditory processing disorder. Without a standard for diagnosis, there is no way to definitively know that the diagnosis is accurate for your child.

The problem with this diagnostic approach is that you have a nice label, but it does not tell you WHY the child is having those behaviors. While there are observable behaviors that fit the diagnostic criteria, how each professional interprets the behaviors is very subjective. One child with attention issues may be given the ADHD diagnosis, while another may be given a sensory processing disorder diagnosis, and still another may be given the auditory processing disorder label. Some may be given a dual diagnosis with two or more of these labels. Of course, there are generally accepted theories about why these issues occur in the brain, but how can you know for certain those theories apply to your child?

For example, it is believed that there is a chemical imbalance in the brain that is helped by stimulants for those with ADHD. Professionals who diagnosis ADHD usually make the assumption that everybody with ADHD behaviors has this chemical imbalance. However there are over a dozen disabilities that can cause attention problems that mimic ADHD. While some people may have a true chemical imbalance, many more have something else causing the attention problems. A colleague of mine, who is a director at a learning center that specializes in diagnosis of ADHD, said only 20% of the children who come to them have a true chemical imbalance. The other 80% have something else causing the attention deficit, such as visual, auditory or sensory processing disorders. ADHD is a diagnosis of exclusion. There is no test that can show the chemical imbalanced believed to cause ADHD. So by ruling out all these other issues, this learning center concludes the child must have ADHD. Can you imagine how many kids are misdiagnosed if all these other processing issues are not checked?!

My older son was diagnosed with severe ADHD when he was 8. He was right at the top of the scales on the Connors assessment (a checklist used to diagnose ADHD). Despite recommendations to medicate, we chose not to. I saw his attention was better at home than at school. To me that was a clear indication that something else was causing the attention issues. On a fluke of fate I took him to get a QEEG brain map with Dr. Barbara Blume (a psychologist in Ventura, California). What she told me was so mind-blowing; I literally sat down and cried from relief. His brain map clearly showed he did not have ADHD, or Autism, or Dyslexia. Instead he definitely had auditory processing disorder. Furthermore his attention problems were caused by post-concussive syndrome. Several bad bumps to the head when he was a toddler had left a lasting impression on his neurological function. He had a brain injury. We got to know Dr. Blume extremely well as we went 2-3 times a week for neurofeedback, and we watched our son improve dramatically.

Remember: It's a diagnosis, NOT a prognosis!

We are obsessed with classification in this world. We like things to fit into neat groups of information. All things in the same pile should have congruent descriptions. Labels help us do that. They tell a parent, 'there is a reason your child has this behavior or learning challenge.' The problem is, there is no consistent agreement as to what the labels represent. Often, professionals will provide a label accompanied by the pronouncement that the child will have lifelong challenges due to this disability. It's not that they *want* to be negative Nancies, they truly believe that the label itself determines a lifelong challenge. The truth is, nobody can predict how a child will manage this challenge.

If we change the way we view this paradigm, and really look at the label as just a description of behaviors or traits, then we can consider the possibility that *something* is causing those behaviors. NOW maybe we can figure out the underlying issue, and in many, many cases, it is something that can be fixed or at least improved.

The biggest challenge for moms is that the majority of professionals do not believe this. They are very attached to the idea that a specific label means the brain is working in a specific way, and it is something the child was born with. They are not open to the idea that a combination of factors may contribute to the symptoms that describe this diagnosis. They are certain there is nothing that can be done to help it, and they hand down a dismal prognosis that can leave you with little hope.

I have met many parents who are very attached to the label. If I even so much as hint at possible options to improve the child's challenges, they get very angry with me. I have been kicked out of support groups for suggesting vision problems could be causing dyslexia or food sensitivities could be the root cause of ADHD. I understand where these parents are coming from; the label gives them a context that explains why their child is different. The challenge is, if you cling to that explanation for your child's difference, you could be missing an opportunity to make school and life easier for him. Would you really want your child to have life-long struggles because you refused to look at other options?

Do not let the label dash your hopes.

The label can throw you into a depressive fog, a fog that is devoid of all hope. I know because I have been there, and it's not an easy place to climb out of. It is very important to remember that a label is only a label.

It does not mean your child will be exactly like others with the same label, nor does it mean your child will have the exact same struggles.

A good analogy is heartburn. What causes heartburn? There are so many causes of heartburn. According to Mayo Clinic, frequent causes of heartburn could be eating too close to bedtime, eating too much at once, drinking too much alcohol, eating fried foods or being overweight. If you have heartburn and you believe the only fix is antacids, you may be missing an opportunity to fix the root cause of the problem.

Find some famous people with the same disability as your child, and use that as a way to remind yourself to stay positive. List 2 or 3 people and what they have accomplished despite the label they received. When you hear your thoughts going to that OMG place, think of these people and what they achieved despite the label. Do not let the label drag you down. It is simply another tool to help your child.

For me that famous person is Scott Barry Kaufman. As a young child he was diagnosed with auditory processing disorder, a disability that can severely affect reading, writing, speech, executive function, memory and social skills. He was in special education classes throughout elementary and middle schools. When he got to high school, a substitute teacher changed his life. She saw his abilities. For the first time in his life he was encouraged to reach further. He graduated high school with honors, and went on to get a PhD in cognitive psychology at Yale! He is a regular contributor to *Scientific American* and *Psychology Today*. He has written seven books. He is a professor at the University of Pennsylvania, and he is also the scientific director of the Imagination Institute. He is a highly sought after specialist in the areas of positive psychology and the science of intelligence and creativity. Wow, talk about impressive! He was the role model who taught me in no uncertain terms to put the label into its proper place!

So how can the label help you?

There is an up side to the labels — they can help you get services at school. For example, if a doctor diagnoses your child with ADHD, your child now has a medical diagnosis. **Since the school cannot provide a**

medical diagnosis, they cannot refute this. They should help your child under the 'other health impaired' qualification category if his 'medical' condition interferes with his ability to participate in school.

You can also use the label to investigate case studies of similar diagnosis and compare your child's symptoms. Then you can research to find out if there are ways to help those symptoms through accommodations in school, specific IEP goals or ways to manage daily life.

You may find cases where the symptoms are similar to your child's, and an underlying cause has been identified. Then there may be a way to remediate it. Remember that the label covers a set of symptoms, but it does not give you the reason your child exhibits those symptoms. For example, a child with a dyslexia diagnosis may have strabismus. This is a visual processing issue that causes difficulty focusing and sometimes double vision. It can be fixed with vision therapy.

Not every solution you hear about will help your child. By the same token, your child will not experience all the life difficulties of people who share the same diagnosis. Through investigative research, you may uncover a problem that can be improved or ways to help your child compensate for his challenges.

The label is a launching point to start your investigation to figure out why your child is having the symptoms and what could be done to help. For example, there is new research that shows that there are three types of dyslexia:

1) Dysphonic Dyslexia:
Also known as Auditory Dyslexia, this person has difficulty with phonological processing. They will often resort to memorizing words as pictures because they struggle with phonemic awareness (difficulty associating sounds with letters). This person cannot sound out new words and may just skip over them, or guess, to compensate. Learning to read is usually very difficult. Spelling will always be a challenge.

2) Dyseidetic Dyslexia:
Also known as Visual Dyslexia. This is the traditional understanding of dyslexia, where the person flips letters. The brain has difficulty with encoding of the letterbox cortex, an area of the brain that remembers letter/

sound combinations (early = erle). They do not struggle with phonics, but instead have difficulty with visual processing. Non-phonetic spelling of words are difficult for them to recognize, and this decreases their reading speed. They will struggle with spelling unless they find a reading method that helps them memorize challenging letter/sound combinations.

3) Dysphonedetic Dyslexia:

Also known as Mixed Dyslexia, is a combination of auditory and visual processing challenges. This is the most severe form of dyslexia and will need extra support for all language arts tasks.

Most people believe that dyslexia is a life-long disability, but there can be medical reasons or learning styles that cause symptoms of dyslexia. For example, auditory dyslexia may be caused by excessive ear infections, which caused auditory processing disorder. Listening and cognitive therapies can improve auditory processing, and thereby improve the 'dyslexia.' A visual-spatial learner will also have great difficulty learning to read phonetically, so finding a program like DM Easyread, a visual approach to learning phonics, will help. DM Easyread uses characters to represent sounds. They put the characters above the words to help the children learn to sound out words. Over time, children begin to associate phonemic sounds with specific letter combinations. Over several months the child will have used his visual-spatial ability to learn phonics.

Similarly, Visual Dyslexia could be caused by a visual processing deficit, which can be fixed with vision therapy. Our younger son lost all symptoms of dyslexia after a year of vision therapy. Did he ever have dyslexia? He did until it was fixed.

So if your child had a disability that could be fixed, would you fix it?

That is exactly how the label can help you. Labels and assessments can pinpoint a collection of challenges. Once you have the label, you investigate to see if there is an underlying condition that could be causing the symptoms. You would then investigate to find therapies or approaches that could help improve the underlying condition.

POINTS to PONDER

- What labels has your child received?
- What do these labels say about your child:
    - Their brain is wired a certain way.
    - Your child will never be able to learn something.
    - Parts of life will always be a struggle.
- How do the symptoms of this label show up in your child right now?
- What preconceived notions about this label can you let go of?

Nobody said being brave
is suppose to be easy.

www.ParentTees.com

5

Cry Over Assessments

"To weep is to make less the depth of grief."
~ William Shakespeare, King Henry VI, Part 3

I hate that dreaded feeling of reviewing assessments during a special education meeting (or with a private assessor). Especially during the triannuals! OMG, you look at that pack of paper, which is often 10 or 12 or 15 pages long, and you just know it focuses on everything that is wrong with your child. There might be some good things, like academic strengths, but those are always glossed over quickly. The focus of the meeting is on helping your child's weaknesses, and so you have to sit there for an hour or more, and listen to them tell you everything that your child doesn't do like a typical child.

How many assessment reports have you had to review? How many times have you eagerly come to the table, *happy* to read these test results that paint a picture of your child's struggles? Don't you always have an awful feeling in your stomach as you review the data? I think I'd rather get a root canal without Novocain than have to read another one of these. Seriously!

I have lost count of how many assessments I've had to read over the past decade. With one kid in special education for over 12 years, and another one for over seven years, I've estimated that it is over 60. I just know that every single time I have to brace myself, knowing that I will be a jumble of intense emotions when I should focus on being present and truly listening. There's a horrible, nauseated feeling in the pit of my stomach that brings up so much fear for my child's future. And the special education team rarely seems to realize the emotional turmoil I am experiencing. It's not that they are heartless. They are there to do a specific job, and coddling mom's emotions isn't really part of that job. They aren't there to talk about how great he is, they're there to talk about how to help with the things that are hard for him. Understanding that this is the way they have to perform their job doesn't make it any easier.

I've learned over time to brace myself for the meeting, knowing that I must be in the right frame of mind to help my child as part of the team. I sometimes try to deal with it by hoping against hope that maybe this time when they review the information, they will tell me my child no longer has issues. I know it seems like a fantasy, but somehow it gets me through those dreaded minutes of listening to them tell me he can't do this, d or he struggles with that, and as a result, he doesn't fit in. They do often point out where he has improved, but that information seems to be gone over quickly as they need to gather the nuts and bolts to plan his IEP. Of course that means looking at where he needs help.

If you are lucky enough to be in a school where they really are focused on helping your child (like our current district is), then you know these meetings are focused on results. They are just trying to get the information out on the table so they come up with a solution to help your child succeed academically. It really doesn't register for them that this is an emotional experience for the parent. They have a job to do, and they are streamlined in doing it. I totally get that.

If you are unlucky enough to be in a district that works hard to deny services (like our previous district was), then you have to contend with a whole other set of emotions as the assessments are usually skewed more positively. And now you are playing a different ballgame where you have to swallow the anger that rises up knowing that these tools are being used as a means of denying services to your child. Not only are you reminded that your child does not do well, but now you have to control the urge to stand up and punch one or more people at the table. This kind of upset can seriously affect your health, so you need to be emotionally prepared and supported when the meeting starts.

It is important to process
the emotions that come up.

When the assessment review meeting is over, it is important that you don't try to push all these feelings out of your mind. It is REALLY crucial that you allow yourself the opportunity to process the emotions that are triggered by the assessment process.

I'll never forget that visit to the neuropsychologist who told us that our son would end up in group home care when he was an adult. There couldn't have been more devastating news, especially when I was expecting her to tell me that he was gifted, and with some specific help, he would be okay. So I wasn't expecting a punch in the stomach. This pessimistic information wasn't in alignment with my intuition, and I did cry for several days. I processed the emotions connected with this information because I knew holding it in would only increase my anxiety about my child's difficulties and interfere with my remediating them.

After I got all the tears out, then I got angry. How dare she predict my child's future! My love and devotion for my child were the impetus for taking charge, but the anger I felt towards this woman fueled my determination. Come hell or high water, I was going to prove that woman wrong. And I did!

> **One thing that has always helped me through assessments**
> **is realizing that these tools are a reflection of**
> **my child's baseline, not his full capability.**

It is very important that you understand that the results they come up with only show the *minimum* your child can do. It does not reflect the possibilities that he can achieve because the tests can only measure so much. In addition, these tests are biased. The biases originate in the circumstances surrounding the testing situation:

- The assessments are completed by a professional who may not know your child.

- The testing room and materials are usually unfamiliar, and that can increase the anxiety and distractibility of your child while he is taking the test.

- Your child was off that day, physically or emotionally.

- The unique connection, or lack of connection, between your child and the assessor.

- Particularly crucial is understanding that your child's disability must be taken into account when the assessor is writing the report. The assessor must articulate very specifically how your child's disability profile can affect the outcome of the assessment.

Obviously the assessment process is not a perfect scenario. Unfortunately assessments are the only tools we have, so we have to work with them. They are only a snapshot of the day and circumstances in which they were administered.

I am stressing the inadequacy of assessments so that you realize that your own research, and your own familiarity with your child, adds to the importance and significance of your input.

Getting the Emotions OUT

How do you process these tense emotions that bring up fear, anxiety, sadness as well as anger? It's important to find a way that works for you. For me I always go through a period of great sadness. I let myself cry. I know that I have to go through this process of cleansing the feelings from within me. If I did not do this, I would be stuck in the sinkhole of fear about my child's future. I know I need to overcome the fear and regain my hope so we can keep moving forward.

The interesting thing is that it used to take me a week or more to process this upset, but as I gained experience, the time needed to get to the other side has decreased. Now it takes me 1 to 2 days to work through the crying and intense emotions. I purposefully respect my need to do this. Sometimes I even facilitate the sadness by listening to sad songs or remembering times past when the assessments had even more dire results.

When you have major emotional upset in your life, what do you do to process it? What is the best way for you to get your emotions out? Do you journal? Do you like to exercise? Do you like to walk in the park out in nature and commune with that which is not created in a specific way?

You need to find your avenue for releasing your feelings. It is really important you do this with purpose. You need to plan the time and space so you can move through it in the way YOU need to.

Ideas for Getting the Tears Out:

- Exercise – it doesn't have to be long, just get your heart pumping
- Calling a close friend who is a good listener and can be empathetic
- Share with your special mom support group
- Visualize a red fire and see it burning and releasing your emotions.
- Write a list of things that are causing your emotional upset and do a fire ceremony (outside of course) to burn the list and release it.
- See a therapist who understands the stress of a parent with a special needs child.

Remind yourself that these are just passing feelings. They will fade into the background again. Realize that you do not have to remain in a constant state of emotional upset in order to process the feelings. It can take 20 minutes or an hour to work on releasing these feelings, and then move onto regular tasks as a distraction from the upset. It is taxing to experience these intense emotions 100% of the time, so give yourself permission to take a break and return to it later.

It is also critical that you do not make important decisions regarding the IEP or 504 in the midst of an emotional upheaval. Unless there is a deadline, refrain from responding to the school or approving the direction or next step to be taken for your child. You did not have to sign the IEP or 504 at the meeting, and you do not have to get it back to them right away. If you live in a state that requires your signature on the IEP, do not sign until you have a chance to reflect on it when you are clear headed. If you feel that you disagree with the IEP, but the school can implement it without your signature, be sure to request a Prior Written Notice to get clarity on the changes in the IEP.

When you feel centered and able to make a good decision, THAT is when you act!

POINTS to PONDER

- How have assessments helped your child get services in school?
- What was the most difficult assessment report you ever had to review?
- What are three ways you can express your emotions around assessment?

Mourn the Child
You Dreamed About

"Motherhood: All love begins and ends there."
~ Robert Browning

It seems like not too long ago I was pregnant with my older son. I was so scared to be a mom. I had never been one of those people who took care of kids, or babysat, or who worked with kids in any way. Actually, being around little kids made me nervous. So I wondered if I would ever know how to do the things I needed to do.

Then that gorgeous little baby was born. He was not very big, 7 pounds, 1 ounce and 18.5 inches long, and he was so beautiful. I will never, ever forget the first time he was put in my arms and my heart just opened in a way it never had before. That unending expansion of unconditional love was bigger than anything I had ever known in my life. I knew in that very moment my whole life had changed in the most fantastic way. I never ever could have imagined how big a change it was.

As I stared at his beautiful, angelic face, I knew that I would do everything I could to make his life as good as possible. I began to dream of what that meant: he would play sports, he would excel at school, he would have friends, he would grow strong, and he would know that he was loved. I just couldn't wait to dive into being a mom.

For the first year and a half that is how it was. He was such a precious baby. He met his milestones, he was beautiful; people would stop and he would smile at them and they would say "Wow, what an angelic child!" For the first year and a half there were no concerns.

As soon as he turned 18 months old, something changed. I still don't know what it was, all I have is theories. At 14 months he had his first ear infection. At 18 months he had a DTaP shot. At 18 months we had the time change to daylight savings time. I don't know what the trigger was, but all of the sudden he couldn't fall asleep, he was hyper and sensory issues began to surface.

This was the child who slept through the night at 9 weeks old, and putting him to sleep was a piece of cake. We would just lay him in his crib, and he would fall asleep. That's all we had to do. Then all of a sudden at 18 months he couldn't fall asleep to save the world. He didn't want to nap anymore, and getting him to bed at night was like... It was horrible! Literally, my husband and I would drive him around in the car for 30 to 40 minutes. To get him to take a nap we had to rock him for 45 minutes to an hour. He could not fall asleep without movement.

Everything changed after that. He had walked the day after he was a year old, so he was already walking and running everywhere. He should have been saying his first words and pointing at things he wanted, but he wasn't.

As the days turned into weeks and months, his struggles with sleeping and talking continued. Also he had ear infection after ear infection. For 22 months they were almost chronic. Worse yet, I had no idea that the medical care he was getting was inadequate to prevent long term problems. I also did not realize at the time that the child that I had dreamed of having – that all-American kid who could play sports and do well at school and have lots of friends – none of that was going to happen. With each passing month of ear infections, our son was slipping into the world of special needs.

As he progressed to age two, then three and then 4, he was still years behind in speech. He exhibited fine and gross motor difficulties, sensory processing overload, and extreme meltdowns. As he approached 5 years of age, a deep sadness settled over me as I became aware that he was not the child I had dreamed of having. He was a handful of unexpected mothering tasks that exhausted me on a daily basis.

In those early years I never imagined my child would be the one who would run off without any warning, or in a split second go from happy and playful to shrill shrieking and writhing on the floor. I never thought he'd be the child who the kids avoided on the playground, and disrupted birthday parties with his uncontrolled meltdowns. At some point, when he was about 5 years old and going into kindergarten (which was the biggest disaster ever), I finally had to face the fact that I had to mourn the child that I had hoped to have, and fully accept the child that I did have. I did love him, don't get me wrong, I loved this boy with all my heart. Never for a moment did I feel angry or resentful towards him; maybe at God, but not at him. He was such a joy because he was so loving and he relished exploring the world and experiencing new things. It was not all stressful meltdowns or managing special education.

Even with the good moments, slowly, and with a sad heart, I realized I had to go through a process of letting go of what I had hoped he would be. I knew if I didn't do that, then I could never fully embrace the role of mom to this amazing little boy. If I couldn't mourn that dream boy, then I knew I would always wish he could be different, and my heart would not be 100% free to love him and guide him just as he was.

And so I did just that. I went through this journey of mourning. I had to mourn the dream and I had to mourn the child that would never be. It's really critical that as moms we own up to our desire, or our dream, or our hope of what we expected our child to be. That expectation shapes our approach to our children. It's not fair to them to hold them to a ghost image. It's not fair to hold them up to a standard that they could never live up to. This is true of any child, not just a child with special needs.

So I went through this mourning process. I can remember spending many nights crying, angry at God, asking over and over: "Why? Why my son? Why did HE have to be different? Why did he have to struggle? Why was school hard? Why couldn't he talk to me? Why did he seem to not understand when I spoke to him, yet he could understand if we spoke in sign language?" I would have these conversations with God. I had to go through this fight with Him because He delivered something that I wasn't anticipating, and it was so, so hard, and I wasn't happy about it!

I had to go through a process of mourning just as if that dream boy had died. If you've ever read anything by Elisabeth Kübler-Ross you know that there are five stages of grief:

1. Denial

2. Anger

3. Bargaining

4. Depression

5. Acceptance

I had been in the denial stage for many years before I finally realized that I had to go through the grieving process. So I did. I would cry, I would get angry, I would feel sad and I would ask God if I did charity work or in some way gave back, would he then please heal my son. It was a private experience. I did not join a group because I could not find a group that understood this process. I did this all privately. I had to come up with my own way of doing it. The best way for me was to write about it in my journal, or just to have these heated conversations with God about it. With each round of emotions the pain of loss decreased, and over time I finally felt like I had grieved and let go of this phantom child.

What I realized over time was that while grieving the childhood he wasn't going to have, and the parenting experience I wasn't going to have, I discovered what an amazing and joyful child he was. Letting go allowed me to focus on the boy in front of me every single day. Even though I let go of that dream, it was still hard to let go of the wish that he could have been neurotypical. That sadness still crops up nearly 10 years later, and I still have to do more journaling or crying, knowing that like any grief, it passes when it's ready to go, not because we make it go.

Mourning process

The following exercises can help you through the process of mourning the child you dreamed of.

How do you feel right now?

Look at each sentence starter and write the first thing that comes to mind to complete the sentence.

- When I think of my child, I feel...

- I feel most frustrated when...

- If I could have one wish for my child, it would be...

- I feel saddest for my child when...

- The biggest dream I had for my child (but know it won't happen)...

- When I think of me as a mom, I feel...

Your Stages of Grief

Where are you in the grieving process? Look at each stage and think back on your emotional reactions to your child or the situation. Have you moved through the stages of grief? Are you stuck in a particular stage?

- **Denial:** My child is fine. There are no problems.

- **Anger:** How could God (or doctors, genetics, etc) do this to my child?

- **Bargaining:** If I am perfect, volunteer, really research well, God will make my child better.

- **Depression:** I am so scared that my child will always have problems. How will I manage this?!

- **Acceptance:** My son is amazing just the way he is. I know he is never meant to be anything else.

Goodbye Letter

Write a good-bye letter to the child you had wished for. To release the idea of the child you idealized, consider burning the letter to release all the energy around it. Write from your heart, but here are some ideas to get you started:

- I am releasing the dream of you because...

- Saying goodbye to you makes me feel...

- I always dreamed you would be...

Even if you do not burn the letter, make sure to destroy it. It's not some-thing you ever want your child to find by mistake. Even years later as an adult, it can be very shocking if your child were to read how you wished for him to be different.

Get Over Your Stuff

"Instead of resisting any emotion, the best way to dispel it is to enter it fully, embrace it and see through your resistance."
~ Deepak Chopra

I don't know who said having a child is the best way in the world to work through your childhood traumas, but it's one of the more accurate things I've ever heard about self-healing. Being a parent really brings out our own inner angst about the times in our childhood when we struggled. As our child grows and reaches certain milestones, we are very often triggered by our own memories of experiences that we had at those same ages.

For example, as a child I was very accident-prone and I have broken all my limbs (one at a time of course). When my children were young, I would stress a lot when they climbed and did things that could potentially cause them to fall and hurt themselves. It took my husband telling me over and over: "You must let them have those experiences. They have to learn to explore and take chances. If they get hurt, they will learn from that." Each time I would see them start to climb, I had to take a deep breath and let it go. I recognized that it was my own fear due to my own experience as a child. Their experience was not necessarily going to be the same. That turned out to be mostly true. We have two boys and had four concussions and one broken finger between them. No major broken bones.

Don't dump your stuff on your child.

The emotions from your own childhood are going to be particularly potent if you suffered from a learning challenge similar to your child's. Watching your child go through the experience is going to trigger the memory and all the psychological repercussions. Your first inclination is to want to protect your child. You don't want her to have the same painful experience you had. Please remember, your child is a different person in a different time. Her experience is not necessarily going to be the same as yours. There are a lot more resources and solutions today, and a lot more can be done to help children who are struggling.

If you have a lot of unresolved trauma (stuff) in your childhood cupboard, and you don't clean it out, you're going to impose it onto your child. I've seen this in my sons. I was raised in a family where academics were very important. When my son started in middle school, he achieved mostly A's. As the classes got harder, it was more difficult for him to continue getting A's. Then he improved to the point he no longer needed a 1-on-1 aide, and it became even harder for him to get A's. I found myself pushing him to try harder and get all A's. I really had to take a step back and say to myself: Wait a minute here, who really wants these A's? This is a student who is just learning how to work on his own. He is doing his work, and he really is putting in his full effort.

I was sending him a message that his efforts weren't good enough. And whose problem was that? It wasn't fair to put that much pressure on him. He was learning how to manage executive function on his own. He was learning to be academically independent, and he was doing an amazing job!

I had to take a step back and say to myself: What can I do to make sure he's getting all the support that he needs? How can I make sure he is okay if he doesn't get those straight A's? I had to talk to myself, and then I had to talk to him and admit to myself and to him that I was pushing him too hard. He needed to know that I saw that he was putting in a full effort. If that did not manifest in his getting straight A's, that was okay with me. I didn't want to be a mom who made him feel less than. The kid is brave, smart, and grades don't really reflect the areas where he is gifted. In his last term of 8th grade he got four A's and two B's, which is really awesome! I was very proud of him and of myself. I had let go of some of my baggage so he could do this his way, not my way.

One of the best books I've read on healing old emotions is *Breaking the Habit of Being Yourself* by Joe Dispenza. He explains in great detail how memories trigger emotions, which then leave a biochemical imprint in the mind and body. He emphasizes the patterns our emotions generate not only internally but externally. Our bodies literally get used to the biochemical imprint, and we get stuck in the habit of re-experiencing emotions, which recreates similar experiences throughout our lives. We literally become habituated to these emotions, and without conscious effort, we find it difficult to break free of them.

If you find yourself stuck in your old patterns, or old emotions cropping up when parenting your child, it is important to find a therapist or self-help approach that will assist you in getting beyond your history. Doing this allows you to parent your child unencumbered by past experiences, and you can also move forward and change the outcome of your future.

What were the most stressful ages for you?

As your child reaches certain ages, it is important for you to pay attention to what triggers you. I have a friend who lost his sibling in a tragic accident when he was an adolescent. When his son reached the age of adolescence, it triggered alarms in him. He wanted to have more conversations with his son and make sure that nothing was upsetting him. He wanted his boy to know that sometimes in life tragic things happen. It was almost as if he wanted to prepare the child in case something bad happened. All it did was freak out his son. It made his son worry, "What bad thing is going to happen?"

The truth was that this dad did not have the emotional support when this tragedy of losing a sibling occurred. Instead of dealing with the grief, the family moved into blame and anger about why it happened. So this young man was left on his own to deal with the intense emotions of losing his sister, and having parents who were now very sad and angry. While he wanted very much to prevent his own child from having the same experience, this was not happening to his son, and there was no reason to prepare or alarm the child.

Find a therapist who can help.

It may be a good idea to seek out counseling to help you work through the difficult emotions that come up when parenting. If there were particularly traumatic areas of your childhood that you need to resolve, a therapist may be helpful so you do not teach worrisome thought patterns to your child. In chapter 12, *Ask for Help*, I outline specific steps to find a therapist who will work for you.

The biggest issues I had to overcome.

Sometimes it's hard to sort out what is a parenting issue and what is an issue from your past. I'm sharing some examples from my childhood so you can get an idea of what sort of childhood emotions can affect your parenting.

My biggest challenge came from that conversation when the neuro-psych told us that my would need group home care as an adult. My first thought was, "Oh my God, what if he can't take care of himself?!" Maybe it's a good thing that concern came up because it definitely spurred me into helping him. At the same time, there was a lot of anxiety and fear around this because to me the idea of not being able to be independent is worse than anything. While I continued to hold the vision of his recovery, I also learned to accept whatever outcome may result from this journey. I had to accept it in order to let go of the anxiety so I could focus on what needed to get done.

Another huge issue for me was having a child who was not going to show up as an excellent student. School was never a problem for me, and it just seemed inconceivable that a child of mine could be like that. I had to work on recognizing that intelligence comes in many forms, that if intelligence doesn't show up academically in school, it doesn't mean that somebody isn't bright or even gifted. A lot of kids who are visual-spatial learners don't do well in regular academics. Their intelligence doesn't show up until they get to use their hands and they can make things. Then suddenly people say: "Wow! Look at how talented you are!"

It was a huge adjustment for me to learn and understand that intelligence is more than a report card. If I had not made that shift, I would have felt like my son would never be successful in life because he didn't fit into a certain mold. Once I got over it, I learned how to foster his strengths outside of school.

Also, in IEP and 504 meetings I was constantly reminding teachers and therapist what my child WAS good at. I had to remind the team that maybe reading was hard, but look at his amazing imagination. Word problems were difficult, but look how easily he grasped math concepts. It really helped me to be okay with the situation when I accepted that everybody has strengths and challenges.

Another issue I had to let go of was the need for social relationships to look a certain way. As a girl I grew up wanting to be popular and have a big group of friends. When I had problems with friends, I did not have good skills to manage the situation, and it made it difficult for me to maintain friendships. I had some friends, but never a big, fun group to hang out with. I struggled with this until college, and it was always a point of deep sadness for me.

My kids on the other hand are not so hung up on having a group of friends. Maybe it's because they are boys, but neither is concerned with how many kids are at their lunch table at school. It was my older son who asked me one day, "Why are you so concerned about my socialization?" I had to wonder when he said that. I had wanted a big group of friends as a child, and I assumed they wanted the same thing. He is happy with a couple of good friends, and I knew I needed to let him decide how many friends should be in his group.

It's very important that you understand that your own history influences how you parent. If you have a lot of trauma, or issues from childhood, this is going to color your way of parenting. It is important to pay attention to what is triggered in you so you can resolve it before it affects how you parent your child.

POINTS TO PONDER

- What were the 3 most challenging aspects of your childhood?
- How do you see childhood challenges affecting your parenting?
- How can you reframe these challenges so they do not effect how you parent your children?
- Who could you reach out to for help if you need to?

Visualize Healing

"Make sure you visualize what you really want,
not what someone else wants for you."
~ Jerry Gillies

Five years ago I was in a board meeting for a non-profit, and we were visualizing the future of the organization. One of the steps in that process was to visualize what God's plan was for me. And so I sat in silence allowing images to come into my mind. Then I saw something amazing.

It was me, standing in front of an audience of over 500 people. I was basically telling them what is in this book. The idea for this book did not even cross my mind until 5 years later, but here I saw myself sharing exactly what I am writing. What came next made me cry. I still get tears when I think of it. In the vision I introduced my older son, and he walked up on stage. He was fully grown and dressed in a college graduation robe. He was going to share his story from his perspective. I saw in that moment that my son was totally healed.

A lot of people will tell you that creative visualization is metaphysical hooey. They might say it's a waste of time to daydream your life away. However science has shown that visualizing an event is just as powerful as actually experiencing it. Physiologist Edmund Jacobson found that athletes who visualized practicing actually developed muscle memory for the activities they were visualizing. The most famous study to corroborate this was done by Australian psychologist Mike Richardson.

Dr. Richardson found a basketball team where none of the players had ever done visualizing. He measured the free throw success of each player before beginning the experiment. He then split the players up into three groups. One group went onto the court and practiced free throws every day for 20 days. The second group practiced free throws on the first and 20th days. The third group also practiced free throws on the first and 20th days, but in between they did 20 minutes of free throw visualizing every day. If they "missed," they "practiced" through visualization until they got the next shot right.

After 20 days he re-measured the free throw success of each group. The first group had a 24% improvement in free throw success. The second group showed no improvement. The third group, which spent the same amount of time on the court as the second group, showed a 23% improvement in free throw scores!

Imagine yourself on a diet. You are working towards a healthier, slimmer body. When you have a craving you are fighting, you can visualize your end result to bring your purpose back into alignment with the here and now. Creative visualization is that simple. You just have to see the goal you are reaching for. You do not need to know the how of reaching the goal, you simply have to know the what.

Before I had that confirming vision in the group visualization session, I regularly envisioned my son healed. I would often visualize him in a college cap and gown, receiving a diploma on a stage during college graduation. I would see him in a college classroom, doing his work, having no challenges. I would see him married, with children, with a job, always functioning with no cognitive issues.

Every time I had to read another assessment, visit another specialist or go into an IEP meeting, I would take time to envision my fully healed son. In this continuous, repetitive visioning, I was consistently reinforcing the end result. When I was in that visualization circle, and I received the gift of seeing him lecturing in a college graduation robe, I was not surprised. I saw it as confirmation of what I had felt all along. My son was destined to be just fine.

How do you visualize?

Many experts will tell you the "right" way to do visualization. I'd suggest you find the way that works for you. I will explain various visualizing techniques, and you choose the ones that are easiest for you. Feel free to try them all and mix and match.

Visualization can be used for short term goals or for your child's 15-year goal. If your child is working through a therapy and you hope to have a specific result, visualize that. You can even create a specific visualization you use every time you go into a meeting with the school or a specialist, seeing a cooperative meeting with a positive outcome. Whatever you choose to visualize, just make sure to focus on the end result, as if it has already happened.

1) Quiet meditation.

Sitting quietly in meditation helps to silence the mind and allow your subconscious to suggest the information that you need. Sit quietly for at least 5 minutes, 10 or 20 is better. Once you have found the quiet space within you, allow your visualization to surface.

Sitting in meditation without words running through your head is a challenge to some. What helps is to use a mantra that can occupy your mind. Make it a mantra that helps you get into the energy of the visualization you are seeking. The mantra should be in present-tense, not future tense. For example, a mantra for me would be "My son is healed" or "I see my son healed." I would not say "I hope he is healed" or "I will see him healed."

If meditation is really difficult for you, try investigating other options of movement combined with meditation so you will have a distraction for the mind while a calming for it as well. Zentangle™, a doodling drawing technique is an excellent way to do this. While doodling random pictures, the mind can relax and find a calm space. Tai Chi would be another example of a great way to give yourself 'something to do' while calming the mind in a meditative way. While doing these activities, you can visualize the outcome you want to achieve.

2) Add depth to your vision.

Adding detail to your vision brings it to life. Experience all 5 senses and then add feelings to make the image as rich and real as possible. Adding taste, smell, touch, feelings, color, sound and dialogue increases the potency. For example, if you have a non-verbal child, you might see the child say a full sentence to you. Imagine the tone of her voice, what she would actually say. Then hear yourself responding. What would you say? Most importantly, how do you feel when you hear her say a whole sentence? Add as much detail as time will allow. Visions with depth are much more potent.

3) Create a vision board.

This is a fun project that can bring in your creative side while spending an entire afternoon visualizing healing. A vision board is a collection of images, words and drawings that you create to hold the vision of what you want to achieve. Everything in the board should be present-tense, as if it is happening right now. You can do magazine cutouts to create your board, or you could use a program like Google draw to write words and pull in images. You could also draw the whole thing by hand. You can find examples of vision boards by searching in Google images.

Print out your vision board and hang it on your wall. Look at it daily and say something to ingrain the vision. For example, you might look at the board and read something on it. You might look at the board and say an affirmation such as, "I know my child has everything necessary to be successful."

4) Write a story.

Create a story that illustrates a positive future for your child. Write this story down and read it weekly. While reading, visualize the story in your mind. The story does not have to be true or even believable. The objective is to really KNOW that your child is going to be okay. The story reinforces this, and gives you a prompt for visualizing it.

5) Write affirmations to go with your visualizations.

One of the reasons people who meditate use mantras is because the mantra becomes associated with a calm state of mind. By repeating the mantra every time, they hasten their ability to get into the tranquil state of meditation. Affirmations can work the same, becoming a catalyst into the feelings and ideas of the visualization.

For me the affirmation was simple. I would visualize my son in a cap and gown receiving his college diploma, and I would say, "I am overjoyed to watch him cross the stage at his college graduation." The affirmation not only reinforced the visualization, but it also put me into the feelings I would experience when the event occurs. It deepens the experience, adding another depth of description to make it feel all the more real.

How often should you visualize?

I did not keep a schedule for visualization, but instead visualized whenever I was challenged by something in my son's journey. When we were in the thick of trying to get him services at the former school district, I visualized several times a day. I used it as a tool to grasp hope and to help me through the strong emotional challenges that were pulling me down. After we moved to our current school district, and finally he was getting all he needed, I cut down to two times per week.

You need to find the rhythm that works for you. If you are desperate about the situation, I would recommend visualizing at least once daily. You might have a quick visualization that you can do in 30-60 seconds, plus a longer visualization that you take 10-20 minutes to do. Use the quick one when faced with a challenge, and the longer one when you have time.

How do I know if I am doing it right?

There is no right or wrong when it comes to visualization. It's really just a matter of taking the time to do it. Also, during your visualization, make sure to add as much detail and emotion and sensory experience as you can. Even if you don't believe it can work, by doing this you are also focusing on something joyful and calming. It is worth the few minutes a day to help you stay in a positive mindset.

POINTS to PONDER

- What do you want to visualize for your child's future?

- Describe this event or experience in as much detail as possible (add input from all 5 senses plus how you feel).

- How do you feel when you visualize?

- Write one affirmation that you can say to help you recall your visualization: I feel _ _ _ _ _ _ _ _ _ _ when I see him/her

  _ _ _ _ _ _ _ _ _ _ _ _ _ _ _ _ _ _.

9

Ignore the Naysayers

"Those not chasing their dreams should stay out of the way of those who are."
~ Tim Fargo

You are on a mission to help your child, but there may be people in your life who cause you to question your ideas or methods. I call these people naysayers. They are the people who always seem to focus on negative outcomes, taking the joy and hope out of daydreaming of a better tomorrow. In order to successfully help your child, it is critical that you identify the naysayers and remove them from your daily life.

Some are easy to cut out of your life. For example, the pediatrician who wouldn't give me a lab slip to check our son for folate receptor antibodies. He said it was a bunch of hogwash, and refused to help me. Turned out to be on of the best things we ever did for our son, but that pediatrician will never know that. We switched pediatricians when he refused to help us find medical causes for our son's challenges.

Some naysayers are harder to eliminate from your daily interactions. It might be people at school, family members, or maybe even your spouse. Obviously you cannot just cut family members or a spouse out of your life. But you can change how you interact with them so you can reduce their an impact on you and your goal of helping your child.

Identify the Naysayers

The first step in eliminating naysayers is to identify them. Think of somebody in your life who you are uncomfortable interacting with. Ask yourself the following questions:

- Do you dread talking to this person?

- Do you feel tired or drained after talking to this person?

- Does she criticize you often?

- When you present a new idea, does this person always come up with a negative "Yeah, but you know what could happen..."?

- Does her advice go against your own intuition?

- Do you find yourself defending your child's issues or diagnosis?

- Does this person complain a lot, but never does anything to change the circumstances?

- Is this person talking from fear or indifference?

- Do you find drama and chaos are always around this person?

If you answer yes to any of these questions, you may be dealing with a naysayer. For both your own sanity, and your child's sake, you must decide how to eliminate or ignore them.

Determine what is best: eliminate or minimize.

Don't feel guilty for changing your relationship with this person. You need to do this for peace of mind and for your child's success. You can do a gradual withdrawal or simply stop talking to them altogether. If you decide to eliminate them from your life, remember to remove all traces:

- Remove their contact information from your phone.

- Unfriend them on social media accounts.

- Don't answer emails, phone calls or messages from them.

If you can't eliminate them, then you have to find ways to ignore them. Consider the person's background. Do they have expertise in this area or are they armchair diagnosticians? Once you realize they aren't experts, it's easier to ignore anything they say.

There are a lot of things you can do to reduce contact or ignore somebody. This will minimize the impact of their negative dialogue.

- Set rules of conversation. Tell the person you don't want to discuss certain topics because you don't like arguing/disagreeing with her.
- Don't talk about your child's challenges or progress around her.
- Keep your ideas and hopes to yourself.
- Do not engage in discussions where you have to debate or defend your point of view.
- Never feel like you must justify yourself to her.
- If you feel really uncomfortable in a situation, you can ignore her or walk away. Just cut the conversation short!
- Change the subject if you cannot get away.
- Reduce contact as much as possible.

Be wary of 'experts' who squash your hope.

As I have traveled through the realm of special education for the past decade, it is amazing to me how many doctors and therapists are ready to predict how a small child will be in 10 or 20 years. I have had many people tell me my son would never improve and I should just accept it. The UCLA-trained neuropsychologist was the worst of the lot when she condemned him to group home care as an adult.

I worked with a mom whose 13-year-old son was diagnosed with an intellectual disability. He did not have a chromosomal abnormality, but he had scored very low on the IQ test administered by a neuropsychologist. The mom was crying when she called me. She was so upset at the thought her son would never have an independent life.

The mom mentioned that he had severe auditory processing disorder (APD) too, and this seemed like too much for him to handle. I asked her which IQ test was administered, and it was the WISC (Weschler Intelligence Scale for Children). The WISC is a verbally administered IQ test and the assessor must provide accommodations if the child has APD. The neuropsychologist did not provide any accommodations, which means the test results were probably invalid. When I explained this to the mom, she was incredulous. The doctor had taken all her hope away, and here I was saying to not give up on it.

The mom began her own journey of healing her child, and today he is in college and managing just fine. That doctor had no right to rob her of hope. She could have said she had nothing to offer, but that does not mean somebody else wouldn't have a solution that would help.

It is dangerous to listen to these experts when they tell you nothing can be done to help your child. They are experts ONLY in their own domain, and not in the vast array of options available. Take any prediction with a grain of salt, and move on. Nobody can foresee how a child will change and grow, and it's just cruel that they believe they can see the future.

Surround yourself with positive-attitude people!

- Like-minded moms who support your quest to help your child.
- People who make you feel good about yourself and your decisions.
- Supporters who will encourage you when you have to make big or scary choices.
- People who will not criticize you for mistakes you make.

In chapter 10 (*Find Your Tribe*) there are ideas on how to connected with like-minded people who will support your journey.

POINTS to PONDER

- Who in your life is a naysayer?
- Can you eliminate this person or ignore them?
- What can you do to bring more positive people into your life?

10

Find Your Tribe

"Stick with the people who pull the magic out of you, not the madness."
~ Unknown

Special Ed Moms are often too busy taking care of hundreds of details to reach out for support. We can easily become overwhelmed by the day-to-day experience of special-ed parenting. That is why it is important to find a support group. Through connecting with other parents who are having a similar experience, it can provide a place to commiserate, find inspiration and know you are not alone. I call that group of people 'your tribe.' They provide a sounding board for your experience.

Why join a support group?

1. Meet local special education parents and possibly make new friends.

2. Learn how others have managed to work with the school district. It can help you in choosing schools or understanding the personality of your child's school administration.

3. Learn about new and handy resources to help your child.

4. Share challenges and solutions.

5. Find playmates and friends for your child.

There are two main kinds of support groups: in-person and online.

In person support groups could be one you create yourself or groups that are sponsored by schools or local non-profits. Online support groups can be found on subject-specific websites or on social media platforms.

Nearly 9 years ago I had no idea how much my journey would change when I stumbled across an auditory processing disorder (APD) group on Facebook. It was in that group that I was first exposed to the idea that therapies could help improve APD. I also learned what kind of support I should be asking for in school. 8 years ago I took over as administrator for the group, and I continue to share what I've learned.

Since that first group, I have joined dozens of other Facebook groups, and each has provided me ideas and information that has helped me forge a positive path for my children. By being part of these groups I have also seen how much information parents need and how little time they have to find it. That is what inspired me to write this book.

I have found less benefit from in person support groups, but that is not because there is no value in them. We live in a rural town, and there are few available, and none pertaining to our children's specific issues. My personality is also better suited to the online groups.

Finding an In-Person Support Group

In-Person support groups have some important advantages. Both you and your children can become friends with people in your community. Parents whose kids are in the same district or region can share local resources while also providing a sounding board for challenges and struggles. You can find a local parent support group through:

- Schools
- Your Local Parent Resource Center (www.parentcenterhub.org)
- Local non-profits focused on special ed, parenting and children
- Local hospitals
- Local advocates

Finding a local support group that you fit into takes a bit of effort. I remember the first support group I joined was for special needs parents, which included all special needs. Some of the kids had developmental delays or learning challenges like my son, but some had life-threatening medical issues. Parents whose children had severe challenges would share their fears for their child. Some of us would be reluctant to talk about our child's 'simple' issues like lack of social skills or struggles with reading. How could we share our struggles when another mom was worried that her child might die? The facilitator of the group had no awareness of the imbalance of needs, and so I left the group. It is important to find a group where the moms and children have similar challenges so you can speak openly and share resources without feeling inhibited or guilty.

Find Online Support Groups

Online support groups are easy to find as they exist on all social media platforms and on some subject-specific websites. If you post a question or thought, hundreds of people might respond. There are support groups for pretty much any topic you can imagine, from broad to specific. **Visit www.specialmomadvocate.com/resources for a list of online support groups.**

It is important to find a group that really resonates with how you think and how you approach your child's challenges. Find a group that offers answers and positive support, not just a group of people complaining or venting about how hard things are.

It's really important to find a group with a similar approach as yours. In the beginning when my son was having attention problems, I belonged to an ADHD support group on Facebook. It was difficult for me to participate because everybody was talking about medication and my choice was to not medicate my child. I wanted to find an alternative to medicating my child. People in the group would say I was an irresponsible parent or I was unfair to my child because I was 'withholding' medication. I would read so much about kids who were on three and four different kinds of medicines. They were talking about side effects and what to take to mask the side effects. I finally realized, "This isn't my tribe because this isn't what I believe in."

Medications do work for some kids, and they work great, but my mother's intuition told me that medication wasn't the right solution for my child. I needed a group that offered a different approach to treating ADHD. When I found the Recovering Kids Biomedical Healing group on Facebook, then I knew I had found a tribe that I really belonged in. This was the approach I wanted to take, and this group brought me the answers that I could work with.

Choosing an Online Support Group

Here are some important things to consider when choosing a support group.

1) Who is in charge of the group?

The group should be overseen by people who have experience with the same disability that your child has. If you have a group that says, "Our administration is pretty lax, talk about whatever," you might find some things that are mentioned will bother you. Admins should watch what's being posted to make sure that there are no trolls. Trolls are people who spam the group, or who oppose the philosophy of the group and want to join so they can argue about things. Administration is really important and really helps to keep the group on track. It also helps to make you feel safe because you know when it gets out of hand, there's an administrator who will take care of that.

You are probably wondering what could possibly get out of hand. In the APD group that I administer, we have had several incidents where people angrily disagreed with what others posted. In our group we believe that people with auditory processing disorder can benefit from therapies. We keep an open mind and we talk about things that can help. However some parents were adamant that nothing will help. They believe accommodations are the only solution for APD and the person just has to learn how to live with it. These people bashed other members who talked about therapy. They said, "You're wasting your time,"

"You're wrong," "There's not enough research." When that happens, many people become very upset because they have personal experience watching their child improve with therapies. It does not feel right to have somebody make a blanket statement that 'all these therapies' have no impact. The bashers insist this is impossible, so they stir the pot, insisting they are right.

If there is no administrator to handle disagreements, people become uncomfortable with these arguments. They leave the group or do not participate in the conversations. People with no experience in using therapies don't know what to think. So instead of a supportive exchange, the group becomes a negative experience, adding to existing stress.

2) Do the administrators allow people to advertise?

Some groups allow advertising, but this may make you wonder what the real purpose of the group is. Is it a sales group, or an honest discussion of options that may or may not work?

I'm not saying professionals can never post about their product. If there is a discussion going on and somebody says, "My child's having a problem with XYZ," then somebody else, "I use this therapy and it works really well for my clients," that's good. Someone asked a basic question about resources, and someone else provided information that might be a good fit. Occasionally a professional joins a discussion and promotes their therapy or product out of context. We don't allow that in the auditory processing disorder group because it's not coming genuinely from the participants, it's just a commercial.

3) What age groups are allowed in the group?

There are groups that are just for parents, and the guidelines state that. Some parents want to talk a lot about parenting issues without concern that children are involved in the discussion.

Some groups have people of all ages. In these groups, everyone learns the first-hand experiences of others. This happens in the APD group all the time. A parent will mention their child is struggling, and a teenager or young adult who has APD can answer questions. Parents might ask, "What was this like for you in school?" Or, "What helped you when you applied for a job?" or "How did you manage going to college?"

It provides an opportunity for you to see what the future might look like with the learning disabilities your child has.

4) Do members tell you what to do or just share their personal experiences?

Group members should NOT be telling you what to do; they should just offer information. This is really important for you to understand because some people will overreach and insist their way is the only way something can be done. There might be ten other options for the problem, but that one person will insist he has THE solution. Since there's no one answer, you want to investigate all the options. Using research and your intuition, try to pick the one that fits your situation the best.

5) Is the group run by one person or a group of admins?

This is really a critical question because people can start support groups as a way to push their own agenda. Often times it is a business agenda. When there's a post that doesn't agree with their agenda, the group owner will delete it. If another professional who competes with them asks to join, the group owner won't let them. Basically, that one person is controlling the information the group members hear about.

A blatant example of this happened in an online support group once. It was run by an audiologist, who did not believe in listening therapies. If anybody posted about listening therapies she would just delete it. Listening therapy discussions often come up in APD, ADHD, SPD and autism groups, so the group led by the audiologist missed out on the opportunity to hear about something that might help.

6) How do they handle things when people start arguing with each other?

This is going to happen. Inevitably people have different opinions. Are the members of the group cordial in their discussion or do they get nasty about it? When people get nasty, what do the administrators do? Do they realize it's no fun to be in a group when people argue like that? It's not a quality group when a few people are arguing and everybody else is turned off and wants to leave.

What do you want out of a support group?

If you are used to being the one supporting everyone else, you may have a hard time figuring out what you want from a support group. Often this is the reason 'supporters of others' do not seek one out, because we don't really know how it will benefit us. So it is important to look at your life and see what support you already get. To do so, consider the following questions:

- Do you feel alone?
- Do you have people you can talk about your parenting challenges?
- Do you feel worn out as a Special Ed Mom?
- Do you wonder if you could be doing something else to help your child?
- Have your regular friends fallen away since you became a Special Ed Mom?
- Do you have difficulty making new friends?

If you answered yes to any of these questions, it provides the impetus for deciding to find a support group. Remember, it does not have to be in-person if you feel you are strapped for time or are not comfortable sharing with local moms.

I would encourage you to find your tribe.

Seek out other Special Ed Moms who are living the same journey. They can be the most amazing source of support and encouragement. It really makes the whole process easier. I can honestly say that this has been the single best thing I did for myself throughout the entire special education process.

If you would like to meet me in any of the online groups, feel free to send me an email at hello@specialmomadvocate.com. I will email you a list of the special education groups I belong to. I can also send you a list of the local support groups I run in Southern California. I would love to see you there!

POINTS TO PONDER

- What kind of support do you want from a group?

- What local agencies could refer you to a support group?

- What social media platforms do you use where you can join a group?

Section 2

Take Care
of Yourself

We hear it over and over,
but how often do we put ourselves first?

11

You Are a Caregiver – Treat Yourself Like One!

"If your compassion does not include yourself, it is incomplete."
~ Jack Kornfield

The *Merriam-Webster Dictionary* defines caregiver as: *A family member or paid helper who regularly looks after a child or a sick, elderly, or disabled person.*

Just by being a parent you fit the definition of caregiver. Being a parent of a child with special challenges complicates this role, making it more difficult and more exhausting to be a mom. According to the National Alliance on Caregiving (2009), there are approximately 8.4 million parent caregivers of special needs children in the United States. They include caregivers of all forms of disability including physical, cognitive or emotional disability. The National Alliance on Caregiving also found that parent caregivers spend an average of 30 hours per week caregiving, 11 hours more than caregivers of adults. This is nearly as much as a 40-hour a week job!

No matter what kind of disability your child has, whether mild or complex, you have extra parenting duties that parents of other children do not have. Moms of special needs kids work at least twice as hard as moms of typical kids, and this extra responsibility can create physical and mental fatigue that can lead to burn out. While this role can be very rewarding, it can also be very stressful. It also affects your mar-

riage and other mother duties, making you feel spread so thin you feel you are dropping balls in all areas of your life. The ups and downs that come with this role can be extreme. You need to be aware of the extra demands it places on your time and energy. You will find your daily routine is impacted way more because of atypical parenting tasks:

- Helping children with tasks of daily living beyond the age they would normally do these things for themselves. (e.g. helping a 5-year-old get dressed).

- Teaching tasks or repeating information many more times than needed for the average child (e.g. teaching a dyslexic child to read).

- Managing extra therapies or services outside of school.

- Extra meetings with school personnel to make sure your child is getting proper support.

- Managing extra financial burdens for medication, supplies or therapies beyond the needs of a typical child.

- Planning and preparing a special diet.

- Researching the child's disability and finding ways to help the child.

- Planning contingencies for everything in life, including the child's future.

- Living in a state of chronic stress, always anticipating the unexpected and making sure you are prepared for those surprises.

- Monitoring behavior for unexpected behaviors that need intervention (e.g. regular meltdowns).

- Hanging onto your patience when your child's challenges delay you or cause havoc while getting out the door or attending an event.

- Taking phone calls from school no matter what you are doing because your child needs help right now.

- Finding people to watch your child when you are not available.

It is important to accept that we are a mom first, and a caregiver second.

Accepting the caregiver role helps you realize the importance of taking care of you.

What challenges do you face as a caregiver?

The role of caregiver has many routine aspects, but it also presents many unexpected challenges and demands. Recognizing those challenges and finding help can alleviate some of the caregiving stress. Common challenges reported by parent caregivers include (but not limited to):

Personal/home challenges:

- Managing personal stress
- Managing financial burden
- Finding time to rest or rejuvenate
- Balancing work and home life
- Getting respite help
- Keeping your marriage healthy
- Finding support or someone to talk to
- Taking care of your other children

Challenges with helping the child:

- Researching information about the child's disability
- Communicating effectively with medical professionals
- Managing the school/special education process
- Managing child's behavior
- Managing toileting issues
- Keeping the child safe
- Transporting, lifting or moving the child
- Helping with homework
- Helping with bullying/social issues

You need to be well to take care of your child.

We've all heard the instructions to put on your own oxygen mask first. It's hard to listen to though, isn't it? That immediate and desperate need to help your child seems to override all logic. It is difficult to accept that we must take care of ourselves first. But think for a moment, and remember this well: If you are not in good shape, who will care for your child? Caregiver burnout is a very real possibility, and that is why it is critical for you to ensure that you can keep it up for the long run.

Don't underestimate the difficulties
or overestimate your strength!

Give yourself permission to care for yourself. As caregivers we can feel guilty taking time for ourselves, and if this is your mindset, you need to let it go. Taking care of yourself is not selfish, it is mandatory in order for your entire family to function well. It is important that you feel good about taking care of you. Again, let me repeat this, it is NOT selfish. You are needed as a caregiver, not as a sacrificial lamb.

Monitor your emotions. Address the emotional needs of being a caregiver. It is okay to be upset, have resentment or feel overwhelmed by the constant demands. Talking to a therapist or support group is a good way to gain suggestions for how to process these feelings. Experienced caregivers often have great suggestions for how to manage things better or where to get more help.

Know your limitations. While you may want to do everything for your child, sometimes it is better to cry uncle and bring in more help. While you may not have the finances to pay a professional, seek out support from local organizations who may have suggestions on where to get help that is covered.

Accept help from those who offer it. Even if it's a mom who casually says, "Let me know if I can help." Ask her to help if you find a way she can do that. If you truly have nobody who can help, then seek out respite care. Respite care is usually a county or state-funded service provider who can come to your home and watch your child so you can get a break. They are trained to care for children with special needs so you know your child is left with somebody who knows what to do in case an issue arises.

Take care of your physical needs. Daily stress not only wears our patience, it can affect both our bodies and minds. It can lead to poor endocrine health which can cause weight gain and sleep issues. This further taxes our bodies. It is crucial you find time in your day to calm your mind and body. Even if it is only 5 or 10 minutes, it is an oasis in the chaos. You also must get regular checkups and visit your doctor if you feel unwell in any way.

Do nice things for you. Find some time to engage in activities you love, or buy simple things that bring a smile to your face. A bouquet of flowers or a pedicure can change your whole attitude on a day when things feel tough. Go to coffee with a friend or take a class in a subject you enjoy just to do something fun. Find ways to bring joy and ease into your life so you have a change of pace from the hectic days at home. Some of the things I do to bring joy into my life include:

- Taking a bath in the evening after everybody is in bed and the house is quiet.

- Putting images of positive quotes up around the house so I am reminded to keep a positive mindset.

- I spray my room with lavender because I love the scent and it helps me feel calm. I also use essential oils on my skin because I love the smell and the calmness they bring.

- I go to paint-your-own pottery with my kids.

- I visit a local meditation retreat and walk the labyrinth.

- I create Zentangle™ drawings and color them in.

- I paint in a fun, non-directed way that brings freedom and self expression into my day.

Watch out for caregiver burnout.

If you find yourself positively exhausted, difficulty concentrating and often angry, you may be headed for caregiver burnout. This is a very real concern if you fail to take care of yourself first. Prolonged burnout can lead to health challenges which will not only make it difficult to function, but will add to your stress. If you find yourself venturing into this territory, it is important to seek professional help through counselors who specialize in working with caregivers.

If you reach the point of burnout, you will not be able to function well. Really think about how this will affect your child, and how it will effect your relationship with your child. Not only will your fatigue make routine tasks more difficult, but you will be more likely to convey frustration and impatience. This will impact how your child sees the situation, and he may internalize a sense of guilt because he recognizes that his issues are causing you more problems. The fatigue factor can have such a huge impact on how you go about your day, and that could defeat the whole purpose of your efforts to help your child.

Getting support as a caregiver.

It is important to reach out and find ways to support yourself as a caregiver. The chapters *Find Your Tribe* and *Ask for Help* give ideas for finding help. I have found online support communities to be a great way to get support any time of the day, and they are also a wealth of ideas for making things easier. It is important to check in regularly with your support groups, even if you feel like things are going well. Staying in touch and supporting others helps you maintain that positive space.

POINTS to PONDER

- List your caregiver duties.
- How do you support yourself when caregiving becomes a challenge?
- What local or online support groups can you join to get ongoing support?

Ask for Help!

"Ask for help not because you are weak, but because you want to remain strong."
~ Les Brown

Special education is a complex process, especially if the school is resistant to providing support. While we all want to feel we are capable of handling it, our ability to think clearly is compromised when our emotions are charged. It is really important you are honest with yourself about when to ask for help. This is especially true when you are just learning the ropes, because your brain is trying to assimilate a lot of new information while your heart is filled with anxiety. The brain's ability to think is severely impaired when under stress, so trying to learn new things while running the show can be asking too much!

Remember you are your child's primary advocate. If you are not able to navigate this complex path, who else will make sure your child gets the necessary supports? It's important that you work smarter, not harder.

Get emotional support for special ed meetings.

In the very beginning you may not feel you need an advocate or lawyer because the school is cooperative and your child is getting help. Even so, it is an emotionally charged experience, so it is good to have somebody to help you maintain focus and calm during IEP or 504 meetings.

During the special ed meetings, you are going to be talking about your child's challenges and where she is falling behind. Having a friend, fellow Special Ed Mom, or a family member attend the meeting with you is highly recommended. The person does not have to say a word, just being there is calming. Ask the person ahead of time to touch you gently if he feels you are becoming over emotional. He can help you calm down and refocus, resulting in your being more effective throughout the meeting.

This same person can also be an objective voice after the meeting, giving you a reality check on your experience. You can ask them to take notes so you can review them afterwards and see if they jive with what you remember. This person is not meant to police the meeting, simply observe and be a source of emotional support for you.

Hire a Special Education Advocate

The special education process can be overwhelming for even the most calm and logical person. Don't think you are failing if you need to ask for help. An advocate can be a valuable resource even if only to help validate your perceptions and guide you in the process. Advocates are not lawyers but they do have extensive knowledge about laws regarding special education. An advocate works with you to identify the needs of your child and then strategizes on how to get the schools to provide the proper support. You can ask an advocate to come with you to special education meetings or act as a consultant, guiding you through the process.

Advocates do not have any kind of license or regulating body, so you must be aware of this when hiring one. It is your job to do your homework and find somebody who is reliable and effective.

It is important that an advocate have a calm, proactive method of working with schools to achieve results for the child. The advocate must know and understand special education and disability law, and how to respond when the district becomes uncooperative. The advocate should have experience in your specific district and understand your district's personality and know how to handle obstacles that may come up.

Advocates usually charge anywhere form $75 per hour to $300 per hour. They tend to require a retainer and an agreement that will stipulate what constitutes chargeable time. Usually they are paid for any time spent on:

- In-person, email or phone conversations with you
- Reviewing records, assessments or other school documents
- Making phone calls to the school or other agencies
- Writing reports, emails, editing IEPs/504s
- Research
- Attending SST, 504 or IEP meetings (usually charge for travel time as well)

Where do you find an advocate?

Finding an advocate takes time but it's not too difficult. Here are several resources you can use:

- Search on the COPAA (Council of Parent Attorneys and Advocates) website (www.copaa.org).
- Call local special education attorneys and ask for advocate referrals.
- Ask other special ed parents
- Search online for an advocate in your county
- Call your state Parent Training Center (www.parentcenterhub.org/find-your-center)
- Check the Yellow Pages for Kids (www.yellowpagesforkids.com - managed by Wrightslaw.com)
- Contact local organizations or non-profits that support children with your child's challenges

How to choose an advocate.

Choosing an advocate is an important process that you do not want to rush through. Unfortunately there is no certification for advocates (state or national), so you must use other means to verify specific experience. Here are ten questions to ask when hiring an advocate:

1. **Have you done any training courses?** There are no licenses for advocates, but there are many training courses available. Wrightslaw.com and Council of Parent Attorneys and Advocates are two worthwhile starting points. Ask your advocate what sort of training she has and what sort of continuing education she participates in. If she claims to be licensed or certified, know that this cannot be true; therefore this person would not be a reliable advocate to work with.

2. **Do you specialize in specific disabilities?** Some advocates are generalists and cover a wide range of disabilities. Some are more focused and have expertise on handling specific disabilities. Find out if your advocate has experience with the specific disability your child has.

3. **What districts do you work in?** Each district has a distinct personality and way of doing things. While it is true an advocate can work in any district where they are familiar with the laws, you may want to find an advocate who knows your district. If you have a difficult case, this specialized experience will make a huge difference.

4. **What experience do you have as an advocate?** You want to find out how long she has been advocating and what sort of clients she has helped. Many parents become advocates after struggling for years with their own children. This kinds of hands-on experience can be invaluable because she will see things from your point of view.

5. **Why did you become an advocate?** Knowing this will tell you if the person is doing it from the heart, the head or the purse. Special education teachers may become advocates because they want to make a bigger difference for kids. Parents become advocates because they see other parents floundering and they want to share their knowledge of how they helped their own child. This is why I became an advocate. Some people may choose to be an advocate because they find it interesting to do. Knowing why an advocate made this choice will help you gauge if she has the right attitudes, methods and motivation to help you and your child.

6. **What do you think is the main goal as an advocate?** You want an advocate who is enthusiastic about making a difference for you and

your child. She should be focused on achieving results that makes school easier for your child, and at the same time empowering you to advocate for your child. Their goal should not be about sticking it to the school district. If you feel the advocate is often badmouthing the district or out to show them who is boss, please realize that approach is adversarial and is not going to get good results.

7. **How often do you review IDEA and Section 504 of the Americans with Disability Act?** While we hope everybody can remember everything, the truth is we do not deal with all parts of the law on a regular basis. Reviewing federal laws that govern special education is an important part of keeping up on being a good advocate.

8. **Do you have any references?** While of course the advocate is only going to give you positive references, it is a good way to find out how the advocate works. It can also give you an idea of some of the specific cases the advocate has handled and how a solution was achieved. You can also gauge how the advocate works with a parent, and what will be required from you while working with this advocate.

9. **How do you handle my child's paperwork?** You want to find out if the paperwork is stored in a secure place and who has access to it during the process. Also, what happens to the paperwork once you are no longer using the advocate?

10. **Have they ever had a case that did not go well?** While it is hopeful to think that every case ends up perfectly, that is not the way it really happens. An advocate who can admit that a case may not have had the best outcome is someone who will be honest with you about the process.

11. **Have you ever referred a case to an attorney?** Many advocates insist they can handle the entire process from start to finish, no matter how difficult things become. When districts become especially challenging, it may mean due process is the only recourse. While there are a handful of advocates who have extensive experience and can help you through these steps, it is often in the best interest of the client to refer to an attorney. It is important for an advocate to know her limitations and to know when to refer the case to a lawyer.

How do you know you need an advocate?

You may be wondering how you will know if you need an advocate. It will be up to you to determine if you feel like you need extra help with your child's case. Some of the common reasons for hiring an advocate:

- **You feel emotionally overwhelmed by this process.** It is difficult to separate the emotions when it's your child who is struggling. An effective advocate can help you face the special education team, and can guide the process without getting emotional.

- **Learn the special education process faster.** A good advocate will teach you what needs to be done; empowering you to be the best advocate for your child.

- **Not knowing how to respond to the school.** Has the school told you they cannot provide services for your child, even though it is obvious your child is struggling? When the school refuses to help it is very difficult to know what to do. An advocate can help you make the right decisions for moving forward.

- **Are you confused by assessments?** An advocate can help you make sense of all the assessments, teaching you how to interpret them in order to figure out what support your child's needs.

- **Do you know how to plan for your child?** Is the school presenting you with a 504 or IEP without any input from you? Do you know how to write goals, choose accommodations and plan for your child's future? An advocate can help make sure this is done correctly and optimally for your child.

- **If your child is not making progress, what do you do?** An advocate can help you brainstorm and plan alternative courses of action. The advocate then works with you and the special ed team to make those plans a reality. Having another person on your side to help you plan will often be the one thing that sways the IEP/504 team into trying something different.

Most advocates charge from $75-$300 per hour for their services, and you can decide how much help you want to receive. Some advocates will require they be in charge of the process and attend all meetings, and that might be more expensive. Others are willing to coach you, guiding you through the process but allowing you to be in charge. Others will be a blending of the two, leading the charge at first, but gradually teaching you how to do it on your own. Each model offers different levels of support and of course different price tags. Even just having a coaching advocate can make a world of difference in the results you achieve when negotiating with the school.

An advocate can significantly reduce your stress and hopefully shorten the time to get your child support. While it is an investment of funds, it could make the whole process easier and more effective.

Hire a special education attorney

Whether you go straight for an attorney or use an advocate first is going to be based on the complexity of your case and the personality of your school district. After fighting for nine months in our previous district we went right for an attorney instead of an advocate. We had limited funds and the district was resistant to helping our son from the start. We figured if we went for the big guns, we'd get quicker results.

Our strategy paid off to an extent. Our son did get everything we asked for within two months of hiring the attorney, but the school treated us like we were pariahs. The attorney we hired had a reputation for winning big so that intimidated the district. I'm not sure an advocate would have had the same results without a protracted fight. It would have ended up with the same cost in the long run, but our son would have had to wait for help. That meant he would fall further behind, and endure more challenges, while we would be stressed trying to get the school to comply. You need to think about the pros and cons when deciding to start with an advocate or go straight for an attorney.

How do you know you need an attorney?

- **You are moving into mediation or due process.** If you have reached a point where you need to fight the school in a legal battleground, an attorney is your best choice for a good outcome.

- **The school has brought their own attorney onto your child's case.**

If the school mentions discussions with their attorney, or brings an attorney to meetings, then you have no choice. You need legal representation. Remember their attorneys will be experts on how to say no by quoting the law. You need your own expert to rebut these refusals.

- **The district has a reputation for playing hardball.** If you find that your district's first response is no, an attorney may be your only hope of getting help for your child.

- **The district keeps giving excuses that are against special education law.** If you find pronouncements by district personnel are in direct conflict with special education law, you may need an attorney to help clarify the law. It is common for schools to misrepresent the law in an attempt to manipulate parents into giving up. How much they misconstrue determines if you need to bring in your own legal guns.

- **Your child has complex needs.** If your child needs a lot of services, or there are disagreements about placement, a special education attorney can help navigate these negotiations. Schools will often do whatever is necessary to avoid footing the bill, including telling you the law does not require them to do what your child needs. Having a legal expert on your side can help the discussion move in a more positive direction.

- **You are not sure if you have a good case.** You have done your research and you know what your child needs, but you are unsure if you have a good case against the school district. Getting advice from a special education attorney can help you know which avenue to pursue in obtaining services for your child.

- **The school district has filed a due process complaint against you.** When you go to due process, it is a formal hearing that is similar to a court. The purpose of the hearing is to determine if the evaluation, qualification and educational placement are appropriate for your child. Usually it is a parent who files due process because they do not feel the school has done enough. There is one case when the school can file due process against you. If you request an Independent Education Evaluation (IEE), and the school feels that they have done everything necessary to evaluate your child, they can file a due process complaint against YOU. In this case, the district has initiated a legal proceeding, and it is best to have legal representation to help you navigate the process.

- **The school has failed to comply with the IEP.** If you have to fight the school to comply with your child's IEP, gaining their compliance will be easier and smoother with a legal expert to help you with communication, meetings and hearings.

How do you find a special ed attorney?

To find an attorney you use the same resources I listed for finding an advocate. When hiring an attorney, ask the following questions:

1. How long have you been a special education lawyer?
2. How many special education cases have you handled?
3. Do you specialize in specific disabilities?
4. Have you ever handled a case similar to my child's? What was the outcome?
5. How much do you think it will cost to pursue this case?
6. What will my role as parent be in the case?
7. Who will have access to my child's records while handling my case?
8. How will you keep me informed on the progress?

Find a therapist if you need extra support.

It's important that you find the courage to say: "This is damn hard, and I'm struggling with it. I need help!" If you can't do that, you may spiral into depression or anxiety. In some cases, if your child has severe behavior or health challenges, you can end up with PTSD. You really need to be able to admit and say, "I need a counselor to help me with this!" It is not a weakness to need help. It takes courage to admit it!

Finding a therapist does not have to be hard, but it is very important to find one that will offer the support you need. Someone who is not a good match will add to your stress. Here are some strategies for finding a suitable therapist:

- If you feel comfortable, ask friends or family for a referral.

- Refer to your insurance provider list. Then research the therapists to help you decide who will be a good fit.

- Use Google to find information on therapists. Find reviews, visit their websites and try to determine if they would be a right fit for you.

- *Psychology Today* (www.psychologytoday.com) has an extensive database of therapists. Each one has a description of specialty areas. You might even find one who specializes in families with special needs children.

- Interview several therapists. Just because you see them one time does not mean you are obligated to go back. Ask them questions. Trust your intuition about whether or not she is the right therapist for you.

Find respite care.

Finding somebody who can provide a break is essential to surviving the special education process. What sort of break you need will depend on the challenges your child faces. For example, if you find yourself getting increasingly frustrated helping your child with homework because of dyslexia, finding a tutor would be the right respite care for you. If your child has serious behavior problems, you might need a babysitter with experience handling these challenges.

Getting a break at least once a month is crucial to helping you find time to be quiet, relax and regroup. Family and friends are often the best source of respite care. Unfortunately that is not always an option. If you do not have friends or family who can help, there are agencies you can turn to for free respite care.

- ARCH National Respite Network (www. archrespite.org)

- Your local chapter of The Arc (www.thearc.org)
- Your county department of mental health
- Your state department of developmental disabilities
- Ask your local children's hospital.
- Ask your local hospice organization.

If none of these agencies have services in your area, use Google to search for "respite services for special needs" to find local services.

If you do not qualify for free respite care, you have no choice but to hire somebody to help. You can find respite help through people you know in the community:

- Trade respite care with another special education parent who understands your situation.
- Ask your religious organization such as a church or temple.
- Ask your child's teacher or other special education team members.
- Look into ARC programs that provide daycare for individuals with special needs.
- Check on www.care.com

Of course anybody you hire or find to care for your child should be interviewed and have references checked to ensure they are the right person for the job. As with any childcare worker, do your homework, including a background check, to make certain your child is in safe hands.

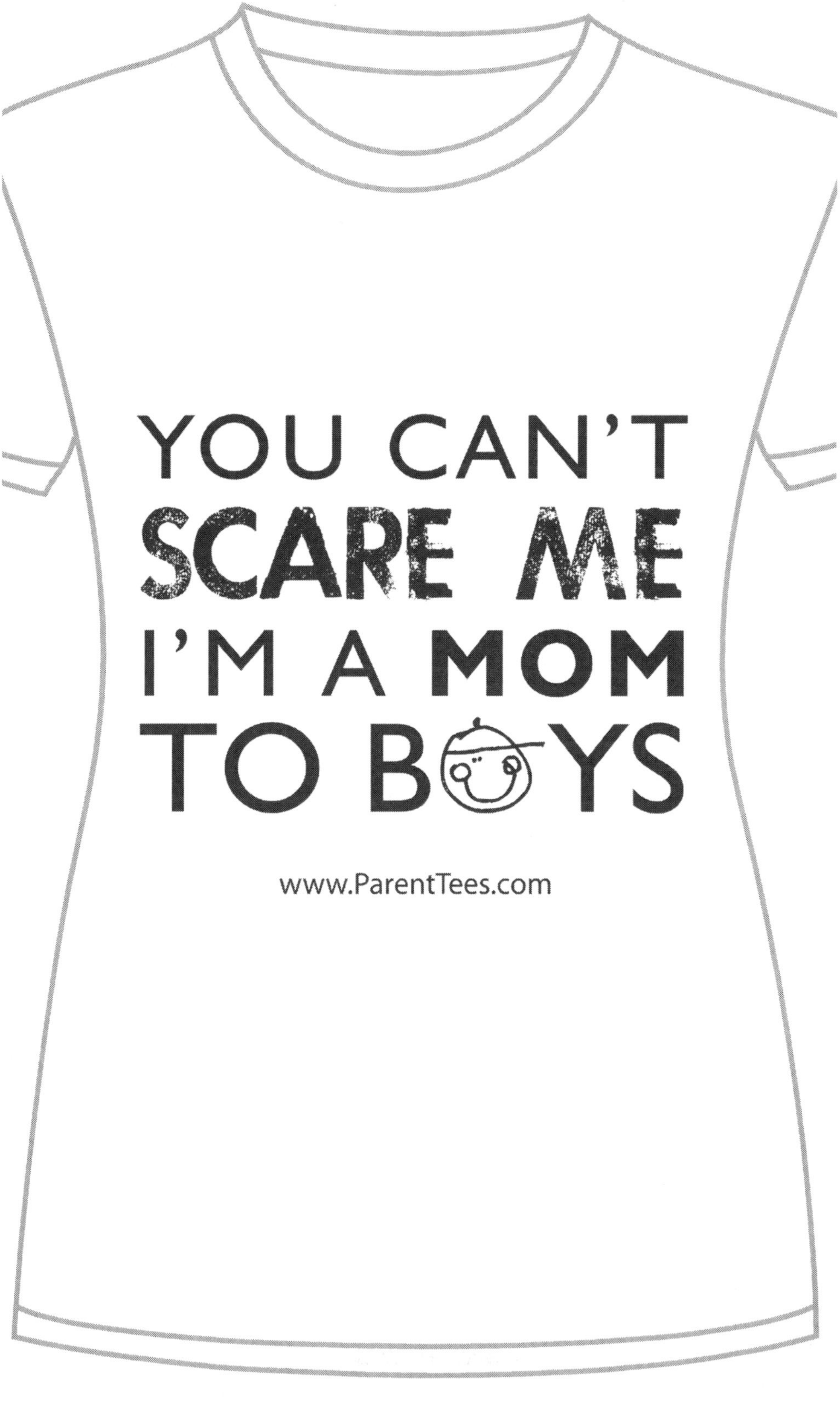
YOU CAN'T
SCARE ME
I'M A MOM
TO BOYS
www.ParentTees.com

13

Manage Your Stress

"The greatest weapon against stress is our ability
to choose one thought over another."
~ William James

I wish I had listened to all the people who told me to take time for me, to get away, and not put every ounce of my time and energy into this responsibility. It is difficult when you are scared for your child, angry with the school and exhausted from the process. If you take away only one message from this book, it is: TAKE CARE OF YOURSELF!

Stress not only affects your physical health, it affects your mind and your ability to function. If you are worried and anxious all the time, you cannot be there for your child in the way you are needed.

How Can You Manage Stress?

I know your time is spoken for, and when you do have time, you're too tired to do anything that requires effort. Find things that you can do in 10-15 minutes, or plan small escapes so you can get a break. Here are some effective strategies I have used to de-stress so I am not over-whelmed all the time by everything:

1. **Breath:** I know it sounds simple, but when we are stressed our breathing is shallow, or we hold our breath. Taking time to con-

sciously breath deeply can be incredibly calming for the body and mind. If you find yourself in a particularly distraught state, take 10 deep, slow breaths. Doing this will reset your autonomic nervous system and help you become calm and centered.

2. **Ground Yourself:** Grounding has become more popular as people have realized the calming benefits it provides. It's basically about becoming aware of your body in space and bringing your mind into the present moment. The easiest ways to ground is by touching water (washing hands, shower, swimming, etc.) or being in contact with nature (take a mindful stroll, walk barefoot on the grass, hold some stones, etc.). I created *Ground for Life*, a deck of 52 exercises for grounding, to help people learn simple ways to become more present. Each exercise explains how to do grounding and provides modifications for children. You can ground yourself in 60 seconds or 60 minutes, making it one of the easiest exercises to bring you to a calm space.

3. **Zentangle™:** This doodling technique was introduced to me by a friend during a very stressful time of my life. When you sit and doodle in a mindful way, it has been shown to elicit the same brainwave patterns as meditation. You can do it anywhere, on any paper, and with any pen. Setting aside a specific amount of time each day or week will go a long way to calming your inner self. Find out more at www.zentangle.com.

4. **Color:** Like Zentangle™, research has found that coloring is calming enough to induce the same brainwave patterns as meditation. Through slow, calm strokes of your pen or pencil, you will bring a calm rhythm to your mind. There are a plethora of coloring books available on any subject you can imagine, so you can always find images that appeal to you. Whether you use colored pencils, markers or good old fashioned crayons, it doesn't really matter. I have a preference for the Tombow art pens, which are a pen on one side and a brush-like tip on the other. You can blend them a lot like water colors, and create vibrant images.

5. **Unplug:** When you feel overwhelmed from all the demands upon

your time and energy, and you need to calm down, try getting away from all the electronic data smog. Find a quiet place to sit. Even pull out an old fashioned book, or just enjoy sitting in beautiful surroundings. Think of this as an electronics fast that will reduce the 'noise' in your life.

6. **Positive Self-Talk:** I know it sounds silly, but the conversations we have in our head can really move us in the direction we want to go. Find some phrases or affirmations that uplift your mood or help you move away from thinking negatively. Sometimes carrying around a card with positive affirmations or quotes can remind us to re-center and calm down.

7. **Exercise:** I find exercise to be an excellent way to get the stressful feelings out, especially if it is intense. Connect to the frustrations, and use that feeling to motivate you to exercise hard and fast, pumping out the feelings while you strengthen your body.

8. **Laugh:** Research has shown that laughter can be one of the best ways to alleviate stress and elevate mood. Watch a funny movie or do something fun with your kids to help bring the laughter back into your day.

9. **Keep a journal.** It can be very cathartic to have a daily or weekly journal where you write down your frustrations and accomplishments. Even if you only take 5 minutes and write in bullet form, just putting it out there can provide a huge release.

10. **Write a letter.** If you find your anger or stress is aimed at one person, write a letter expressing these feelings. It is not a letter you would send to that person. It is simply a way of processing the feelings. Once done you can release the emotions by destroying the letter. Fire or shredding are great ways to do this.

11. **Meditate.** I know many people are put off by this word, but it really does not have to be so intimidating. I am not talking about sitting for hours on end in a transcendental meditative state. I'm talking about sitting quietly while listening to music and allowing your mind to relax. If upsetting thoughts keep floating in, then focusing on a mental image or mantra can help. Meditation does not have

to be complex; it is just quieting the mind. If you find it hard to do on your own, you can find guided meditations online. You can also find a local meditation group where you can do it alongside others.

12. **Get a counselor.** Sometimes we need a neutral party to hear our challenges and offer some positive suggestions for change. The Ask for Help chapter has some ideas for finding a counselor to assist you.

13. **Get good sleep.** If there is one thing that can take me down in a day, it is a bad nights sleep. When we are under stress it is often difficult to sleep, which is why it is important to be protective of our sleep schedule and to create habits that help us get a good nights sleep. The better you sleep the easier it is to manage difficult emotions, and the less stressed you will feel.

14. **Say no more than yes.** As caregivers we are apt to want to help many people and we end up overextending ourselves. It is important to practice saying no. If somebody asks you for help, and you have any hesitation, then just say no. You need to be protective of your time and energy. Others may not understand, especially if they are used to you always saying yes. You may lose friends over this one. That is okay. You need to make sure you have the resources and time to take care of your family and YOU. Don't give it away just to be nice!

15. **Choose companions carefully.** If the people around you are stressed and anxious, that will amplify your feelings of stress and anxiety. While you may not be able to choose your family members, you have complete control when it comes to who your friends are. You do not want to be around people who are constantly complaining or who hype their personal drama. If you must be around people because of work or family situations, do your best to limit your exposure to them.

16. **Have fun!** What kinds of things do you truly love to do? Are they still part of your daily or weekly life? Bring the fun back so you have moments where you can escape daily stress and revel in the joy of your activity. It could be a solo project or a group adventure, whatever makes your heart sing!

POINTS to PONDER

- List three ways you can manage your stress in 10 minutes or less.
- Make a commitment to:
  1. Engage in an activity to manage your stress at least 3 times this week.
  2. Set a reminder on your calendar or your phone so you remember to do these activities.
  3. Check up on yourself to see if you are following through. You can also ask a friend to be an accountability buddy to help you make sure you do the things you committed to.

14

Be Okay With
Your Breakdowns

"Let your tears come. Let them water your soul."
~ Eileen Mayhew

In an earlier chapter, I recounted an incident where my child was overstimulated and had a meltdown at a birthday party. After that, the other moms avoided me at the party. You could see from their glances and raised eyebrows they thought there was something seriously wrong with our son.

I went home and just cried and cried. I was mad at God for making my son have problems. I was mad at myself for not recognizing the signs and pulling him out sooner. I was mad at the school for not doing more to help him. I was just mad because my son had such a huge struggle with something as simple as a birthday party. Mostly I was mad that the universe made my son this way, and I was scared for his future. The tears would not stop coming.

It is important to let these tears fall.

When you feel this much emotional overwhelm, you just have to cry it out. And when I say 'cry it out,' I mean crying about something that has no other means of release than deep, heart-wrenching sobbing. Crying so hard you cannot breath; the tears stinging your cheeks, and your shirt so wet from the waterfall of emotions. It feels like a gushing release from a popped water balloon. And even though you are thoroughly exhausted afterwards, you somehow feel lighter.

Nearly 10 years ago my husband and I went to a play in the park. We were invited by a very nice couple who I enjoy talking to. Through the course of the conversation, I became pensive and sad. My husband and I ended up taking a walk. The park was by the ocean, so we went to look at the ocean waters lapping in the half-moon light. We saw a small family of raccoons who walked right by – three moms and a baby. As we walked in this charming place, I talked about how I was feeling.

I'm not sure how we got there but the subject of my friend who had cancer became the topic of conversation. My friend, who I loved like a sister, had a cancer that refused to know that it was unwanted despite every effort to get it to stop growing. It had now reached her brain. As I talked about my dear friend, I lost it. I totally and completely broke down. Right there amongst the roar of the waves, where nobody could hear, I sobbed and sobbed and sobbed. I DIDN'T WANT TO LOSE MY FRIEND!!! I sobbed out the feelings of despair; the unfairness of the whole situation. I cried about the anger I felt because I had to go through this; and even more the about rage that I felt because she had to go through this. I cried until my throat hurt. I cried it out, and it felt good!

The next morning my eyes were burning. I'm sure they were puffy, but I didn't even care to check. My heart was still sad, but I felt like a dam had finally broken, and a huge backlog of emotion was released. I had been holding it in for months, and I had been wanting to let it out. With this crazy busy life, I did not have any place to just scream. But that night, the ocean gave me the sound screen, my husband created the space, and I finally understood the concept of crying it out. It truly is a better way to go when the emotions run so deep you can barely keep your head above the turbulent waters.

Honor your tears. They represent your pain.

You had expectations of motherhood. But as a Special Ed Mom, you are reminded over and over again that those expectations have been completely dashed. Nobody can understand the heartache we endure when we watch our kids struggle socially or stick out in a less than becoming way. Tears are part of accepting that your expectations were totally smashed. They won't last forever, but letting them out gives you some temporary emotional release.

Do not judge yourself for these moments of emotional display. They are often unexpected and sometimes happen in front of others. When you cry, remind yourself how important it is to allow the tears space and time to flow. There is no shame in being emotional. You are finally able to unburden some of the pain and angst that goes with this journey. Cherish these moments. They are a gift you must give to yourself.

Breath into the Anger.

A harder emotion to accept is anger. Unfortunately it often comes out in special needs families. Our frustration and exhaustion reach a peak and we pop like a balloon under too much pressure. We need to give ourselves a break and breath when the anger is overwhelming.

I know all too well the pattern of intense frustration that boils inside. I hold it together, hold it together, and hold it together. Then as the day wears on, it gets harder and harder to hold it together. This is even harder if I didn't sleep well. Then some minor thing happens. Something is spilled or a toy is broken, and the ensuing noise and upset pushes that anger button. I find myself screaming, irritated and wishing things could be different. Then I see the face of my child, and wish I could take it all back.

Anger can be a very scary emotion, especially if we try to keep it all inside. Then it comes out in shooting rays of emotions like light coming through a cracked window. It is critical to find ways to express your anger in safe and productive ways in order to avoid the boiling point.

Some of my favorite ways for reducing anger:

- Hitting a punching bag with a baseball bat

- Exercising super hard

- Shredding thick paper and then burning it

- Getting a 10 pound bag of ice and chucking handfuls of it at a wall

- Writing scathing letters to people I'm mad at (but never sending them)

How do you help yourself get the anger out?

Find something you can do once a week or every other week. Plan a half hour or specific time period to give yourself space to get very mad. This is a safe way to release anger, and a positive way to keep yourself in better balance.

Of course there are times when it is counterproductive to get angry. So it is important to come up with some strategies that can help you calm down so you do not go off. Some of my favorite strategies:

- Take 10 deep, slow breaths (resets the autonomic nervous system).

- Take a break. Leave the house and walk around the block.

- Lock yourself in the bathroom for privacy.

- Whisper instead of yelling.

- Ask another adult to take over.

- Clench all my muscles as hard as I can for 15 seconds and then release. I do it over and over until I feel calmer.

If you do get angry, forgive yourself. I used to be hard on myself whenever I became angry. Then I realized I am only human. I can only take so much, and sometimes it's too much. It does not help if you berate yourself for having an outburst.

Whenever I get mad I will always talk to my kids after I calm down. I apologize and explain why I got mad. I let them know that sometimes it is harder for me to stay calm. I explain why I'm extra tired or impatient. I let them know which of their behaviors feeds my frustration. I never pretend that I was okay with getting mad. I always apologize. But at the same time, I use it as an opportunity to let my children know which of their behaviors can be challenging for me.

It's Okay to have Breakdowns

Just remember, this is a very challenging process. Each day presents surprises and demands intense parenting. We cannot be perfect moms every single day. The emotions will wear us down. So be okay when your emotions come gushing out in uncontrollable ways. Its part of the whole deal, and it helps make the next day not so overwhelming.

All fight.
No quit!

www.ParentTees.com

Find the Blessings
in the Journey

"Blessings sometimes show up in unrecognizable disguises."
~ Janette Oke

What helped me most to move through the challenges of being a Special Ed Mom was to focus on the lessons and the blessings that came from this journey. Every opportunity, everything that we experience in life, whether it's positive or not so positive, brings with it an opportunity to learn something. It also brings blessings.

Many people think that's 'new age' thinking, but the truth is, this philosophy has been the reason people often say to me, "How to do you stay so strong?" No matter what happens people see me rising to the occasion and tackling the "stress of the universe." You rarely see me collapse under the weight. It's because when something happens, while I do get upset, I then pick myself up and say: "Okay, obviously there's something in this for me to grow from, and I need to figure out what that is." I encourage you to take this same approach with this experience as a Special Ed Mom.

Identify the lessons you are learning.

I'm sure there have been many lessons that have made you a better person, a better mom, and maybe a better spouse. Focusing on the lessons helps you maintain a positive attitude about the experience. It also helps you to embrace the situation as an opportunity. Here are some of the lessons I have found on our journey:

Probably the number one lesson we all know extremely well is the ability to have patience. Who knew that we could have so much patience? I've always been told I was a patient person, but being the mom of a child who has sensory issues, cannot control behavior, and hits other kids, can try the patience of a saint. I know that for me, much of my energy went into trying to be calm and collected. I had a mantra: don't get angry; don't get frustrated; and don't break down and cry. Patience is a lesson we all share.

Another thing that I learned, without a doubt, is: Wow, I'm one hell of a researcher! I've always loved to read, and I've always loved information, but before I had my special needs child, I never had a need to collect information in such a voracious manner. Friends and family learned of my talent and would call me up asking me to find things on Google for them. I found out that I have this unique skill, I'm not really sure what to call it, for knowing which words to use to search Google. If you read the chapter on research, I teach you the methods I use to figure out how to find things on Google. Before I needed to help my son, I never realized that I had this ability to research and find needles in haystacks. Truly, it proves that necessity is the mother of invention.

I also learned that my capacity to love was greater than anything I ever knew. It is very hard to keep your heart in a loving space and to love a child who is angry or hitting or having a complete meltdown in public. It takes active cultivation and reminding that this child cannot control himself, and he is doing the best he can. My ability to love and my experiencing the giving and receiving of love has expanded greatly. When we had our second son, who has a loving heart as big as the Sun, I was able to feel even more love. I knew it was because I had learned to remain connected despite the challenges.

Find the blessings along the way.

Blessings are good things that happen without the need for effort on your part. Every life experience has blessings that come with it. The key is to recognize the blessings so you can focus on positive aspects, even in the most difficult circumstances.

The biggest blessing for me has been the joy of watching my son grow, learn and improve. Parents of typical children take for granted the successes that we know are so difficult for our child to learn. For example, a child's ability to write words on a straight line. I think our son was in 6th grade before he could do that accurately because writing was really challenging. The ability to champion all the small milestones was such a blessing because we really honored each step instead of just expecting it to happen.

So many kids go to school and do fine in all classes. Their parents never worry that their child may fail or not fit in. I know my parents never worried about me in school. I always did well, so nobody really made a big deal when I got good grades. I'm not criticizing any parent who accepts a child's normal progress in school. I'm just saying that when you have a child who doesn't struggle, you don't focus so much on the accomplishments, and you miss so many joyful moments as a result.

Another blessing that I received was the understanding that I didn't need words to communicate with my child. This was huge! When he was young he wasn't able to speak and my friend, a parenting coach, told me: "You don't need words to talk to him, you need to use your intuition and learn how to communicate without words." Then I had the idea to start teaching him sign language, which helped so much, especially because it showed me that he could communicate, just not with words. It was a huge blessing to know that I could connect with my son non-verbally! I think that brought us closer, and it made it easier because I found a way to get through to him.

Finally, one of the bigger blessings for me is finding a purpose in my life. While I have loved being a graphic designer for over 25 years, it had lost its luster and I yearned to make a difference in the world. As I immersed myself in special ed support groups, I soaked up information like a sponge. I also discovered I was a natural teacher. Helping my child through this journey brought a mission into my life. I knew with my knowledge and abilities I could help other parents find an easier path through this crazy special ed maze. So in mid-life, I chose to get my masters in educational counseling and launch a new career helping special ed parents and their children. The joy I feel in doing this work has been a big blessing in my life!

Your Children Are Your Teachers

What I realized over time is that there are no mistakes in the universe. I worked on shifting my focus from what my child wasn't to what he was. I began to look for the lessons and the blessings in the relationship with my boy, the journey we were on, and the path we were walking together. It just brings tears to my eyes to think of it... Because I realized that God had sent me this child to help me grow. He had sent me this beautiful boy to open my soul and my heart and to help me expand as a person who will help others. It is because of him that I'm writing this book today. He made me a better person by being the son he is.

Our children teach us in profound ways. With my older son, what I have come to realize is that he provided me an opportunity to become a better human being. Before he came into my life I was an intellectual snob. I focused on where people went to school, what degrees they had, and what kind of job they had. That was impressive to me. As he grew I began to realize that not all people manifest abilities in the same way, and yet can be equally as brilliant. Some people aren't destined to go to college; it's just not their cup of tea. They can still have amazing abilities. Somebody might be so brilliant at fixing cars he has a thriving auto repair shop. Just because he didn't go to college doesn't mean he isn't smart. Believe it or not, that's what I used to think! I see people in a whole new way, and I love the new perspective I have.

Some people say, "You have two boys, and you shouldn't give all credit to the older one." So let me I tell you about my younger son. He's all heart, and he taught me in a whole different way. He has brought unconditional love and acceptance into my life. Every day he teaches me to look beyond color or abilities and see others as just people who want love and friendship.

When he was 4, and his older brother hit him during a tantrum, instead of getting upset he said, "It's okay mom, he can't help it." He was teaching *me* acceptance and patience. Every single day — at least twice — my younger son asks if I want a hug. He has been an oasis in this process, helping me focus on the positive despite the desire to scream from the rooftops. He has some minor special education needs that are similar to my older son's reading and writing issues, so he benefited from the knowledge I gained. But make no mistake, he has taught me the true meaning of the soul's journey – to give and receive love in a totally unconditional way. He has helped me heal my heart and grow as a divine being having a human experience, and for that I am very grateful.

POINTS to PONDER

- What lessons have you learned? Write them down and review them to remind yourself of the positive aspects of this journey.

- What blessings have you gained? Would you have gotten these lessons without this journey?

16

The Power of Prayer

"Prayer is not asking. Prayer is putting oneself in the hands of God, at His disposition, and listening to His voice in the depth of our hearts."
~ Mother Teresa

I'm not sure where I would be right now if I had not found my way of praying. It really helps me feel comforted and keeps me in a positive frame of mind. It does not matter what your religion is or if you even have one. It doesn't matter how you believe in God or if you don't believe in God. Prayer is a way for us to put our wishes out into the universe. Who or what answers that prayer is up to your individual belief. The act of praying can bring you comfort and a positive frame of mind.

Positive prayer helped me.

In religious practice, prayer is often done by pleading with God to answer our prayers. Through my own spiritual practice, I have learned the concept of positive prayer. Instead of pleading and asking for something, I actually state my prayer as if it's already been granted. For example, instead of saying, "Please, please, please, help my child get better," I say, "God, I know that you're bringing me the solutions to help my child get better. I am open and ready to receive this information. I am so grateful for this wisdom that will bring him to the next level of healing. And so it is. Amen."

By stating your prayer in positive terms, you are confirming to yourself that this is going to happen. If you pray in a pleading way, you might say, "Please God, please help my child. Please make my child get better!" With a pleading prayer you're putting out the energy that you're afraid that your child will not get better. On the other hand, positive prayer affirms your belief that your child can get needed help and improve. Because of this, I believe it is really important that your prayers be framed in a positive sense. Only use this if it resonates for you.

The answer is not always what you think it will be.

I've heard a lot of people say, "my prayers never get answered." Sometimes the answer is "no" and that could be a good thing. Just because you have something specific in mind doesn't necessarily mean that will be how it turns out. It's really important to be open to other options. When praying you can include: "I'm open to receiving your blessing in whatever way is best." Be open to however the prayer might get answered because the universe works in very mysterious ways, and you never know what could come down the pike.

The answer to a prayer.

When our son was three he was already in special education preschool, but we could not find after school care for him. He had been thrown out of three preschools. Home daycare programs said he required too much attention. Even though we were self-employed, we needed to get work done, and with his non-stop hyperactivity and meltdowns, he needed to be watched all the time. We had tried babysitters, but they could not manage him. I could not find anybody with the right skill set.

So I prayed about it. I put it out to the universe to send me the perfect person to watch our son. Somebody who could work with him, somebody we could afford, and somebody who was available in the afternoons. I told a few friends that I was looking for this perfect person. Then I waited.

Less than 24 hours later, an acquaintance of mine called to ask if I knew of any babysitting jobs in our area. In her office was a friend of a friend who was trying to find a nanny or babysitting position. The woman was a preschool teacher who only worked half days. She needed to find work for the afternoons. Christina lived 20 minutes from our house, and she had a lot of experience working with kids with special needs. When she came and met our son, they immediately clicked, and I knew my prayer had been answered. I found out later that Christina had been fervently praying too, hoping for a position exactly like ours. She was instrumental in helping our son, and we were blessed many times over by her presence in our lives.

So I invite you to consider that prayer be part of your process. In whatever way you pray, know that those prayers can be answered for you. Know that there is some being, some energy, some force in the universe that will respond when you put your prayers out there. In moments of despair, in moments of great anguish, when you look at your child and watch her struggle, prayer can be the way to bring you back into that positive mindset. It's a very useful tool, and I encourage you to make it a regular part of your routine.

My prayer for you.

I know all the answers are there for your child. I know that you have the strength, the knowledge and the resources to find the solutions to help your child manage school and life. I also know you will forgive yourself for your impatience, emotional outbursts and imperfect decisions, and that you will care for yourself as lovingly as you care for your child. I am so grateful to the divine energy in the universe for the blessings of these amazing solutions that help your children be the best he/she can be. And so it is. Amen.

Section 3

Take Care of Your Child

With special education we think about dealing with the school, but it is important to consciously pay attention to how you care for your child.

17

Follow Your Gut

"Her intuition was her favorite superpower."
~ Unknown

Eight years ago, when my older son had just turned 7, I was on a message board about auditory processing disorder (APD). Another mom mentioned that she had done something called primary reflex integration to help with her child's APD. Intrigued, I began researching this therapy, which was developed by a Russian doctor named Svetlana Musgatova. The therapy involves specific movements to help develop neurological wiring that failed to develop during infancy and toddler years. While reading about the therapy, I knew without a doubt this could help my son. Getting the therapy would be difficult because at that time there were only a handful of practitioners in the United States, and most did not teach classes. The closest person who taught classes was in Seattle. I was in California.

I talked to my mom about it and she agreed that my hunch was a good one. She offered to help me get to Seattle so I could take the class. So I registered for the class and told my husband I was going to Seattle that weekend. He had learned to let me go with my intuition. I did a whirlwind 3-day trip to take the Neurodevelopmental Movement Training from Sonia Story of Move, Play, Thrive (www.moveplaythrive. com). Not only did I learn a hell of a lot about how early movement effects brain development, I gained an invaluable tool to prevent or lessen meltdowns. I learned how to assess for unintegrated primary re-flexes and how to develop a program to help integrate them in my son. This turned out to be one of the best things I ever did to help my son, and it was all done on a hunch that it would work!

Mother's intuition is unique.

Intuition is such an amazing thing. We all have it, but it seems to be especially strong in mothers. It's like having a special honing beacon to tune into the needs of our children. I'm talking about having informa-tion that doesn't fall into the usual sensory channels of hearing, seeing, touching and feeling. Nobody can really explain how moms have these moments of knowing. We just know.

I can remember when my boys were toddlers and they would have ear infections. I developed an intuitive sense about their ear infections. My ears would hurt when either one had an infection. I have never had an ear infection, and as soon as I took them to the doctor, my pain would resolve. I knew that if my ears were hurting, one of them needed to have his ears checked. Neither one of them would pull on their ears, have fever, or exhibit any other signs of a problem. So I developed a different way to detect if either one had an infection. I have no idea why or how that worked, but my ear pain became a reliable way for me to make sure that my kids were taken care of.

It's very important for you to develop, follow, and trust your intuitive hits. This chapter will teach you how you receive this intuitive informa-tion. It will also provide some exercises to help you develop a stronger sense of intuition to make it easier to pick up the information that comes into your consciousness. I do want to emphasize that I'm not trying to teach you to be psychic or 'talk to dead people.' I'm not talking future predictions either. I'm simply helping you develop a very effective tool to know what direction to take when helping your child.

6 Steps to Developing Intuition

Intuition is an inner sense of knowing that guides our actions in life. It helps us understand others and assists us in making decisions to lead us to the right choices. Everybody has intuition, but not everybody stops and listens to it. If you feel you do not have strong intuition, you can strengthen it with practice. Here are the 6 steps to develop your intuition:

1. Know how you receive information
2. Ground yourself in the here and now
3. Quiet your mind
4. Listen to your body
5. Distinguish between intuition and fear
6. Practice

1. Know how you receive information.

1. What do you notice when you first meet someone?

a. Their appearance: clothing, hair, shoes, and general attractiveness

b. The sound of the person's voice or laughter

c. How intriguing they are, or if they share common interests?

d. How you feel with the person. Do you feel comfortable, uncomfortable? Do you feel safe? Do they seem agitated or calm?

2. Upon returning from vacation, how do you describe it to your friends?

a. You describe how beautiful it was or tell about something specific you saw.

b. You talk about the amazing sounds you experienced while on the trip including the sounds of nature or the general sounds of the location or special music.

c. You share history or facts about the place you visited and what you learned about the people.

d. You describe how the vacation made you feel or how specific experiences made you feel.

3. Think of a movie you love. What comes to mind first when you think of it?

a. How the actors and actresses looked, the locale setting it was in, the photography, or the costumes.

b. You can hear the accents of the characters or the quality of the music

c. You remember the underlying message of the script or the life lessons the characters learned.

d. You feel the emotions the movie brought out in you.

4. Think of a discussion you had with somebody recently. What stands out most about the conversation?

a. The look on the person's face and how they were moving their hands and arms.

b. The tone of their voice.

c. The words they said.

d. How you felt being on the receiving end of the person's words or behavior.

Write how many of each letter you chose:
a_____ b_____ c_____ d_____
My Primary Type (letter chosen the most) _____

The 4 Ways Intuition is Received:

1. Clairvoyance: visual images

2. Clairaudience: auditory input

3. Claircognizance: Just knowing, the thought popped into your head

4. Clairsentience: Feeling other's feelings as if they were your own

Based on the quiz, your primary type is the way you most often receive intuitive information. It does not mean you do not use the other intuitive methods, it just means it's the easiest way for you to receive intuitive information.

Recall a recent experience when a strange coincidence occurred or you suddenly knew exactly how to handle things. You had nobody to tell you or no information available, you just got a feeling or simply knew exactly what should happen. Review the experience in your mind, and then answer the following questions.

- Describe what you remember from the experience.

- What intuitive senses did you use during the experience (seeing, hearing, feeling, tasting, smelling or just knowing)?

- What stands out most about the experience?

Does this match the primary input method from the quiz? The more you analyze how you received your intuition AFTER a situation, the better tuned in you will be to intuitive input in the next situation.

2. Ground yourself in the here and now.

You are a physical person living in a physical world yet you have the ability to "travel" away from your body in the form of thoughts or daydreams. When you are engaged in an activity like watching TV, your attention is not focused on your body, but instead on the TV program. The same can be true when you are in a mall shopping for gifts. Instead of focusing on walking, you are thinking about what stores you want to go to and what you want to buy. When you are focused on things outside of your body, you can become ungrounded.

Being ungrounded means being out of touch with your physical self. When we are ungrounded, it causes an unconscious anxiety in the body.

How Grounded Are You?
Check all that apply.

- ☐ Hunger often comes on very suddenly.

- ☐ You have difficulty falling asleep.

- ☐ You absentmindedly bump into people or objects, or you find bruises on you and don't know how they got there.

- ☐ It is easy for you to ignore pains in the body (i.e. headache).

- ☐ You must frequently manage anxiety.

☐ When you engage in a frenzy of activity, such as house cleaning or exercise, it helps you feel calmer.

☐ You recently had a lot of very stressful experiences.

☐ You daydream often.

☐ It is hard to stay focused on one task at a time.

☐ Crowds cause you to feel unsettled and anxious.

☐ You are very empathic and feel overwhelmed by highly emotional people.

☐ You are easily startled.

☐ You easily lose track of time.

☐ When driving you do not remember how you got from point A to point B.

☐ You sit for long periods of time (i.e. desk job).

Score your results by counting the number of checks:

- 1-3 Excellent! You are present in the here in now.

- 4-8 Good work! With some daily exercises you will become more grounded.

- 9 or more: Needs improvement. Grounding is crucial for you. At least twice a day you should do grounding so you can be more centered in your body.

How to do Grounding

Grounding is a very simple process that requires you to pay attention to your physical self. There are many ways to do grounding, so try several and find ones that work best for you. You can do grounding for one minute, five minutes, or more. Choose both a strategy that will work immediately, and one to use when you have more time. Here are some suggestions:

- Feel your body. Close your eyes and feel your body in space. Feel the surfaces your body is touching or become aware of how your body is positioned.

- Use your eyes to take in the visual surroundings

- Use your ears to take in all the sounds around you

- Walk barefoot in the grass

- Use a weighted blanket

- Get a strong hug

- Take a shower or go swimming

- Do some intense exercise

- Go for a walk and feel the sensations of walking and the environment around you. This is called purposeful walking.

I wrote and published *Grounded for Life, 52 exercises for grounding*. It is a deck of cards that describes 52 exercises for daily grounding. You can purchase a copy on my website at www.specialmomadvocate.com.

3. Quiet Your Mind

Find techniques to help you quiet your thoughts. There are many methods, so choose one that works the best for you. It is important to find a tool that helps you get out of your analytical mind and get into the non-verbal space of being. Intuition is most apt to come through in this non-verbal space in the mind. Some suggestions for quieting your mind include:

- Meditate to calm your mind. It's not always easy for everyone, so using a guided meditation might help. Joining a local meditation group may also help.

- Use a calming visualization, such as imagining a rose opening slowly, or feeling yourself floating in a boat down a quiet stream.

- Do Zentangle™ drawing or coloring

- Walk purposefully, which means walking while paying attention to everything in your surroundings and how you feet hit the ground.

- Listen to calming music you really enjoy or listen to music with words and sing along!

- Escape into a creative hobby that does not require words, such as art or crafting.

- Hug or pet your cat or dog, or take it for a walk.

4. Listen to Your Body

The stomach is called the second brain and actually generates more neurotransmitters than the brain. Intuition is often felt first in the body before the thoughts reach the mind. That 'knot in your stomach' or that 'gut feeling' are examples of intuitive body signals that are trying to get your attention. When you receive intuitive information, pay attention to how it comes through in your body. It could be tightness in your chest, or pressure behind your eyes, or even a sudden electric-like feeling coursing through your entire body. Any sudden or unexpected sensation in your body could be a clue that your intuition is kicking in.

⌐. Know the Difference
Between Intuition and Fear.

It is difficult to be intuitive when in an anxious or fearful state. When your body sends you feedback, it is important to distinguish between intuition and your own anxiety. The following chart can help you determine if your 'intuitive' hits are truly intuition or anxiety. Think about what you are sensing and look through the two columns on the chart and determine which best describes your sensations.

Intuitive information is...	Anxiety-based information is..
Neutral/unemotional	Emotionally charged
Focused on the present situation	Based on anxiety of a previous experience
Feels peaceful, good and positive	Fearful and provokes more anxiety

Clear and specific thoughts	Muddied with chatter
Like you are watching a movie. It can feel like a third person perspective.	Very personal. It feels like it is happening to you.

6. Practice

You need to practice regularly to strengthen your intuitive muscle. You can practice by intuitively sensing who is calling when the phone rings (without looking at the phone number). Sense what people are thinking or feeling and then verifying it with them. The more you use it, the easier it will be to 'hear' the information that you sense. It can become the most valuable tool on this journey!

A worried mom does
better research than the FBI.

www.ParentTees.com

Knowledge is Your Strength

"The good life is one inspired by love and guided by knowledge."
~ Bertrand Russell

Research is one of your strongest tools when it comes to helping your child. For so long we have put our trust in the doctors and professionals who diagnose our kids. In the world of special education, things are changing super fast. We have to stay on top of these changes. Experts these days are the people who continuously read and stay updated on new information. These experts are hard to find. YOU need to become the expert on your child's challenges so you can find ways to help. Research is how you gain that expertise.

When my older son was in Kindergarten, his teacher and a school psychologist talked to me about his attention issues. The school psychologist suggested I take him to the pediatrician to get him some medication (I found out later it was illegal for her to suggest that). They kept saying he was clearly ADD (attention deficit disorder). Since I had never thought of him as having ADD before, I decided to do my own research. This initial research forever changed my way of helping my child because it led me to find the first piece of his complex puzzle.

I started the research by looking for symptoms of ADD and found an article that compared ADD to APD (auditory processing disorder). The article talked about how similar the two diagnoses were and how often APD was misdiagnosed as ADD. As I read the list of APD symptoms, a massive light bulb was turned on. It had such an impact on me, I can still see the article in my mind. I read the symptoms of APD over and over. This is what my son had – I just knew it! Even though it took nine more months to get a definitive diagnosis, my mother's intuition told me I was right. This one experience taught me the value of research in helping my child.

Support Groups are Great Catalysts for Research

Do you wonder how you should start your research? It begins with your paying attention to what people say, and then investigating further to get a deeper understanding. Most of my ideas for research come from online support groups. While many groups are established to provide emotional support, many also share the latest research and information on disabilities. In addition, support group members tend to ask questions in different ways. They sparks ideas in your mind and give you other directions to explore. Dozens of times I've had posts by others in support groups spur a research bug in me that led to something that helped my kids. Read *Find Your Tribe* (chapter 10) for more information on how to find support groups.

Talk to Professionals in their language.

You need to learn the lingo in order to talk to doctors and specialists in their language. If you're going to see specialists, spend time beforehand looking up what they do and what they call it. Do some research on how to interpret their tests so you can ask intelligent questions. It will show that you are paying close attention to the process. Most professionals enjoy talking about their work. So they will teach you more about what they do if you show a curiosity about it.

I remember when my son had his first audiology exam I wanted to know what the charts and numbers all meant. I found *Essentials of Audiology* by Stanley Gelfand in Google Books. This audiology textbook taught me how to interpret audiology results. I sat with my son's report, reviewing and learning, and next time I went to the audiologist, I was able to ask her about some of the testing results she had not mentioned before. It helped me pinpoint my son's challenges so I was better able to find solutions that would work for him. The audiologist was very experienced, but not in the challenges my son had. If I had relied on her recommendations, we might not have found the right path to help him. This is why it is so critical that you do your own research!

Search Engine Strategies

Search engines index information at an amazing rate, but sometimes finding that information can be tricky. Results can vary with simple changes in words. Even adding an 's' to make a word plural can completely alter search results. It is important you know how to find the right information based on the information you input. The following suggestions are focused on Google because it is so popular, but the suggestions apply to any search engine.

- **Keywords:** Think of as many search terms as possible. Think like a professional as well as like a layman. The most common mistake people make is when they only search one or two ways and then give up figuring they can't find what they are looking for. You must persist! Think about not only formal terms (e.g. auditory processing disorder), but informal terms (e.g. trouble understanding what is heard). Consider acronyms (e.g. APD) and complementary phrases (e.g. difficulty understanding teacher in class). Also think like a professional (assessing auditory processing disorder) and like a parent (what are the signs of auditory processing disorder). The more keywords you can think of, the better luck you will have finding what you need. If necessary, use www.thesaurus.com to help you find similar words.

- **Different forms of words:** I mentioned changing a word from singular to plural can sometimes change the search results. Also consider changing from the active and passive forms of words (assessing vs. assessment). Also think of different ways to say the same thing ('how to' vs. troubleshoot).

Notated Search

Adding some notation to your search can help narrow or expand your results.

- **Quotes:** Search engines search for any word you put into the search box. If you want to search for a specific phrase, you must put it in quotation marks. For example, if you search for "auditory processing disorder," the search engine will search for that phrase in its entirety instead of each word individually.

- **Minus sign:** If you type a minus sign before a phrase (-ADHD), it will not show any links that have that term in it. A good example of this was one time we were searching for daycare for our children, and a bunch of doggy daycares came up in the results. So we searched again but put in –dog, and we got results with child daycares.

- **Number range:** If you want to look for a number range, put two periods between the numbers (e.g. 2015..2017). This is especially helpful for looking for information in certain time periods. You can do this with any numerical measure just by adding the unit of measure ($100..$200 or 45..75 lb).

- **Asterisk (*):** The asterisk creates a wild card word in your search and is very useful if you are not sure of all the words in a phrase. For example, "auditory * disorder" will return all results that have a phrase that starts and ends with those two words.

- **Google Tabs:** Google will automatically search its entire repository, but if you know the specific type of information you are looking for, using the tabs at the top can help you narrow it down. The tabs are: news, videos, images, shopping, maps, books, flights. You can also use the tools option to narrow the search by date. For example, you can search for results that have only been published in that last year.

- **File type:** If you are looking for a specific type of content, you can add the file suffix to find it. For example, if you want to find Acrobat documents, you search for them by including the 'pdf' in your search. Here are some common file type suffixes:

  - pdf: Acrobat PDF

- ppt: Powerpoint

- doc or docx: Microsoft Word document

- xls: Excel document

- jpg: JPEG image file

- png: PNG image file

- gif: GIF image file

- **Google Scholar:** If you are searching for research studies, try using Google Scholar (scholar.google.com) instead of the regular Google site. Google scholar is an index of scholarly literature such as books, academic research papers, dissertations, journal articles, etc.

Research is Part of the Process

While research is tedious, it really is indispensable to helping your child. You must become the expert on your child so you can talk to school personnel and professionals in an educated manner about current challenges and possible solutions. It is worth all the time it takes to acquire this valuable skill that will enable you to gather the information necessary to be the most effective advocate for your child.

19

Get to the Root Cause
of the Challenges

"Don't dwell on what went wrong. Instead, focus on what to do next.
Spend your energies on moving forward toward finding the answer."
~ Denis Waitley

Many people believe that once a child is diagnosed with a learning or cognitive disability, that disability will be a permanent challenge throughout the child's life. What if I told you that there could be an underlying cause that is fixable? This is not true in all cases, but what if that possibility existed for your child? How would that change your view of the diagnosis?

When my son was 6, I used to take him to a learning center that specialized in diagnosing ADHD (attention deficit hyperactivity disorder). During one of the visits the director told me that of all the kids who came into that center, 80% of them had something other than ADHD. These kids had all the symptoms of ADHD, and they had previously received a diagnosis for it. But when the learning center did their series of screenings, they would find underlying conditions that caused symptoms that looked like ADHD. The kids definitely had serious attention problems, but they were not due to chemical imbalances in the brain, which is the assumed cause of ADHD. Often they had already tried medication and it didn't help, and they came to the learning center to find a solution. The learning center evaluated for visual, auditory, and sensory processing, as well as unintegrated primary reflexes, vestibular issues and cross-lateral integration. The center had developed special therapies to improve whatever the processing deficits were, and the children's attention problems improved. The director of the learning center was the first person to tell me that my son did not have ADHD, he had auditory processing issues. He turned out to be right. He also offered us the first therapy that brought dramatic results.

We have to remember that 'diagnosis' of these issues is done based on observations and checklists. Doctors do not use a biological marker that can measure ADHD, dyslexia, autism or many other cognitive disabilities. Unless you do a QEEG brain map, it is a subjective diagnosis because it's based on the observation, opinion and experience of the assessor. If the person has no knowledge of alternative diagnoses, they are not going to recognize the signs of a differential diagnosis.

This was the case with the UCLA neuropsychologist who diagnosed our son with PDD-NOS when he was 6. I told her I suspected auditory processing disorder, but she said she checked his auditory processing and it was fine. He did have severe auditory processing issues, but this professional did not have the right training to diagnose it. Four months later he was diagnosed with severe auditory processing disorder by an audiologist. Clearly the neuropsychologist was mistaken. Because *she* didn't know she was wrong, it was so crucial that I knew she was wrong! Because it meant that all the verbal assessments she did were most likely invalid, and so her final diagnosis was also invalid!

When my son was 8 he had a QEEG brain map done by Dr. Barbara Blume in Ventura, California. This gave us our first glimpse into the real cause of his attention problems. It showed that he had very low theta brainwaves and very high beta brainwaves. Individuals with true ADHD have an opposite pattern, high theta and low beta. Theta brainwaves are present right before you go to sleep, when you wake up or when you are in meditation. This is a very calm, almost drowsy kind of a brainwave activity. ADHD brain patterns indicate the brain is not getting enough stimulation. That's why stimulants work because the stimulants help activate the brain. In our son's case, he didn't have

ENOUGH theta wave activity to help his mind calm down so he could relax and go to sleep. He also had too much beta wave activity, so his brain was going way too fast. He was thinking so fast he couldn't even grab the thoughts in order to utilize them.

Even though he had a diagnosis of severe ADHD (based on checklists and observation), he clearly did NOT have ADHD. If I had accepted that ADHD was his diagnosis, he probably would have ended up on medication, and that could have made it worse since his brain was already over stimulated. The QEEG brain map showed that he had post-concussive syndrome (PCS). Thankfully Dr. Blume is one of the leading experts on neurofeedback, and she was able to remediate the PCS with twice-weekly neurofeedback sessions.

I really want you to think about this because it applies to all diagnoses, including autism, dyslexia, and auditory processing disorder. All of these diagnoses could have another cause for the child's symptoms. If you just accept the diagnosis and say "this is my child's diagnosis, and she's going to struggle with it for the rest of her life," you may be missing an opportunity to fix the root of the problem. **The school is never going to look for a root cause, so it is up to you as the parent to take the reins and investigate the possibility!**

The diagnosis is a clue.

It's important for you to really look at the diagnosis as just a description of a set of symptoms. It's like a series of clues that help you hone in on what might be causing these issues.

Make up your own mind

I know parents who don't trust this approach. Many people talk about how crucial it is to accept a child the way he is. I do honor that, but again I ask you to think about whether or not you are willing to a turn a deaf ear to fixing an underlying issue.

I used to work for DM Easyread, a reading program that uses a visual approach to teaching phonics. They cater to kids who are visual-spatial learners, many of whom are diagnosed dyslexic. Learning to read is very difficult for children with dyslexia. I remember a parent telling me about her conversation with the pediatrician. When she told him that her son was diagnosed with dyslexia, the pediatrician's response was: "Oh my goodness, I'm so sorry. Your child's whole life is going to be a struggle because of the dyslexia."

The mom was in tears while telling the story. She was so worried her child would suffer. The child did brilliantly with the visual approach to reading. Through the process it was discovered he had a visual processing issue. Using the reading program and getting vision therapy allowed the boy to move ahead by leaps and bounds. But the mom was still worried. The pediatrician's words haunted her. Every time I talked to her, she would ask anxiously, "Is he going to get better? Is he going to be okay?"

The fact of the matter is that you will do everything you can to help your child. Clearly you want to find solutions; otherwise you wouldn't be reading this book. You will find ways to help him learn to manage his challenges. But, if you could help him overcome them, not just accommodate them, wouldn't that be even better?

In the world of autism, there are two polarized camps. There are the people who say, "Autism is just the way they were born. It's just the way their brain works." Then there's the other camp who says, "Autism is something that happens environmentally or physically to the child. These factors injure the brain, causing autism symptoms. If you can change diet, add supplements, and sometimes therapies, then the brain can get better."

I belong to a biomedical healing Facebook group that has over 35,000 parents in it. I have seen hundreds of stories where the children have dramatically improved or even completely recovered from 'autism.' They improved because the parents weren't willing to just say, "This is the way my kid was born." They followed their gut, and set out to investigate.

The whole world of biomedical healing is opening up because there is an epidemic of kids being diagnosed with autism and ADHD. Medical professionals are starting to wonder if maybe something else is going on. Maybe they're not just born with it. There are autistic adults who get upset when people talk about this. I don't mean to offend them. I am merely presenting an idea. You can take it if it resonates with you, and ignore it if it doesn't. I am speaking here to parents who wonder if there could be an underlying cause for their child's challenges. I know there are many who wonder if there is more they can do to help, but do not know where to turn for answers. It is these parents I am talking to. If you wonder if there is a root cause to your child's difficulties, then keep reading.

5 Steps to Uncovering the Root Cause

In my work with children I have found five stages to discovering underlying causes. It's important the first four stages be done in the proper sequence because one builds on the previous. I'm giving a brief overview of each one here, but you can do more research to learn about each step in depth.

STEP 1: Chemistry: Is the biology balanced?

Using the approach of functional medicine, consider if your child's biology is in some way out of balance. Looking at food sensitivities, vitamin deficiencies or intestinal health issues can start you in the right direction. You can have DNA analysis done that can give you clues on how your child's body is working and make appropriate adjustments to diet and supplements. You can do testing on the gut biome and body chemistry to see if there are imbalances that need correction. This approach is called biomedical healing. Through looking at the biology, you can heal the body, including the brain.

When people say that the learning challenge runs in the family, this is a huge clue that it could be in your DNA, or have something to do with lifestyle or environment. In our family we have MTHFR gene mutations that effect mood and cognitive functioning. The fix is easy diet and supplement changes. Yes, it runs in the family, but that does not mean it cannot be fixed.

STEP 2: Wiring: Is the neurological wiring in place?

If the biology is in balance, then look at neurological wiring. Even if your child has not had a head injury, there is a chance the neurology was not properly developed or was somehow interfered with. For example, children who have excessive ear infections often have malfunctioning vestibular systems. The ear infections impair auditory development, thus causing the vestibular system to not develop properly. There is something called the vestibular-ocular reflex that sends information to the eyes when the body moves. This information helps the eyes develop neurologically. This reflex is often absent in people with vestibular processing issues. The absence of this reflex would mean the eyes may not get the right information, and it could result in a visual processing disorder.

Primary reflexes are another example of body movement contributing to neurological development. When a baby moves, the movement sends information to develop the brain. Bouncy chairs, car seats and baby exercise saucers deprive many babies of critical movement in infancy. This prevents the primary reflexes from integrating and can hamper the neurological development.

Crawling is one of the most critical movements for a child because it helps develop the corpus callosum, the area of the brain that allows the two hemispheres to communicate. It also integrates the symmetrical tonic neck reflex (STNR), which is instrumental for proper learning. In a forward-thinking study by Miriam Bender, it was found that 75 percent of children with learning disabilities also did not crawl enough to integrate the STNR primary reflex (Bender 1976). In this same study she found that children with no learning disabilities all had a fully integrated STNR. Children with unintegrated STNR reflexes often have problems with sitting still, visual processing, reading, and writing. In addition they suffer from poor posture and clumsiness.

When I first learned about primary reflexes from Sonia Story at Move, Play, Thrive, I was amazed to discover the reason I was so accident-prone. I have broken all my limbs, and I often bumped into things, and I just thought I was clumsy. In learning about primary reflexes I discovered that my tonic labyrinthine reflex (TLR) was not integrated, and when I would move my head, my body would follow. At 43 years old I was able to do simple exercises to integrate this reflex and my clumsiness resolved. So even without a learning challenge, I still had under developed neurology that was affecting my coordination and caused me to be clumsy!

STEP 3: Processing: Is the neurology functioning properly?

So the wiring might be there, but is it working right? This is a common issue for kids who have had excessive ear infections as toddlers and end up having an auditory processing disorder. They were born with a functioning auditory cortex, but lack of stimulation caused by ear infections prevented it from functioning properly. Through therapies to stimulate the auditory system, it is possible to get it working again, resulting in auditory processing that will be significantly improved or even normal.

Sometimes it is difficult to determine if the issue is lack of wiring or lack of processing. You may have to go to several professionals to look at the problem from several perspectives before finding which one it is. Many times you will not know where the problem lies until you try a therapy and see results (or not see results). Remember that you are your child's expert, and it is your job to synthesize the information from multiple sources. Remember to follow your intuition, do your research, and learn as much as you can.

STEP 4: Knowledge:
Is the understanding there to know how to do something?

So once you know that the chemistry is right, the wiring is there and the processing is working, now the child can learn and retain information. If the child has been delayed for many years, this means that there is a learning gap. For example, a visual processing disorder that makes a child see double results in the child's being delayed in reading and writing. After vision therapy the child can see fine, so now she can get busy learning how to read and write.

Often when we find the root problem, we hope that simply resolving the issue will make everything better. Unfortunately the child will probably need some time to catch up, so focusing on learning and retaining information is the final step of the healing process.

STEP 5: Methods: Are the teaching methods in line with the child's learning style?

One big caveat is making sure you child is being taught in keeping with his learning style. A learning style is the optimum way for a child to take in information, and therefore the easiest way for the child to learn. General consensus says that there are three basic learning styles: visual-spatial, auditory-linear and kinesthetic. Most people have a combination of learning styles, but one dominant style. In some cases, a person can have a prevalent style and hardly use the other two at all. I would recommend getting your child evaluated to determine what your child's dominant learning style is. Even if your child has learning disabilities, teaching in the style that is his style will improve academic performance.

School is taught in a mostly auditory-linear fashion, so students with visual-spatial or kinesthetic styles are often at a disadvantage. Auditory-linear learning used to be the most prevalent learning style, but visual-spatial is becoming more prevalent as children are exposed to technology from an early age. Kinesthetic is the least common learning style so the least used method for teaching.

To understand your child's learning style, and find ways to teach to it, I highly recommend *Discover Your Child's Learning Style: Children Learn in Unique Ways - Here's the Key to Every Child's Learning Success* by Mariaemma Willis and Victoria Hodson.

Become an investigator.

If you are open to this idea of looking for a root cause, then you need to put on your investigator's hat! Search every corner and under every rock to find answers. Be open to new ideas, and if something strikes you intuitively as an idea that might help, follow up.

When our son was 6 we were told he would need group home care as an adult. Last year he finished 8th grade as an honor student. In high school he is taking general education classes and will receive accommodations, but no longer has a one-on-one aide. In his IEP meetings everybody talks about plans for college. None of this would have happened if I had not pursued the underlying causes of his cognitive issues. I can tell you from personal experience, there is nothing like that moment of realization that an issue is totally behind you!

20

Schools Can't Share Medical Concerns

"Nothing and no one is perfect. It just takes a good eye to find those hidden imperfections."
~ Daphne Delacroix

I'll never forget the day my younger son told me he saw double. We were playing a board game, and I was contemplating my next move, and he said, "Look mom, I can see two of you!" He thought it was so cool, but when I looked up at his face, I saw one eye turned in towards his nose and the other eye looking straight. I did what any rational mom would do — I freaked and did my best to hide it!

I knew about visual processing disorders, but I didn't know anything about seeing double, and definitely nothing about eyes turning inward. I gave him the third degree to find out all the details. How often it happened and what kind of problems it caused. It turned out it had been an on-again, off-again problem for many years, and we never had a clue. Suddenly it made sense to me why my son avoided soccer and baseball and refused to ride his bike. A trip to a behavioral optometrist diagnosed alternating, intermittent strabismus, and the doctor prescribed vision therapy.

What really amazed me though was he had serious problems with reading and writing, and not a single person at the school mentioned that he might have a visual processing disorder. He worked with an occupational therapist for writing, and a resource teacher for reading. Their approach to fixing his challenges was more repetition of the same process they had been doing for years – and with minimal improvement. Nobody ever even hinted that there might be an underlying reason for his difficulties. And of course, as the tiger mom that I was, I wanted to know why. And so they got the third degree too. I **discovered one of the most crucial reasons why it is YOUR job to lead your child's team:**

The school cannot tell you about possible medical problems.

There are three reasons why the school can't tell you about a possible medical problem your child presents symptoms of:

1. It is unlawful to practice medicine without a license.

All states have a law that says it is unlawful to practice medicine without a license, and diagnosis is one aspect of practicing medicine. School personnel can recommend seeing your family doctor, but they dare not mention the diagnosis they suspect. Similarly, when a child fails a vision screening, they can only state that the child should see an eye doctor. On the other hand, if they suspect the child has a visual processing disorder, they are not allowed to refer the child to a behavioral optometrist for vision therapy. That would be reaching into diagnostic territory.

Of course when I first heard this I thought to myself, "How ridiculous is that?!" I mean, if they know of a disorder, and they know of somebody who may be able to help the child, they are required to ignore that information or withhold the information from the parents? But the reasoning behind this law is sound. Unless a school employee is a doctor (which is rare), they do not have the training to diagnose medical conditions. As such, while wanting to be helpful, there is a high probability they err on a diagnosis and therefore on their recommendations. Just look at the number of teachers who are quick to label kids ADHD because they can't sit still in class.

In my younger son's case, if he had failed his vision screening, he would have been referred to an optometrist or ophthalmologist. Unfortunately those kinds of doctors do not usually diagnose visual processing disorders. Visual processing issues seem to be the primary domain of behavioral optometrists. But even if a teacher or school staff suspects a visual processing disorder, it is against the law for them to tell you to take your child to a behavioral optometrist or to obtain vision therapy to correct it. A behavioral optometrist is the only kind of doctor who can actually correct the problem, however despite this, school staff could face disciplinary action if they tell you about it.

By the same token, the school is not allowed to suggest medical treatment for your child's problems. That means EVERYBODY in a school who is not a medical doctor cannot even whisper the suggestion that your child should be on medication. Unfortunately this is a common problem in the schools where teachers are desperate to insure classroom discipline and teaching are easier. A teacher or school psychologist can NEVER suggest medication to help your child with behavior or attention problems.

This happened with a parent I was working with whose son had serious problems focusing and doing his schoolwork. He tended to get very agitated when there was a lot of loud noise, and he often acted out by having a temper tantrum. The teacher was new on the job, and she was completely ineffective at controlling the students, let alone a hyperactive child who appeared to not listen. It was actually the school psychologist who did some testing and found through the Connors scale that the boy qualified for a diagnosis of ADHD. She didn't actually diagnose him, but she did tell the parents they should visit the pediatrician, show him the results of the assessment, and ask for a prescription.

This was advice from a district that refused to give the child any support that would help him with his disruptive behavior. They just wanted the parents to get a pill to fix it. The parents could have reported them to the California Board of Education, as it is 100% against the law for the school to do this. Instead the parents chose to use this as a negotiating tool, which led to getting the accommodations he needed.

2. Medical services are outside "appropriate" education.

IDEA (Individuals with Disabilities Education Act) states that the schools provide "appropriate" education, not maximize the potential of the student. Appropriate education means education that is commensurate with non-disabled students, which does not include medical care. So they are not required by law to provide services that are found outside of the typical school setting.

I have a colleague who works as an occupational therapist with children who have physical disabilities such as cerebral palsy or severe brain injury. Her job is to help the children with gross and fine motor skills. She also has some students who have severe difficulty eating. Outside a school setting swallowing and eating therapy falls under the domain of an occupational therapist, but because this therapist works in the school, she is not allowed to perform swallowing or eating therapy. Many of her students are tube fed and want to learn to eat with their mouths, but she is not allowed to help them to learn to eat food that way. It is beyond the scope of 'appropriate' education.

Similarly, mental health services are not considered 'appropriate' education. Psychological challenges such as depression, anxiety or other mood disorders can significantly impact a child's ability to participate in school. Thankfully some lobbyists (both at state and federal levels) are working to add mental health services to regular school services. If your child exhibits mental health difficulties, the school will provide you a list of resources outside the school, but it is not required to have resources in school. The students whose IEP qualification is under emotional disturbance (ED) can receive mental health services in school. That qualification means that the problem has a significant impact on the students' capacity to access the curriculum. But the ED qualification is only for the most severe cases, and it is not easy to get, so don't count on in-school help.

Some schools receive grants from local non-profits in order to provide services to non-disabled children with emotional challenges. In our town a local non-profit provides these services to students who contend with traumatic events such as divorce, death of a family member or homelessness. These programs are the rare exception, and so it is difficult to prove the school must provide these services when they do not fall into the 'appropriate' education category.

3. The schools don't want to foot the bill.

If the school does refer your child to a specialist, and the doctor or therapist finds the child needs therapy or special treatment, the school may have to foot the bill. While there is no specific law requiring this, there have been parents who have sued the schools. In some cases, the court ruled that because the school suggested the doctor visit, they have to pay for it. So while this is not specified in Section 504 or IDEA, case law establishes the precedent. As a result, schools avoid giving out referrals to physicians in order to avoid being stuck with the bill. You would probably have to sue to get reimbursement, but with precedent already set, you have a good chance of prevailing.

It is your job to research medical challenges.

These three reasons are why it is SO critical that as the parent, you take up the gauntlet, do your research, and find out if there is any underlying medical issues that could be causing your child's learning challenges.

In the case of my younger son, a year of vision therapy, and $6,000 later, his problem has been permanently corrected. He has become an avid reader and he reports he can now see the lines he has to write on. His handwriting improved dramatically and he is willing, and at times eager, to do his schoolwork. He also loves to bike ride now. Imagine that! Had it gone on, his brain would have turned off vision in his left eye, he would have lost binocular vision, and he would have had serious depth perception problems the rest of his life.

If you want to read an amazing case of vision therapy improving vision, I highly recommend *Fixing My Gaze: A Scientist's Journey Into Seeing in Three Dimensions* by Susan R. Barry.

21

Choose Alternatives
Beyond the Schools

"The things that have been most valuable to me I did not learn in school."
~ Will Smith

When my older son started third grade he was reading at a Kindergarten level. The school's suggestion was to increase his resource time, which meant he would do more of the same reading routine. They were certain more effort and repetition would catch him up. I was not convinced. It just didn't make sense because in the past three years, more repetition had not helped. I looked outside the school for something we could do at home. I found DM Easyread, a reading program done at home that used his visual-spatial strengths to learn to read phonetically. Eight months into the program our son was reading at grade level.

When our younger son exhibited phonics challenges at the end of Kindergarten, I immediately knew what to do. We put him on the same reading program in June of his Kindergarten year. By the time he started first grade he was reading at grade level.

You need to take charge
of your child's education.
....

As parents we all expect that the school will handle all the learning needs of our children, but the truth is, they often cannot or will not. No matter what the circumstances are at your child's school, you should be looking for options outside of school for ways to supplement your child's education. This is especially true if the school is making it difficult to get services. As you struggle with that battle, your child continues to fall behind.

I know many are saying, "Wait a minute, I'm the parent, not a teacher!" Truth be told, you are your child's ultimate teacher. You are the one who will stay with her from infancy until adulthood. It is up to you to ensure your child's academic success. So yes, it is your job to help your child in ways the school won't. Maybe you will get lucky and the school will step up, but until that happens, you need to take on the task of helping your child to keeping moving forward.

Be aware of the emotional toll on your child.

From an academic standpoint it is hard for your child to have a learning disability. Over time it becomes an emotional issue as well. As the child's sense of frustration grows, and peers are doing things better with less effort, the child's self-esteem can begin to plummet. She may begin to feel stupid and ineffective, and school becomes something to be hated and avoided. The further your child falls behind, the harder it will be to catch up. This compounds the emotional issues.

You need to choose your battles when the school is uncooperative.

Fighting a school district takes time, and during that time your child is not getting the support she needs. If you find yourself in a protracted process, you may consider alternative schooling options until you work things out with the district. Many moms pull their kids and do homeschooling, or temporarily move the child to a private school. Some parents will pay for an aide to come work at the school, which could bolster the case for needing a full time aide for your child. Others hire after school tutors to provide specific programs or just help with homework. Many undertake the tutoring role themselves.

Find alternatives.

Of course the ultimate hope is that the school will provide the support and services that are needed. In the meantime, consider how you can help your child so she can continue to learn. Research and find teaching programs that you can do at home:

1. Join support groups online and ask other parents what they have done to help their child.

2. Research homeschooling curricula for your child's specific challenges. You can use homeschool educational materials even if you don't homeschool because it provides additional instruction to help your child.

3. Investigate programs that are directed towards your child's learning issues. For example, DM Easyread, a reading program geared towards children with dyslexia; or Math-U-See which is uses physical manipulatives to teach math to students with dyscalculia. There are many alternative teaching approaches that can be used to help your child understand the material that is being taught in school. Just do your research, read reviews and find other parents who have used the program to make sure it is a good fit for your child.

Helping your child improve skills.

Sometimes the best help you can give your child is to find therapies that will improve her skill deficits. For example, if a child is having difficulty sitting still, seeking out occupational therapy or brain development therapies can make it easier for them to stay on task in school. Skills therapies come in many different forms, including:

- Occupational therapy
- Listening therapy
- Movement therapy
- Social skills groups
- Brain training

- Assistive technology
- Cognitive behavioral therapy (counseling)
- Biomedical healing
- Vision therapy
- Sensory integration therapy

Not all programs are going to work for all children, so be diligent in your research.

1. Ask parents in your support groups about therapies that have worked for their child.

2. Investigate therapies that were specifically created to address your child's disability.

3. Research homeschooling curriculum or activities that are focused on helping kids with learning issues.

4. Find programs where you can be trained to administer them at home for less than the cost of seeing a practitioner.

5. Avoid programs that either promise to 'cure' your child's learning challenges, or those that insist they are the only program that can achieve results.

Do your homework before you sign up.

Many learning and therapeutic programs will rave about how successful they are. It is important you investigate thoroughly and make certain it is a right fit for your child. Many of these programs can cost a lot of money and take a lot of time, both of which are precious in helping your child. You want to make sure your investment is going to get the results you are seeking.

- Use a search engine to find reviews about the program. To do this, type "program name" + review in your search engine. As an example, if you wanted to get reviews for peanut butter therapy (obviously a fictitious therapy), you would type this phrase: "peanut butter therapy" + review.

- Search for "program name" + Scam. This may seem harsh, but it is very important to see what negative comments have been written about the program. Even if you don't believe the negative comments, they should become part of the information you use to make your choice.

- Ask online and in-person support groups if anybody else has used the program and what the outcome was.

- Look for case studies of other children who had success with the program. Note if the child in the case study had similar symptoms or challenges as your child.

- Research the science behind the programs you are considering to make sure it is valid. Some programs will not have research. But do not discard them because of that. Some of the best things that helped our kids did not have formal research to back them up. I'm just saying if they do provide research, make sure the research is administered by an experienced researcher.

- Find out how the program administrators respond if your child is not progressing and how they would remedy the problem.

- Find out what kind of support they provide if you are struggling to do the program at home, or you do not understand how to implement certain parts.

- Find out if there is a money back guarantee. Some programs do provide this because they realize not all programs are going to work for all children. This makes it easier to give it a try.

The early years are the best years to help your child with out-of-school options, but no child is too old to gain improvements from therapies. I encourage you to accept your role as the your child's master teacher, and find ways to supplement your child's public education. The more you can do to help now, the easier it will be for your child in the future.

22

Help Your Child Understand His Disability

"I choose not to place 'DIS' in my ability."
~ Robert M. Hensel

I worked with a middle school student who was having many angry outbursts in class. She started to skip classes and even hid in the library because school was such a challenge for her. When she explained what was going on in class, upon checking her IEP, I realized the teachers did not offer her the accommodations spelled out in her IEP. She did not know she could ask for them. Worse yet, I discovered that she did not even know about her IEP plan, and she had no idea she had a learning disability. When I explained what it was, she got very agitated and expressed dismay at the thought that something was 'wrong' with her. She was in 8th grade and nobody had ever talked about her learning disability or why she had an IEP!

Why we avoid talking about disabilities.

Not talking about a disability doesn't mean it isn't there. Many disabilities are hidden disabilities, and parents choose to not tell their children because they believe the information may be difficult for the child to hear. Your child will know on some level he is different, and he is already in pain due to his challenges in school. If nobody is talking about it, he may interpret it as something 'really bad.' You may be afraid to tell your child about his disability because:

- You believe the information will cause him emotional pain.
- You believe it will damage his self-esteem.
- You think he will use it as an excuse to not complete work.
- You think he may become upset when he finds out he has a disability.
- You do not want him to feel different.

Why you have to talk to your child about his disability:

Your child has a challenge, and you need to share it with him. If your child had physical illness, would you explain it to him? Of course you would! Then why would you not explain an intellectual or learning disability to your child? You need to talk to him because:

- **It is crucial he understands his disability so he can self-advocate for the support he needs.** Withholding this information is not going to protect him. On the contrary, it will in fact make school much harder.
- **Your child probably notices he has challenges in school that other students don't have.** He will have a lot of unanswered gnawing questions. Talking to him about it provides an opportunity to get these questions answered.
- **If your child understands his disability, he is better able to self-advocate** and get the support he needs.

If you consider the topic too touchy, perhaps a counselor can help you work through your concerns. It may feel overwhelming at first, but with professional help you can overcome your uneasiness and feel comfortable addressing the issues.

When should you tell your child about his disability?

Not all children are ready to hear about their disability. Depending on the age, maturity and communication skills, you may not choose to have an in-depth conversation. If he is young, perhaps first or second grade, you may talk to him about his challenges without giving it a specific label. If he is in high school, he may want to hear all the details.

When he questions his challenges, the time is ripe to share information. For example, if he talks about not working as fast as the other kids, or about getting in trouble for behaviors he cannot control, it is time to explain to him how his disability effects him. If you avoid telling him, it can amplify the child's anxiety and possibly impact his self-esteem.

If the child is struggling in school and you see it affecting his self-esteem, it is time to enlighten him about why he is having a difficult time. It is not good to keep pushing him to try harder, when more effort is not really going to resolve the problem.

If the child is being teased at school about his disability, then it is particularly important to help him understand his differences. Consider doing some disability awareness training in his class to help the other students understand that everybody has challenges.

It is important that you be the first person to talk to your child about his disability before he accidentally hears it from somebody else. Teachers and staff at school are not always cognizant of their words. If a child overhears the teacher talk about his disability, it will be shocking if the child has never heard it before.

Talking to your child about his disability.

Talking to your child about his disability requires you to balance your child's need to know with his ability to comprehend what you are sharing. You want to be positive in your approach, always focusing on the balance between strengths and challenges. You should use age-appropriate language so he understands what you are explaining. It may be a conversation that happens once in a while and evolves over time into a more detailed explanation.

For a younger child you may never even use the word disability, but instead just talk about his challenges and strengths and how everybody has things that are easy and hard. For a child in middle or high school, you may go through all the steps, and he may ask to read more about his disability or request in-depth explanations. You know your child; use your intuition about how much or how little to share.

I've talked to many kids about their disabilities, and this is the general sequence that I use to share the information:

1. The first step is to have a conversation about things that are hard at school. Talk about how his challenges affect his ability to do his schoolwork, and reassure him that he is not the only student who has difficulties in school. There are a lot of people who have these kinds of issues, so it's important to approach the conversation in this way. Make sure your child knows that he is not the only person in the world with these difficulties.

2. Ask what sort of things help to make the challenges easier. For example, perhaps taking tests in a quieter room will help if he is sound sensitive. Help him to see when he gets help and support the challenges are not as monumental as when he is left solely on his own.

3. Remind him that everybody has strengths and weaknesses. Talk about different family members and their strengths and weaknesses. Emphasize that no matter the challenges, he has the ability to succeed in school and in life. If you have the same disability, it is particularly important that you share this with him. If you withhold it and he finds it out later, it could imply the disability is something shameful.

4. Explain to him what an 504 or IEP plan is (depending on what he has). Go through his plan and show him the information about the support he is meant to receive.

5. Talk to him about what a disability is. The Merriam-Webster Dictionary defines disability as: *a physical, mental, cognitive, or developmental condition that impairs, interferes with, or limits a person's ability to engage in certain tasks or actions or participation in typical daily activities and interactions.*

   Provide your child with examples of obvious disabilities, like a person who can't walk and uses a wheelchair. Then provide examples of less obvious disabilities, like a person who has a hard time hearing. Perhaps there are other children in school who have more obvious disabilities, or characters in TV shows that the child watches. Help him see that disabilities are not uncommon.

6. Talk to him about his specific disability. If it is age appropriate, share the formal name (dyscalculia, dyslexia, sensory processing disorder, etc.). Talk about the general description and how it effects him in school and in life.

7. Give him examples of people who have had the same challenges but went on to be successful.

8. Ask if he has any concerns or questions about his disability.

9. Find age-appropriate books about his disability so he can see that other children have similar challenges and how they cope and overcome their issues.

Remember that you are embarking on new territory with your child, and there is not just one way to handle it. I have merely offered guidelines. Use your own intuition and consider the age and personality of your child to determine what, when and how much to say. Keep reminding yourself that something is better than nothing because it keeps the door open for communication

POINTS to PONDER

- What have you done to help your child understand his disability?

- Are you comfortable talking to your child about his disability, or should you seek some support for this conversation?

- When would be a good time to talk to your child about his disability? Set a date and time at a place where you will not be interrupted. Perhaps plan a walk in the park, a special meal or a favorite place to visit to open the conversation.

23

Foster Your
Child's Strengths

*"Disability is a matter of perception. If you can do
just one thing well, you're needed by someone."*
~ Martina Navratilova

Focus on what your child can do, not what she can't do. If you always focused on where your child struggles, she will internalize this negative thought pattern. I know it's difficult when you see other parents with neurotypical kids and they have none of the challenges you and your child have to contend with. It feels unfair! If you fixate on fairness, or that someone else's child doesn't have to deal with all these problems, you will be miserable.

While with special ed kids, I have noticed a trend with Special Ed Moms. They are so intent on helping their child succeed, they become hyper focused on the problem. They completely forget about the good things. Parents often do not realize that their words and actions make a lasting impression on their child. When you focus on fixing the 'problem,' the child internalizes the message: "I am broken. I need to be fixed."

I know personally how hard it is to keep the big picture in mind. A majority of your time is spent on making sure your child gets the right support. You need to focus on the details in order to get the proper help, and to make sure the school follows through on it.

Unfortunately the 'I need to be fixed' message the child gets from home is blended with the child's experiences at school. This sense of being different is amplified as he compares himself to peers. It is the adolescent and early teenage years when a sense of 'I am different. I need to be fixed' thought process can manifest as anxiety or depression. This compounds the actual school challenges.

Be proactive to make sure your child understands why you are so focused on helping him with school. Help him understand that he is not broken, he just needs an extra boost.

Teach about being different.

While we do have to focus on finding solutions, it is important to take time to explain to your child that everybody is different in some way. Differences do not make us broken or bad or in any way less than other people. Differences are what make each of us unique. Point out some of the differences you see in their world. For example, your child may be great at sports and other kids struggle with it. Some kids speak with accents and others may have difficulty speaking clearly. Kids can be a wizard in one subject and bottom of the class in the another. Everybody has a variety of strengths and weaknesses.

Ask your child:

- What can you do really well?
- Are there kids in school who aren't good at that?
- What is really hard for you or you aren't good at?
- Are there kids at school who are really good at that?

Help your child understand that her differences aren't bad or something that makes her broken. Everybody is good at something, so her strengths make her stand out. The sum of her strengths and weaknesses make her unique.

Teach her about her disability.

It helps to educate your child about her challenges. Read Chapter 22, *Help Your Child Understand His Disability*, and find ways to talk honestly about it. If your child had diabetes, would you hide that from her? No, you would inform her about what she needs to know so she could make proper choices to take care of her body. The same is true of a learning challenge, sensory issue, behavioral difficulty or physical challenge. Help her understand that everybody needs help with something, so it is okay to ask for help when she needs it. In other words, just because she needs help doesn't mean she is broken or less than somebody else.

Reinforce their strengths by creating a dream.

While it is rewarding to compliment our child on what he is good at, it can become old to keep saying, "Wow, you are really good at such-and-such!" Instead find ways to demonstrate positive outcomes that result from your child's talent.

Both our boys are very skilled in math. I help them understand the value of this skill by talking about how math impacts the world. I talk about architecture or engineering, where math is a necessity. I found math puzzles and math games that I thought they would feel successful as they played. I showed them fractals and explained that each design actually comes from a mathematical equation.

Help your child get excited and intrigued by her strength so she realizes the value of it. Show her how her strength can morph into something wonderful. This will help your child develop a positive self image despite her learning challenges.

Help your child find her niche.

I work with a boy named Jordan, who is in 9th grade, and has a very good sense of self. He's okay being different and not always fitting in. He has a lot of interests in math, engineering and the environment, but not so much sports, music or girls. As a result, he often feels left out of conversations with peers. He realizes this makes him different.

When I asked why it doesn't bother him that he isn't always interest-ed in the same things as his peers, he said it's because his parents taught him that he would find peers who would have mutual interests. Even if he didn't fit into these everyday conversations, he knows he can talk to other friends about mutual interests, and then he is one of the gang. As long as he knows he can find this group, he's okay when he doesn't join conversations with other peers.

Help your child find that group. It could be a sport, or extra curric-ular activity or even a specific class in school. Help her find other kids with similar interests so she can feel a part of the group. This will help her to cherish her strengths, and to understand that she is not broken, just unique.

24

Do Not Compare
Your Child

"Learn not to compare yourself to other people
because comparison will clip your wings and shoot you down."
~ Euginia Herlihy

As a Special Ed Mom, I know the desire to compare is always there. Whenever you see her with others, or discuss her progress in school, you want to know if your child is on par with other students. It is very difficult to resist the urge because comparison seems like the best barometer of your child's progress. Also, if your child comes out ahead, then you feel you have earned some bragging rights.

Comparing is okay if it is merely a tool to help you measure current progress. It is a problem when comparison is used as a yardstick to push your child to improve or to compete. This may cause your child to feel inferior. It can then affect her sense of self-worth.

If you measure her against typically developing children, you are never going to get an accurate measure. One typical child is vastly different from another, so which comparison is accurate? Think about that for a moment. Which child should you hold up as the yardstick since they are all so different?

The same is true if you compare her to other children with disabilities. I've heard it said many times that if you've met one kid with autism, you've met one kid with autism; it's the same with ADHD, dyslexia or any disability. The challenges and reaction of a disability are so varied. Don't generalize just because the diagnosis is the same. People respond very differently even with the same talents. Do you think all singers are the same just because they can sing well? Can you compare one painter to another, or are they all equally good but good in different ways? Comparison is a very inaccurate method for determining if your child is measuring up.

Comparison erodes self-esteem

It is typical for a child to compare oneself to her peers. Your child will notice the things she does differently or inadequately, and that may lead her to question her self-worth. Even though this is a natural tendency, teach her to measure herself against her own past achievements. You can teach her this by making sure she knows that you value her individual growth, not by comparing her progress to the herd.

When you measure her achievements against others, you are implying that you wish she were different. She already struggles with school structure that demands she fit in, so don't send another fit-in message. That message also teaches her that how she stacks up against others is more important than her own progress. Because her focus is now external to herself, she will not pay attention to her progress or achievements. She will also forever feel inadequate because there is always be somebody who can do it better. For a child with learning disabilities, this can be very self-defeating because there will be areas where she will not be able to keep up with peers, let alone surpass them. It may cause her to give up all together because no matter how much effort she puts in, she cannot perform better than the other students. So what is the point of trying?

Avoid creating undue pressure

Your child is already struggling to keep up because of learning challenges, and the comparison to peers increases the pressure to 'try harder.' This creates even more stress for the child who is already under pressure to put in extra effort to get things done. Research has clearly shown that stress diminishes the brain's ability to process information, so increasing pressure to improve is not going to help. If anything, she will have an even greater challenge and will likely perform worse.

Comparing focuses on the negative.

When your child measures herself based on the performance of peers, she automatically focuses on where she is falling short. Instead of focusing on those areas where she is doing well or excelling, she will focus on where she is doing poorly. This negative focus causes her to feel like she will never do well enough, and she may internalize an ongoing sense of failure.

When a child is competing with other children, this can also create an atmosphere of rivalry. If you are constantly telling your child to be the best or to try harder, she may begin to resent the children she is trying to perform better than. If they weren't so good, she wouldn't have to try so hard. As a result, your child may begin acting out against these other kids. In siblings you'll see it come out as bickering or fighting. In school it may come out as teasing or bullying. Children who feel they do not measure up will often find ways to make their rival feel bad.

Rivalry is particularly keen between siblings, especially when the achievements of one sibling are measured against the other sibling. Avoid saying, "You should be more like your brother/sister!" While it is natural that parents see the differences in their children, never verbally measure one child against the other. This will set up a life-long rivalry that is difficult to overcome.

Lack of achievement can become a self-fulfilling prophecy.

Constantly telling your child she does not measure up may eventually lead to your child's believing you. That belief could cause her to stop trying – just give up altogether. If children with learning issues fall further behind as they get older, you are making the problem worse if you keep emphasizing the differences.

Instead of comparing, foster achievement.

Give up the need to compare your child with a general yardstick. Instead, focus on helping her utilize internal measures for success. Here are some suggestions for fostering positive achievement:

1. **Compare against previous success.** Look at the past measures for your child. Use them as a way to help her improve. I'm not suggesting you use grades, but instead the volume and quality of work. This is the approach used when setting goals in IEPs. For example, if she is not good at sports, but she is required to run a mile once a month at school, encourage her to improve her running time. Even if it is only a ten-second improvement, it is still an improvement.

2. **Acknowledge her strengths.** Acknowledge the subjects and tasks that come easily to her. Don't focus on what she cannot do. Be happy about what she excels at. Those moments of success will counter balance the moments that are difficult.

3. **Keep your expectations reasonable.** How much she improves or achieves should be measured based on her capabilities. If you expect too much, you set her up for failure and she may give up. If you do not expect enough, she will not try harder.

4. **Teach your child to ask for help.** All children struggle at times, so remind her that it is okay to speak up when she encounters difficulty. She must learn that it is okay to admit when she cannot do something on her own. Recognizing the need for help, and not feeling ashamed to ask, is in itself a measure of achievement for her.

5. **Provide unconditional support.** Whether your child achieves her goals or not, remind her that you are there to support and cheer her on. Dealing with disappointment is just as important as having success, so it is crucial she know she can come to you no matter the outcome. It's the effort, not the result, that counts!

POINTS to PONDER

1. Identify the areas that you compare your child to other children.

2. What areas does your child need to improve? What measure has been used in the past that you can utilize to show progress in the future?

3. What areas does your child have some success? How do you acknowledge these areas of success?

THE ONLY DISABILITY in THE LIFE is A BAD ATTITUDE

Scott Hamilton

www.ParentTees.com

Teach Your Child
to Self-Advocate

"I learned a long time ago the wisest thing I can do is be on my own side, be an advocate for myself and others like me."
~ Maya Angelou

Working in the schools, I am amazed how often a student is not aware of the accommodations he is entitled to in his IEP or 504 plan. The teachers are aware that an IEP or 504 is in place, but often the teachers fail to implement those accommodations. I have seen situations where teachers need to be reminded many times about accommodations. Sometimes teachers even outright refuse to provide them. It is very apparent that special education students need to learn how to self-advocate so they can make sure they get the proper support that has been approved for them.

Please don't think I'm bashing the teachers. I know how hard these teachers work. They're not denying accommodations to hurt your child. Although not all teachers are the same, most are doing it because they have too much on their plates. They're really doing the best that they can. Sometimes there are teachers who do not understand how important the accommodations are to your child. In that case you must babysit them. Document issues and create a paper trail to help, and if you have to, go to the case manager. In some cases the teacher says no because it is an inconvenience. Some will say, "It's not fair if I do that for you, then the other kids are going to want it." All these refusals to provide accommodations are illegal. Your child needs to know he can ask for them. He also needs to know what to say and what to do when the teacher resists. This includes learning how to report it to somebody at school who can help fix the situation.

Self-advocacy is a skill that the child has to develop over time. They are never too young to start. Even in kindergarten and first grade you can help your child learn what support is needed in order to get his schoolwork done. For example, let's say you have a child with ADHD, and he has difficulty sitting still. He needs movement breaks. If the teacher keeps saying "get in your seat, get in your seat," he must learn to say to the teacher "I'm allowed to move around." It doesn't matter what age the child is, you need to teach him that he has a right to get what he needs.

How do you teach a child to self-advocate?

There is a step-by-step process that I have developed and use very effectively with students. I'm referring here to children who have learning disabilities, have an IEP or 504 with accommodations, and who have the ability to know when to ask for what they need. The age and capability of the student is going to determine whether or not you can implement all or some of these steps. You cannot teach all these steps in one day. Find a pace that works for your child. You have to repeat steps over and over again before it sinks in, and that is okay.

1. Teach him about his disability

I'm sure that your child is already aware of challenges he has in school, but he may not know why. In chapter 22 (*Help Your Child Understand His Disability*), I go through a series of steps that you can use to teach him about his disability. It is an important conversation to have because it can help your child feel okay with his challenges. It also sets the stage for understanding why he is allowed to ask for extra help.

2. Explain his 504 or IEP plan to him.

Step two is talking about what a 504 or IEP is. Again, the age will determine the depth of this conversation. For a younger child, it may be a very simple conversation, "In school when things are extra hard for you, they have a plan to help." You don't have to go into details about it. With a high school student though, you show him the IEP or 504 plan. Talk about his difficulties in school and explain that this is the reason the plan was created. If it is an IEP plan, show him the goals that have been created. Help him understand the value of these goals. Explain how any services he receives help him achieve his goals.

3. Talk about the accommodations in detail.

Pull out the accommodation sheet in the 504 or IEP plan. Ask your child how the accommodations help at school. Ask him if he knew he was allowed to ask for them. Every student I worked with had no awareness they were allowed to ask for this help, so don't take it for granted that your child knows it.

If your child can write, have him write down the first accommodation on a separate piece of paper. If he can't write, then you write it. Once the accommodation is written, ask him why he needs this accommodation. You have him put into his own words why this helps him. It is really important that the child understand how this accommodation is helpful in school. Not only is this educating the child, but it helps create memory triggers: "Oh, this is when I can ask for help."

Now ask him how he can get the accommodation. In most cases he will have to ask the teacher for the accommodation. Some accommodations may have some procedures or limits. For example, he may get to take movement breaks, but the breaks are limited to three breaks per day. Implementation of the accommodation may require a specific action; the student shows the teacher a colored card, and then gets up and walks out for a break. He may have the right to take tests in a quiet room, but only if he requests it. If he doesn't know how to get the accommodation, talk about how he would ask for it.

Go through each accommodation. Write down what the accommodation is, have him explain why it helps, and have him write down how to request the accommodation.

4. Inform teachers about the accommodations.

Now you want to make a copy of the list both of you made in step #3. The original list should stay in the student's notebook so he can have it as a reference. The copies should be given to all teachers or staff who work with your child in a learning environment.

If he is in elementary school, then you can take the copy to the teacher. Bring your child with you so he is present when you tell the teacher, "We have reviewed Sam's accommodations so he understands when he's allowed to ask for help. He knows that there are certain accommodations (point to items on the list) you will give him automatically each day. He won't have to ask you for these. There are other accommodations he knows he has to ask for, and he knows how to ask. Please remind him if he forgets to ask. This is written in his own words so you know that he understands what he needs." The teacher has been put on notice that the student is aware that he is supposed to receive these accommodations.

In middle school, if the child is mature enough, he should take the accommodations list to each teacher and basically say the same thing: "These are my accommodations. I know why and when I'm allowed to ask for them. I wanted you to know, if I do ask for them, they are on my IEP/504 plan."

Most kids in high school should be able to do this on their own, but not all of them. If the child needs assistance in high school, ask his case manager, school counselor or a familiar teacher to assist the student. Having somebody besides you help approach the teachers will facilitate more independence for your child.

5. Check in with your child.

Check in with your child, perhaps once a week, or perhaps every other week. Do not check in every day because it will drive him crazy. When you check in, ask him:

- How are things going in class?

- Do you have any difficulties with any of the assignments?

- Have you had to use any of your accommodations?

- Has the teacher been providing your accommodations?

If he brings up something that was difficult in school, ask him if he requested his accommodations. In the beginning, be prepared for him to say no. Even though you went through a whole process of teaching about the accommodations, he may not remember, and he needs reminding. Do not get upset or be judgmental if he forgets. In a nice way, remind him, "Remember on your list of accommodations, you have a right to ask for so-and-so. Did you forget that?" Then discuss ways to help him remember.

If he forgets twice in a row, then it is time to email the teachers. If the student is in K-8th grade, then you email the teacher. If the student is in high school, the student should email the teacher and CC you. The email should specify when the student was struggling and accommodations were not given. Be sure to copy the case manager so that person is aware that the student forgets to ask for support.

6. Call out the teachers who refuse accommodations.

Hopefully you will never have to use this step, but it is important to know if you need it. Unfortunately, I've seen this happen a lot, even in districts where the special education services are good. For some reason teachers think they have a right to say no to accommodations that students should receive. I have seen teachers say, "You cannot leave" to students entitled to a movement break. The result: the student's frustration escalates into a behavior problem, and then the student gets in trouble. Of course, the teacher then tries to blame the student for the incident.

Teachers rarely get in trouble for not giving accommodations. This is why it is really, really important to keep checking in with your child. If you find that a teacher is not providing accommodations, you need to inform the case manager in writing. If the student is in high school, the student should email the case manager and copy you on the email. In this way the case manager is notified and is aware that you know too. Ideally the case manager will check in with the teacher and explain why the accommodations must be given. Hopefully that will resolve the problem. If it does not, then you call a team meeting to make sure your child gets what is due.

If your child has to beg for his accommodations, this requires a different approach. While some teachers will outright refuse, others will create an obstacle course for the child. For instance, let's say a student has an extra time accommodation for assignments. Despite that, every late assignment is docked. The student then has to go to the teacher to change the grade. This is an indirect pattern of refusal of accommodations. It requires the student to work extra hard to get the accommodations. The teacher is not abiding by the rules of the IEP or 504.

A student should not have to beg or keep reminding the teacher that he has a right to this extra support. He should not be made to feel inadequate, or inferior, or bad because he needs these accommodations. That is essentially what the teacher is doing by forcing the child to beg for them.

If a teacher displays an ongoing pattern like this, then you must report, in writing, to the case manager. Even if your child is in high school, you need to be the one to take this to the special education team. Let them know that there has been a refusal to implement the child's plan properly. If the case manager does not help, taking it up with the principal is the next step. You need to take the issue up the chain of command until somebody helps your child get the accommodations in his plan.

That, in a nutshell, is how to teach your child to self-advocate. This is an indispensable part of helping your child be independent. It is equally critical that he learn that asking once may not be enough. He must ask and ask until he gets it. Asking for help is a critical life skill. It is especially important if he has a disability that could impact his future employment.

26

Teach Your Child
to be Resilient

*"Persistence and resilience only come from having been
given the chance to work though difficult problems."*
~ Gever Tulley

I was working with a 16-year-old young man who was coping with many recent changes in his family situation. He had been living with his father, but was devastated when his father died suddenly in a car accident. He was very close to his grandfather, his father's dad, but right after his father's death his mother insisted he come live with her. He was estranged from his mother, but legally she still had rights as his mom. The mother was a recovering drug addict and her parenting was erratic and emotionally abusive. The boy struggled to grieve his loss and keep going with day-to-day tasks like school and homework. More and more he would flee his home to get away from his mother, and he began ditching school.

After six months the mother was reported to child protective services, and finally the court decided to give the grandfather custody of the boy. He moved to another state, another school, and began again. That is when I started working with him.

I have never met a more cheerful, positive young person. Despite a devastating and shocking loss at a young age, and a harsh living environment, he always looked for the positive in situations. He worked hard to allow his grief to flow as he was eager to get past it and back to being a regular teenager. He came to every session with a checked off to do list from last week. He was the epitome of a resilient spirit. Through talking to him, I learned that his father had taught him how to overcome difficult circumstances. No matter what the situation, the boy believed in his ability to overcome the situation. I was impressed with his progress.

You don't want your child to hurt. You watch her struggle with school, friendships, behavior and sometimes everyday tasks. You want to magically make it better. Perhaps you even plan around events or experiences hoping to minimize her challenges so that everything will be happy and as positive as possible. This is not the best strategy for the long term! Every child needs to learn how to navigate and rebound from challenges. This is known as resiliency. If she doesn't develop resiliency, she not only becomes dependent on you, she will also have great difficulty getting over even minor unpleasant experiences.

A key component to building resilience is the ability to handle many small stressors. A 2015 report by the Center on the Developing Child at Harvard University (National Scientific Council on the Developing Child, 2015) talks about the components needed to build resiliency. Active skill building and at least one supportive relationship were found to be the primary requirement for building a resilient personality.

Active skill building means learning how to handle many little stressors in life. Somebody who's handled a lot of small stressors will be able to handle a big stressor. Kids who are protected and sheltered from small difficult experiences are the very ones who struggle when faced with a big challenge. Children who are NOT supported through the experience of managing small stressors will fail to learn critical life skills.

A parents' desire to shelter and protect their children is a pattern with all parents, not just parents of special needs kids. Parents have a tendency to swoop down and fix things. They don't realize that they are making it difficult for their child to learn how to find their way through hard experiences. Sometimes the phrase "helicopter parenting" or "over protective parenting" is used to describe this tendency.

Kids give up when they can't manage stress.

Research has shown that in 2014 the rate of depression and anxiety was much higher for all children than it was in 2000. This is resulting in a sharp increase in suicides in kids.

According to the Centers for Disease Control, suicide amongst children 14-17 tripled between 1999 and 2014 (Curtin SC, Warner M, Hedegaard H., 2016). In the 2010-2011 school year, the Los Angeles Unified School District (LAUSD) reported 255 incidents of suicidal behavior amongst all students in the district (LAUSD, 2016). An incident is a student who has self-injurious behaviors (i.e. cutting), is contemplating suicide, has a detailed plan on how to commit suicide, or has made a suicide attempt. In the LAUSD 2015-2016 school year, over 5,000 incidents were reported, and 347 of these were actual suicide attempts! This is nearly a 20-fold increase in incidents from 2010-2011! This is not just high school students. 9.1% of these reports came from middle school students. Children's inability to manage challenging life situations has become an epidemic.

I know suicide may seem like an extreme measure of resiliency, but it is enough of an epidemic that schools are adding suicide prevention to staff training.

I recently talked to a school counselor who shared how problematic this has become in her high school. As the head school counselor, she is the first line of help when a student shows potential suicidal behaviors. She said students were contemplating suicide because they broke up with their girlfriend/boyfriend, or they flunked a test for the first time. These are every day occurrences for millions of teens in the United States, yet these kids could not handle such common aspects of their lives. It turned into a life or death crisis.

I believe these kids lacked resiliency. They have been over-protected from painful experiences. Maybe their parents bent over backwards to make sure that the child was not exposed to experiences that might cause frustration. Parents will often protect their children from everyday unpleasant tasks, like having a shy child ask the waiter for something in a restaurant, or making kids do icky chores such as cleaning the bathroom.

Parents want their kids to have a happy, good, perfect childhood. That is my wish for my children too. However, if you protect your child from having to manage small struggles, you are preventing her from learning how to deal with events she doesn't like or that cause pain.

This extends into our schools and sports too, where every child is given a trophy or certificate just for participating, not for any actual accomplishment. In sports all teams are given trophies, even if they did not place in the top three in the finals. I've heard teachers in school decide to give award certificates so a child wouldn't feel left out; even making up an award just for that child. These children do not learn how to manage disappointment when they are rewarded as a consolation prize.

Your response teaches your child how to handle stress.

Unfortunately our special education kids have more life challenges than a typical child. Not only do they struggle with school, but they feel different than their peers, and they may be treated differently by their teachers. How you respond to the difficulties can make a difference in how they learn to react. It is worthwhile to remember that kids learn from our examples.

Encourage them to talk about their challenges, and then together come up with solutions for overcoming them. These talks should include supporting the child's emotional expression, so the child learns that it is okay to cry or be sad or to express this frustration. Giving them permission to express themselves allows them to release the emotional energy created by the experience. Then you can focus on finding ways to improve the situation.

If you are focused on only avoiding the problem, or if you swoop in to eliminate the problem from your child's life, your child will not learn how to handle this type of situation on her own. Try to find a way to support her through the struggles, not make the struggles disappear. Of course there are definite limits when letting your child learn lessons. If your child is being bullied in school, she may not be able to handle it on her own. For children in elementary school, you will probably need to step in to make sure it is stopped. If the child is in middle or high school, she may try to handle the situation on her own, but if the problem continues, then you may need to talk to administrators yourself.

The same is true regarding their learning challenges. If their agreed upon supports are not being implemented properly, you may need to call a special meeting to help make sure that gets done. This is about you being a leader for your child, and teaching her how to problem solve so she is empowered to *take action*. Sometimes, the action has to come from you. Even then, you are teaching your child how to manage the problem, not just ignore it.

Many people carry scars from childhood because they lacked the emotional support to work through challenges. They stumbled through and clearly managed to move on, but inside they may still be haunted by those experiences. The parent earnestly wants their child to avoid the same pain they experienced. Remember that life's struggles help your child grow and get stronger. Do not let your own experience drive you to become the knight in shining armor. Help your child learn to be resilient, and in time, you will see your child is strong enough to deal with the upsets that come down the pike.

Teaching kids about resilience

These 9 steps for teaching resilience are not meant to done on any particular time schedule. It might take you *several months*, doing one step every couple weeks or even one step every month.

1) What does resilience mean?

Ask your child to define what resilience means to her. If she doesn't have an answer, ask her what she thinks it's called when somebody does really well handling a hard situation. If she still has difficulty, use a rubber band to demonstrate resilience. Show how the rubber band can stretch, but then it goes back to the original shape after it is stretched out. Compare that to how we change when we have a hard experience in our lives and are able to overcome it.

Ask if she can give an example of a family member or friend who has exhibited resiliency. Perhaps there is a situation in school where she struggled, and alone or with you she found a way to resolve it. Remind her of these circumstances when she has been resilient.

2) Why resilience is important.

Once she is able to define resilience, ask her why it is so important to bounce back when things don't go as planned. Talk about how she reacts to disappointment. Ask her to discuss times she was disappointed or upset. How did she feel? How did she handle it? Was she resilient? Do not be judgmental; this is something she can learn from, so reassure her that it is okay if she was unable to be resilient sometimes.

3) People can help you be resilient.

Talk about the adults who are there to help her figure out difficult life situations. Part of being resilient is knowing when to ask for help and who is available to help. Explain why she may need to ask for help from adults, and suggest that her friends may not always have the right answers, especially if she is younger. Help her make a list of people she can go to when she needs help with a problem.

4) How thoughts can help us be resilient.

Explain about positive and negative thoughts. When we have a negative thought that makes us feel bad, call it an ANT (annoying nonsense thoughts). When we have a positive thought that makes us feel good, call that a HAWK (happy, awesome, wonderful knowledge). If we have too many ants in our brain, it can cause us to feel sad and upset. We must squash the ANTs and focus on the HAWKS.

For example, you say "Hi" to a friend, and the person does not say "Hi" back. You could either think, 'Wow, I bet she doesn't like me!' Or you could turn that ANT into a HAWK and instead think, 'Wow, I wonder if she is having a bad day.' Perhaps you are having a hard time with math homework. You can entertain an ANT and think, 'I'm so bad at math,' or you can turn it into a HAWK and think, 'This is hard, but I know I have what it takes to get it done.'

5) Calming down helps to focus.

Stress can cause us to overreact when emotions are intense. It is important to teach your child how to calm down when she feels anxious or upset. This allows her time to think things through and make better choices. Teach her how to take 10 slow breaths to calm down. You can also look up mindfulness exercises on YouTube or get my *Grounded for Life* pack on my website at www.specialmomadvocate.com.

6) Teach active problem solving.

The goal is to help your child learn a strategy for solving problems that seem too hard to solve. Go to Google and find a "problem solving wheel printable." The wheel will have various ways to solve problems between friends, and it is a good tool to show your child. Once you have the wheel, ask your child about a situation at school that is difficult for her. If she cannot think of a situation, perhaps she knows of a friend with a problem. Then go through the problem solving steps:

1. Define the problem
2. Get as much information as you can.
3. Think of all possible solutions. Follow the rules of brainstorming. Take 5 minutes to complete this step. Use the Problem Solving Wheel to help see a variety of options for solutions. Remind her that the wheel is just a start, and she can think of more ideas too.
4. Choose the best solution.
5. Make a plan to implement the solution.

Have her complete each step before moving on to the next step. Have her share the problem and solution she has come up with. Discuss how it feels to come up with a solution to a difficult problem.

This tool even works with younger children. Their ideas will be simpler in some cases, although I have been surprised at the answers my younger clients have provided once they understood how it works.

7) Learn about making choices.

You want your child to understand that she has choices in life; that the choices she makes will affect how she feels and what happens next. Talk about how hard it is to make choices when we have strong emotions. When we get really emotional, it can be hard to think clearly and see the various options to choose from. When we are angry, we can make a choice and react without ever thinking about it. But making negative choices often brings negative consequences. It is important to remember the 4 steps for making good choices:

1. Stop and think

2. Take deep breaths and calm down

3. Recognize your role in the situation

4. Believe in your ability to make a positive choice.

8) Believe in your ability to be resilient.

You want your child to have confidence in her ability to manage problems and find solutions. You want to remind your child what makes her strong and resilient. Give her a piece of paper. To make it more powerful, both you and other family members can join in while she does this exercise. Using pen or permanent markers, ask your child to write down 3 things for each of the following:

1. What 3 activities are very easy for you to do (examples: reading, basketball, drawing, or math)?

2. What 3 things have you done that you are proud of?

3. What 3 things has somebody else given you compliments about?

4. What 3 positive adjectives describe your personality?

5. What are your 3 favorite hobbies?

6. Choose 3 people that you could help. How would you help them?

After they have written everything out, have the child decorate the page while you talk about her answers. You can share with her how each answer reflects a part of who she is.

•   The 3 activities that come easily for her are talents. When something is easy, it is because we have some extra special skills in doing it. We should be proud of our talents because they help us feel successful and may turn into a rewarding career.

- The 3 things she is proud of shows that she cares about what she does.

- The 3 things somebody else complimented her about show that others notice positive things about her.

- The 3 positive adjectives show she has positive thoughts about herself.

- Your 3 favorite hobbies are things that make her happy when she does them.

- The 3 people she would like to help shows that she cares about others and she wants to make a difference in the lives of others.

9) Reinforce your child's resilience.

Once you have gone through all these steps, remember to reinforce your child's resilience. This means stepping back and supporting your child's problem solving. It also means holding her when she cries when a situation has not turned out so great. It also means recognizing when your child has handled a situation really well. Remember this is a learning process, so she will get better the more practice she has.

POINTS TO PONDER

Examine your parenting. Are you teaching your child to be resilient?

- Do you do too much so your child avoids having to manage challenges?

- When the child gets upset, do you help her deal with the emotional overload?

- Are you being a fix-it-mom? Do you run and resolve the problem so she will calm down, or do you sit with her and talk it through or offer suggestions on how to manage the problem?

27

Babysit the Teachers

"If the child is not learning the way you are teaching,
then you must teach in the way the child learns"
~ Rita Dunn

It is important you realize that the teachers are just as overworked as the special education staff. Whether it's elementary, middle school or high school, you've got teachers who are dealing with larger class sizes, changes in curriculum and different kinds of monitoring environments. Often they are so focused on teaching to the test, so they don't have much time to customize teaching for individual students.

As much as they want to try and help the children, teachers are not always on top of helping your kid who needs special accommodations. We all agree that there are inadequate teachers. We all wonder how some teachers passed all the tests to get certified. I believe most teachers intend to do right by the students. Unfortunately many general education teachers don't have adequate skills to implement 504s and IEPs. Consequently, despite their wanting to help, they will not always implement the IEP or 504 accurately and consistently.

While it may feel like overkill, you will have to babysit your child's teachers. There is nobody to conduct oversight except for the parent. In my experience the special education staff will do this if there is a problem, but they do not check in on a weekly basis and make sure everything is okay.

Many schools assign a case manager to each special education child. This is the person on the school campus who is responsible to oversee the students' special education experience. Often the case manager are teachers as well. They do not have the time to be checking every day on every student that is assigned to them. They rarely have an effective strategy to assure that all accommodations are provided or that the students get the extra help that they need.

Some students can advocate for themselves. My experience indicates that many students don't know what they need to be successful, so they don't ask. This is especially true in the lower grades. So it is really left up to the parent to monitor the teacher to make sure that everything is being implemented as planned.

I worked with a student who was in 11th grade with auditory processing problems. The accommodations for this student were very well delineated in the IEP. She was supposed to be getting extended time on tests, permission to move to a quiet environment if the classroom was too noisy, and the option to ask for class notes. She had a lot of accommodations to help with the issues that she was having, but they weren't being implemented.

When I met her, my assignment was to help her learn methods for dealing with her anger outbursts in the classroom. She had a history of blow ups, which the teachers said were unprovoked. She would shout and sometimes throw things. The school thought she had an anger-management problem.

I reviewed her IEP and past assessments before starting to work with her. After reviewing her history I asked her, "Do you know that you have these accommodations on your IEP?" She said, "No, what are those?"

So we started going through her accommodations, and I said: "Did you know that if you're doing independent work in the classroom, and it's too noisy, you have permission to ask to go to the library?"

Her response was, "I can?!"

I said: "Do you know if you don't understand the assignment the teacher's giving to you, the teacher is suppose to explain it multiple times until you understand? He has to try different methods of explanation like using symbols, writing it down, or different wording until you get it?"

Her response was, "Really?!"

As we went through each accommodation, the student was astounded that she had the option of receiving this support. I realized that this student was not using her accommodations at all. It's not that the teachers did not want to provide them; the student did not know to ask. So in addition to addressing the anger issues, I began to include self-advocacy coaching into her counseling sessions. She became the person who would babysit the teachers, and her behavior in class improved significantly.

I have worked in the schools and I've been a parent in the schools. For the most part the teachers and special education staff work very hard at their jobs. They're not doing it to hurt your child; they have way too much on their plate. Remembering all of your child's accommodations is not high on their radar.

For younger children you need to remind them and check up on them. For older children you need to teach them to self-advocate. If you find that the teachers are not honoring the IEP or 504, then you need to start documenting everything and reporting it to the case manager. That way you have a paper trail that can help you when you call a special education meeting to work things out.

Strategies for Babysitting the Teachers

1) Study your child's IEP or 504 plan.

You need to be aware of the accommodations and services your child is supposed to get. Unless you know what they are, you can't make sure they are being implemented.

2) Provide a copy of the IEP or 504 to each teacher.

I remember when my son started Kindergarten, everything went to hell quickly. He went from developmental preschool, where he did well, into a general education kindergarten with ZERO support. It blew up like you can't even believe. His teacher looked like a Barbie doll, and was completely incapable of managing anything out of the ordinary in her class. About two months into the school year she was just complaining and complaining and complaining about my son. She was not providing his accommodations, and when I asked her why she replied, "I haven't read his IEP."

To me that was inconceivable. I was so used to working with the developmental kindergarten staff that specialized in special education children. That was my first "Wow!" moment. I knew I needed to do something radically different to get my son the support he needed.

The case manager is technically supposed to distribute the IEP or 504 at the beginning of the year. Teachers are often so overwhelmed with prepping for school, they don't always have the time to read every IEP or 504 plan. Sometimes case managers will only provide the list of accommodations, so the teacher doesn't have a framework of the disability to understand why the child needs this support. So at the beginning of the school year you want to write an email to each teacher and CC the case manager (email gives you proof you sent it). It can be a simple email that says:

"I just want to let you know I'm really happy that you're going to be working with my child this year. Here is my contact information if you need to reach me about anything. I'm happy to get involved if there's any concerns, I can come to meetings if you need to discuss this in detail. Just let me know. "

It's just a simple letter introducing yourself, but then you let them know you are monitoring everything by attaching your child's accommodations. You could add, "I want you to be aware of my student's IEP/504 plan and the accommodations that may be needed in your classroom." You may call out specific accommodations. For example, "The one about avoiding noisy environments is particularly important. If my child needs to leave the classroom and take a break, please understand that this is really important."

Then you might add a conciliatory note, letting them know that you understand they have to stretch a bit to remember to accommodate your child. You could say, "I realize you have a large class and sometimes it is difficult to remember what each student needs. That is why I wanted to share this information with you. My child does much better when the accommodations are given without him having to ask or justify his needs."

By doing this, the teacher realizes you are watching what should happen, what your child needs, and you expect your child to get the help they are legally required to receive. By emailing this, and including the case manager, the teacher has no excuse for not providing accommodations.

3) Educate the teachers about your child's disability.

If your child has a specific disability, it is helpful if you describe it to the teachers so they know how it shows up in the classroom. Create an informational sheet on the disability (or disabilities if there are more than one). You want this informational sheet to explain:

- This is the name of the disability and the definition

- These are the common symptoms of this disability

- This is how it presents itself in my child at school, at recess or in specific circumstances

- This is how you can support my child with this specific disability

For example, with auditory processing disorder, the information sheet would explain what APD is and what the common symptoms are. Then you might share specific ways it shows up in the classroom:

- He is really sensitive to sound.

- Don't assume that he's not following directions, assume first he did not understand what you said. You may need to come closer and repeat the instructions or write them down.

- If he gets emotional, assume he may be over stimulated.

- If he is slow to start his work, see if he is looking around to observe what the other kids are doing so he can figure out what you said.

The information sheet tells the teachers how to best support your child when doing schoolwork. For example, a student who has dyslexia may get very fatigued if they have to do school work for too long. You might say, "After 15-20 minutes the child might demonstrate frustration. That's a sign my child needs a break. Maybe he could get up and get a drink or go to the bathroom, or maybe you could give him something to run to the office."

The key point about the informational sheet is you're educating the teacher about the disability so she understands why your child has all those accommodations in place. You're basically sending the message, "This is why my kid has accommodations, and he will do much better (and cause you less grief) if you use them."

By giving the teacher "cheat sheets" for helping your child, you are saving her so much time and stress. In addition, you're putting the teachers and the professionals on notice that you expect to have good results for your child. By offering support, you become an ally to the teacher. You will also be seen as a prepared parent if the school does not provide what they should.

4) Ask your child what is going on at school.

If your child is verbal, he is likely to tell you when school has been hard or if he was pulled out of class for a special service. Learn his schedule so on the days he is scheduled to go to special services (speech, OT, etc.), you can ask him about it after school.

Sometimes you have to teach your child how to describe what is going on in school. For example, if the teacher tells you that he talks too much in class, ask him about that. Help him describe what is happening when he is talking, or what is triggering it. Then talk to him about troubleshooting and how he could find solutions to help reduce the issue.

By the same token, help your child learn how to share when he feels he needed help but did not get it. Since you cannot usually be in school, help him become an observer in the classroom experience. You want to teach him when he needs to let you know that he is not getting the proper support. The first step in being able to report this is observation and being able to describe what the challenges are.

5) Check in with the special education team.

You don't want to "check in" with them like you're checking up on them. You want to develop a routine for saying hi and seeing how things are going. For example, once a month, send individual emails to each team member. The email should be a nice note and just say, "I want to check in, see how things are going, make sure nothing is amiss and everything's going well." If there are special assignments or activities, use this as an excuse to email or send a note to check in with the teachers. You could include something about progress you have seen or maybe a comment your child made about working with that person.

It helps to share observations of your child's at-home behavior that relates to the team member's service. For example, if your child "discovered" that he likes to eat with chopsticks, let them know about his new fine motor skill. Fine motor skills are used in writing and many other school activities. If the child achieved success outside of school, it will validate the work of the school's occupational therapist. Perhaps the Occupational therapist can use your child's chopsticks as a tool in her therapy.

If you develop a routine check-in, the special education team begins to expect it. As issues arise, an opening for discussion is created. It also tells them that you are monitoring everything. This check in is particularly important in the upper grades because your child has multiple teachers. By checking in you are making sure the special ed team is monitoring your child's classes and knows if there are any issues.

6) Track interactions with school personnel.

It is really important that you log all interactions with the school. The reason for this is that you want to make sure that you have the paper trail so the staff can't say, "Oh, I didn't know." If you have a verbal conversation, you want to follow up with an email to say, "When we talked today, this is what I understood. Does that sound accurate to you?" In this way you're making sure that both you and the teachers agree on expectations and plans. In chapter 33, *Track Everything and Stay Organized*, I go into detail about effective ways to track interactions with the school.

7) Treat teachers with respect.

Some teachers may get offended when you keep reminding them about what they're supposed to do. Maintain good rapport with all the staff at school. It's not always easy, especially when they're slow to follow through on what your child needs. Don't approach them with a tone that implies you expect them to fail at helping your child. When you're checking in on them you want to make sure that you do it in a way that just feels like you're part of the team; and that you're here for them if they need something.

Avoid sending accusatory emails. Remember there are always two sides to a story. Don't say something like, "Oh, my son said that you wouldn't let him have a break. He was crying because he wasn't allowed to get up from the desk." Instead, you should phrase it as: "Gosh, my son came home upset today. He really needed a break a break in your class. I'm not sure what happened, maybe there was a misunderstanding, but he felt like he wasn't allowed to take a break. Based on his IEP plan, it was my understanding that if he needs a break he's allowed to take one. Can you please get back to me and let me know your side of the story?"

You never want to put blame or point fingers or tell them what they should have done. You always want to leave open the option that perhaps your child did not interpret things correctly. I have seen many situations where kids interpret it one way and teachers have a very different story. After talking to all the people involved, you may find that your child left out an important piece of the story. You want to make sure that your interactions are supportive and open to dialog instead of confrontational and judgmental.

8) Volunteer at school.

Another way that you can keep tabs on what's going on with the teachers is to volunteer at school. This is harder as the students get older, particularly in high school, but in the elementary school it's very easy. There are so many different things that you can do at school to get yourself into the classroom. For me, I volunteered as an art docent and I taught art to the whole class. It provided me a great opportunity to see how my child was doing in class and how he interacted with other students. Also, it gave me a chance to see the situation first hand if my child was having issues with a particular child in class.

I remember one instance when my younger son came home and talked about a kid who was being really annoying in class. The boy was new to the school, so the next time I taught art I observed the child. I saw the kid was flapping his hands, moving around a lot, and getting very upset if things didn't go exactly the way he wanted them to. The student had an aide and clearly had symptoms of autism. Then I was able to explain to my son why this student might have all those behaviors. My son actually changed how he looked at the kid. He was nice to him instead of trying to avoid him because he realized the child could not help his behaviors.

Being in the classroom will give you a lot of information. It also gives you an opportunity to get to know the teachers. There's no doubt that if the teacher knows you, and knows how interested you are in your child's education, that teacher will pay better attention to what is going on with your child. It helps to build rapport with the teacher, which brings a better level of education to your child.

In middle school and high school, volunteering is not as common, and the PTOs are not as involved in the day-to-day classroom experience. So it's a bit more difficult to find ways to observe. Be more creative about it. Maybe you have a specific interest or talent, like woodshop or art; ask the teacher if he might need help with specific projects. Do it in a way that doesn't embarrass your child. Also ask your child if it is okay. If he doesn't want you at school, you need to respect that.

In the middle or high school ages, consider creating a lunchtime or after school club: gardening, chess, Pokemon Go, or playing video games. Many school clubs bring in outside experts to help. This gives you a chance to be on campus where teachers and students can get to know you.

9) Get involved with the PTA/PTO so you can get to know other parents.

Parents who become involved in the PTA/PTO often volunteer at school. They become another set of eyes and ears for you. Many times I had parents approach me and say, "I saw your son get really upset in the classroom and the teacher just ignored him." Or, "The teacher just sent him outside to sit by himself." Or, "I saw this kid taunting your kid." Getting to know other parents who are volunteering in school gives you another perspective on what is going on. When you choose to participate in the PTA/PTO, they know that you're concerned about your child's education.

Let me just clarify that you don't become a member of the PTA to get spies. You do it if you want to support the school in that way. I'm just helping you see that getting to know the other parents can have the unintentional benefit of gaining more insight into what is going on at school.

Don't feel guilty about babysitting the teachers.

I know it may feel like you are spying when you strategize about checking up on the teachers, but don't feel bad about it. Instead think about it like you are helping the teachers. They cannot track everything. This is your child's education, and you must take every advantage to help your child succeed.

Convincing Dad
That This is Real

"Any man can be a Father. It takes someone special to be a Dad."
~ Unknown

I don't know why it is that so many dads have difficulty getting on the special education bandwagon. They seem to be in a state of denial about the situation and will often resist the support the child needs. It's such a pervasive issue that if you bring it up to a Special Ed Mom, she'll often respond with, "Oh, yeah, my husband too." I am not saying all dads are in denial, just enough to establish a clear pattern. If your child's dad falls into this latter group, this chapter is very important for you.

I have a friend whose son of two and a half was exhibiting signs of severe autism. He was non-verbal, stimming behavior, completely blank look in his eyes, not connecting with people at all, displayed sensory issues, and having major meltdowns. The parents took the kid to regional center to be assessed (in California that's what they call the early intervention centers). A regional center neuropsychologist did a preliminary assessment to determine if an in-depth autism assessment was needed. They interviewed mom, interviewed dad, and then filled out surveys on behavior. They determined there was not enough cause to pursue a full autism assessment. The neuropsychologist in charge of the screening said that mom's results showed autism, but dad's results presented as typical. They assumed the mom was exaggerating the symptoms.

It was the aunt of the child, a psychologist, who went to see the neuropsychologist to explain that the dad was in denial. The aunt shared her observation of the child, and the neuropsychologist agreed to allow the aunt to interview dad in front of her. They brought the dad in and the aunt started asking him questions. "When your son spins around and around, and he never gets dizzy, what do you think about that?"

Dad replied, "Well, all kids do that!"

Then the aunt asked, "What about the fact that he's two and a half and he can't say a single word?"

The dad said, "He's just a late talker."

The aunt continued, "Well, what about when you take him to a carnival or somewhere noisy and after ten minutes he has a total meltdown. He's putting his hands over his ears and he runs off because he can't stand it anymore?"

The dad's response, "He's just a sensitive child!"

Every symptom of autism the child had, the dad would explain it away. In his mind his son's behaviors were normal. After observing this interaction between the aunt and the dad, the neuropsychologist realized that the dad's results on the assessments were skewed. He really did see his kid as typical. It was his first child, and he had no experience working with children. He really believed his kid was fine.

Why are the dads in denial?

I've never heard a concrete explanation for why dads have such a strong denial of their child's challenges or need for extra assistance. If you can determine why dad is having a difficult time accepting the diagnosis, it may help you help him to come to terms with it. I have read many theories, but never any concrete research on this topic. However, it is such a prevalent pattern, a lot of writing has been done on it. There are many reasons the dad may deny the diagnosis.

- Probably the most common issue is that the dad does not interact with other children as much as mom does. He may honestly not realize the behaviors are atypical. Maybe the dad works so mom takes the child to the park, etc. Therefore the dad has limited opportunities to see how typical children behave.

- The dad may not understand the medical aspects that cause the symptoms in question or have any reason to suspect a problem exists. Without a point of reference, the dad has no way to evaluate his own child's behavior.

- Sometimes the dad may struggle accepting that something is 'wrong' with his child. It may feel like a blow to his manhood. He may feel helpless to fix it. Men in general are problem solvers, and to be faced with a problem they can't fix can feel extremely frustrating and anxiety producing. Because he feels helpless, he cannot face the problem. So instead he denies it exists.

- The dad has guilt that he passed on sub-par genes to his child. As a result, his child is now struggling. Maybe the dad has the same learning challenges, but cannot bear the thought of his child struggling the same way. The dad still has emotional baggage from his own history of school struggles. Maybe the dad doesn't have the learning difficulties, but other family members do, so he has witnessed what these struggles look like. It is extremely difficult for him to accept that his child may follow a similar path.

- Perhaps the dad has the same learning challenge and struggles to accept it within himself. Acknowledging it in the child means he has to finally come to terms with something he has been denying about himself for a long time.

- Maybe the dad believes that the diagnosis is just an excuse for the child's 'bad' behavior. He may think better parenting or stricter enforcement is needed.

- Maybe the dad cannot face the loss of the child he had wished for. Just like moms, dads have a vision of what being a father is all about. They see themselves teaching their child, playing sports, going on family vacations and all the other things typical families do. When faced with a diagnosis that could have life-long repercussions, many dads cannot face that their dreams have been dashed.

- Perhaps he is angry at the 'unfairness' of it all and cannot come to grips with his strong emotions. As a result he shuts down and ignores the problem.

- Finally, he might have difficulty accepting the change this brings to the marriage, as mom is now hyper focused on helping the child. Parenthood is already a strain on the adult interactions, but when a child requires extra attention, it can widen the gap between couples.

My experience convincing dad.

In the beginning of this journey, my husband also had a lot of difficulty accepting the symptoms our son had. This created a huge challenge because he did not want to pay for therapies. He may have been resistant because we never had a concrete diagnosis. As a result, it was unclear what we were trying to help. Even if we had a diagnosis, the therapies themselves did not have predictable results, so practitioners could not promise specific improvements. Each case was different, and there was no way to predict how the child's brain would respond.

I'll never forget the very first therapy I wanted to try. It was a listening therapy called auditory integration training (AIT). I had read about using it for kids who have auditory processing disorder. Our son was 6 and I knew he had APD, even without a diagnosis. I intuitively sensed that AIT was going to help him. My husband doubted he had APD and he dismissed my intuitive hunch. AIT was a $1,200 hunch, and even though insurance was going to pay some, we were going to pay $600 for it. My husband was reluctant. I showed him case studies that I had found online. I showed him *Hearing Equals Behavior*, the book from Dr. Guy Berard, the guy who created AIT. All this information was too subjective. He needed something more scientific and wouldn't agree to it.

Finally, in tears, I begged him, "Please, please, let's try it because he needs help!" He finally agreed.

The day we were going to start he called the provider and asked, "Can you promise me that this will help my child?" In all honesty the guy said, "I can't. We don't know until we do it." My husband changed his mind. He didn't want to do it. He wanted to cancel the appointment.

I implored him to change his mind, and I broke down in tears. It was the tears that got him to change his mind again.

So we started AIT for our son. It's a ten-day therapy with a two-day break between days 5 and 6. Our son had phenomenal results from it. It was the best result the practitioner had ever seen. Before AIT our son would speak in sentences, but they were all mixed up. He would say, "Water me please mom," when he needed a glass of water. About a week after he finished the AIT his speech spontaneously reorganized. Literally one day his sentences were mixed up, and the next day they were normal.

A month or so after our son finished AIT, my husband came to me and said, "Thank you! Thank you for making us do this for him! I feel like you've given my son back to me."

We found out that he had a conductive hearing loss, so he wasn't hearing properly. In a lot of ways he was in his own little world because his hearing was like a bad cell phone connection. The AIT fixed this hearing loss. He started to connect more socially, and he started to have back and forth conversations. The impact on him was humongous!

A Father's Point of View

I asked my husband to write the following section about his experience coming to terms with our son's challenges. It may help you understand that some fathers need time and understanding to accept the diagnosis of his child.

I was forty-six when #1 son was born. I had just bought a retail business that needed a good bit of work. I was excited because it was a really good fit and I was my own boss. The business was growing and my career path seemed set. My mom had died less than three years before and I was starting to feel settled again in my life.

When my son was born, it was amazing! There is nothing that can prepare you for that. I was really looking forward to enjoying my son and I adored all the cute mannerisms that mothers especially love. I saw him make a mess of Cheerios on the kitchen floor. I saw the dopey look when he snuggled next to the cat for the first time. I had had a good relationship with my father, and my dad was a source of inspiration, life lessons, and fun for me. This is what I envisioned my son and I would have.

I was pretty engaged as a father; I have always considered parenting to be a joint effort. Bonnie comes from a medical family so I didn't spend much time reviewing the medical information when our son showed symptoms. My son seemed normal to me, and I enjoyed watching my wife bond with him. She is more of a detail oriented person. I thought too many cooks in the kitchen would not be a good thing.

As he grew older, I aspired to play ball with him and to show him amazing things in nature. My first big recognition of a problem was when he was around approximately 3-1/2 years old. I called him from another room. He didn't respond. So I went to his room and stood in front of him. I said a few things and waited for a response. My son waited for a few seconds and then turned and walked away.

I was startled. I didn't know what to think. Perhaps my wife's concerns were more valid than I realized. Later that year, I saw him slamming his body against the wall for no apparent reason. By that time, I had learned the term sensory seeking vestibular. I could now believe that he had a medical condition. I could feel my heart sink.

So I did what I thought would help. I engaged him like a typical kid. I signed him up for T-ball and decided I should be his coach! I decided my first-born son just needed more time with daddy. I loved my business, but my kid needed me more.

However my son was not ready for organized sports. He loved hitting the ball, but he was not able to wait for his turn in practice. About the sixth or seventh practice, he wandered off by himself to play on the slides in the adjoining playground. Game, set, match. I handed over my coaching duties to another parent and we quit T-ball.

To this day, my son has happy memories of this time, but it was simply crushing to me. I realized that I did not know how to help him. When I saw my son unable to engage and unresponsive to conversation, I conceded that I needed to look closer at what my wife was suggesting.

Over time, I began to accept that I loved my son anyway. There was no way anything was his fault. Around six years of age, he began to be able to interact socially with me. I began to accept that when he came out of his room to give me monster bear hugs and then go right back into his room, it was all he could do. The one thing that has always made me so proud is that he has done all the therapies without flinching. As I have seen him recover and mature into a wonderful young teen, I know that I love him so very much.

One of the other hardships emotionally for me is that I have missed the bonding with other fathers and families. As many of you may know, if your child is challenged in some way, you lose out on many opportunities to build family friendships. It's pretty hard to have the simple "water cooler" conversations about church, sports, dance, Scouts, etc. if your child does not participate in the usual way in these activities.

Our oldest son required monitoring at social events. He lacked neurotypical coordination in athletic activities until perhaps eleven or twelve. Since he was poorly coordinated early, he did not learn athletic skills and the related social skills of teamwork. His auditory processing disorder left him without the ability to understand social conversations.

Many other parents cared about our situation. However at some point, I tired of updating them on the latest therapy or his "progress." Our son has made great progress but it is socially awkward to talk of his progress. It was emotionally draining to talk about exercises to help with basic coordination when the other parents are talking about winning hits in baseball. It also takes emotional energy to invite peers to birthday parties and events that your child likes and wonder if peers come because they like your child or their parents feel a sense of obligation to support you. As my son got older, there were fewer opportunities that fit. At this point, no one asks us to join their private activities.

I am not a party animal but I love social interaction. With the time we spent helping our son and the lack of social interaction, my life is more isolated than I would like. It is a loss that stays with me always.

Parenting doesn't exist in a vacuum for most men. It is supposed to be a proud, fulfilling and (in a male sort of way) vindicating experience, but not all that life is about. My attitude has necessarily had to shift to be more about others. The only other choice was to leave, and I knew I could never do that.

If you are struggling as a man with your child's development, I can only suggest that you will learn to accept things as they are. It doesn't happen overnight. When I saw my wife's anguish when our son was diagnosed, I could not protect her from that. I believe that most men would try to protect their partners, but sometimes there is nothing you can do to take away the pain. It was really hard to sort things out in the beginning.

I didn't really know what my responsibility was at that point. I tried to maintain our business since we were self-employed. I didn't know how to support my wife emotionally because I was so confused. I initially didn't engage in learning about therapies because I thought this would all blow over. When it didn't, it took me some time to regroup.

So for what it is worth, here are my suggestions:

- **Get close to men you can talk to.** Your wife will not understand you in the same way because men have a different set of aspirations and social interactions. If they have medical issues in their family, so much the better.

- **Do not hate on yourself.** You will never really know why this happened to your child.

- **Do not give up the things that you love.** It is so important to do what you enjoy because you will need the reserve of happiness and satisfaction.

- **Learn what you can.** There is so much that standard Western medicine lacks in terms of helping special needs children. However research is making more information available all the time. Take in what you can absorb and participate when you can.

Helping dad accept the diagnosis

After reading my husband's experience you see that a dad needs time and a lot of information before he can accept the diagnosis. Be patient, because he is struggling with it in his own way. Here are some suggestions that have worked for other moms to help the dads come around to see the light.

- **Be patient.** Dad has to process the information in his own time. You can gently try to talk about it, but do not be pushy about him getting on board. Anecdotal research has shown that most dads eventually do get on board. They just need to do it at their own pace.

- **Have a medical professional explain the diagnosis** and the symptoms in your child that confirm the diagnosis. Having a third party explain it in concrete detail helps the dad accept that it is real.

- **Show him articles that enumerate symptoms** of your child's condition to help him recognize the symptoms in your child. Do not force him to read the articles, simply suggest that he read them.

- **Print case studies of other children** with similar symptoms and the same diagnosis.

- **Bring dad to all meetings** regarding diagnosis or school planning.

- **Have dad take the child on outings to places where other children play.** Over time he will see the differences between your child and the other children.

- **Share biographies of successful grownups despite the same diagnosis.**

- **If dad really struggles to accept the diagnosis, suggest counseling.** He may have to go through a process of grieving the child he had hoped for and accepting the child he has.

This is a complex psychological experience for all parents, and the dad may need time to work out his own issues in order to finally get on board. You cannot rush this as it involves emotions, history and psychological obstacles. Counseling can really help as it can reveal the basis for the resistance. More importantly, it can provide ways to find a solution.

I know you desperately need your partner to be alongside you as you help your child. You may need to accept that this will not happen for a while. If you find yourself pushing and wanting him to hurry up and just see things the way you do, then you may need assistance in managing this sense of desperation. This is a tough journey for the entire family.

POINTS to PONDER

1. What has your child's dad done that makes it clear to you that he cannot accept the diagnosis?

2. Why do you think he struggles to accept the diagnosis?

3. What can you do to help him accept the diagnosis?

29

Do Not Ignore the Neurotypical Siblings

A mother understands what a child does not say.
~ Jewish Proverb

I was heartbroken during a meeting with a mom name Marcie who told me her neurotypical (non-disabled) son, Paul, didn't want to be a part of the family anymore. He said that all the attention was focused on his brother with autism, and Paul felt like he had to be broken in order to be loved by his parents. Marcie felt like she had failed as a mother because she recognized the amount of attention she gave to each of her boys was terribly lopsided. She had unintentionally supported her children unequally, and she felt like Paul had been short-changed.

Typical siblings of special need kids have a psychology all their own. I know because I am one of them. Some of my siblings had physical or learning challenges. I did not have any obvious difficulties. I often felt left out and that my parents didn't care about me because I did not get as much times as the others got.

When I was about 15, I was mad at my mom and I told her I thought she didn't care about me because she never paid attention to me as much as the others. She got really quiet and then she said, "It's because I don't worry about you. I know you are going to grow up and be just fine." It was a real learning moment for me. I didn't feel so bad anymore because she was right. I didn't need her help, even though I wanted it. She made me realize that the attention goes where the help is needed.

Families with special needs children are often organized around the needs or moods of the child with challenges. If resources are tight, finances are often allocated to tutors and therapies for the child with a disability rather than dance lessons or softball for the typical kids. When special kids have behavior problems, a lot of time and energy is spent on calming the child down or limiting what the family does socially to avoid embarrassment. Typical children feel like the family is controlled by the special sibling. This feels very unfair to them.

Challenging feelings about having a special needs sibling.

A neurotypical child (NT) with an atypical sibling is full of emotions. There is a wide gamut of reactions, although not all children have strong negative emotions in the beginning. The challenging emotions may show up many years down the line. Some children become model children, finding a role in helping their sibling. Others may become quiet and withdrawn, unable to express any part of the whirlpool of feelings. Others may become problematic. They act out to gain attention or to work out their frustration and hidden resentment.

It is important to pay attention to what your typical child says and does to see if signs of depression, anxiety or other mental health concerns are cropping up. Take time to talk to your child. Explore how he feels about the family situation. Listen carefully to words that may indicate the situation is creating some strong negative emotions.

Some emotions typical siblings may experience include:

- **Perfectionism:** I have to act like everything is okay so my parents have a 'normal' child. I have to be perfect so I do not cause any more problems for my family.

- **Sadness:** Would my parents love me more if I were disabled in any way?

- **Anger:** I wish my sibling wasn't born this way (or wasn't injured). I hate having to help my sibling.

- **Grief:** Why does my sibling have to suffer so much?

- **Guilt:** I feel guilty that I do not have the challenges my sibling has. I feel guilty when I can do something that my sibling can't. I feel guilty when I resent the attention my sibling is getting. I feel guilty for resenting my parents focusing so much on my disabled sibling.

- **Embarrassment:** I wish our family could be 'normal' (whatever that is!). I don't want to go to school with my sibling.

- **Isolation:** None of my friends understand what I go through at home.

- **Anxiety:** Will my sibling be okay when he/she grows up? Will I have to take care of him/her when we grow up? When will the next 'incident' occur? Will I develop the same disability? Will God punish me for any of these feelings?

- **Resentment:** Why do I have to always help my sibling? Other kids don't have to do the things I have to do. Why do I have to be second in line all the time? Why do I have to be treated like a step-child?

- **Over responsible:** I can't go out with my friends because I have to help at home. How can I move out when I grow up? Who will help my family?

It is important to let your typical child know that it is okay to have these feelings, and it is good to talk about them. They are typical for the NT child to have. Through expressing and exploring the child can process the feelings and perhaps find some better ways to manage family life.

These emotions may not always be manifested overtly. That makes it doubly important to recognize when your typical child is faced with a challenge. Because they will feel bad about their feelings, they will hide them. They withdraw or avoid family situations; or they may behave extremely well to avoid adding to the family stress. They may choose to be loners at school because they can't find other kids who understand them. They may start to struggle with academics and not participate in extracurricular activities.

If you are concerned about something your child says or does, talk to a therapist to get some help. Find someone who has experience with special needs families and can work with your typical child as she processes the thoughts and feelings about the situation.

Strengths a typical child may gain from having a special sibling.

While it's easy to see where a typical sibling may feel short-changed, there are benefits that derive from being in that family. It's good to recognize these benefits because they present opportunities to acknowledge the strength and kindness of your typical child. Some of the positives you may see include:

- **Greater compassion and patience.** Through spending time and helping his sibling, a typical child is usually more caring and kind than other children his age. He is more aware of the needs of others and more tolerant of people who are different.

- **Resiliency towards stress and challenges.** Life with a special needs child is rarely smooth. Dealing with a lot of little, and big, stressors can develop a strong resiliency in your child. While it is not always easy to watch, take comfort in knowing your child will have learned coping skills for his entire life.

- **Less likely to engage in teenage drama.** Typical children of special siblings know what real stress is like. Peer dramatics can seem silly in comparison to their real-life challenges.

- **More likely to ignore negative reactions by others.** If the special sibling has issues that elicits stares from strangers, your typical child will learn how to handle this unwanted attention.

- **May choose a helping profession.** Because of their experience with their special sibling, your typical child may choose to pursue a profession that helps individuals with special needs or just helps other people.

Things you can do to help typical siblings.

- **Spend one-on-one time with each child.** As a mom of one who had severe issues, and one who is pretty much typical, I am very aware of the feelings of my typical child. My typical boy and I talk about it frequently. It's important he feels just as important, and loved, but in a different way. My husband and I make a point of spending one-on-one time with our typical kid so he knows we love him just as much. It's really important to schedule this time in your calendar so it doesn't just happen haphazardly. Remind your child throughout the week that you have alone time coming up.

- **Explain why your special kid needs extra attention.** It's really crucial that you also articulate why so much of your attention is on the other child. Your NT child needs to understand that it's not about loving one child more than the other. It is about helping the sibling so he can have as independent a life as possible. In the long run, this is a positive thing for the NT child because if the special sibling is dependent in adulthood, it is often the NT child who has to step in and help. So the more independence that can be fostered, the easier it is in the long run for the entire family.

- **Teach your typical child about the disability.** It is important to talk openly about the disability and educate your typical child on the symptoms and concerns. When it comes to therapies or doctor visits, your typical child does not participate. This leaves a lot of their questions unanswered and triggers their imagination. Through understanding where the challenges lie, your typical child can then have a better awareness of why sometimes all of a sudden you have to drop things to go help your special needs child. You don't have to get into scientific or technical terms, just talk about how it affects family life. It is helpful to articulate how your special child experiences his disability.

    It is very important that your typical child understand when his sibling could potentially put someone in danger. For younger siblings, they need to know when to move away from a developmentally challenged sibling who is acting angry and go get an adult to help. If he is aware and mature enough, he may recognize what interventions might be helpful in that moment. It is equally important that a sibling realizes that he is not the person responsible for the challenged brother or sister. He must maintain his own childhood while at the same time knowing what to do in an emergency situation. It would be worthwhile to do some practice scenarios with your NT child so he knows how to react in these circumstances.

- **Honor your typical child's emotions.** Your typical child will probably be angry or maybe even feel sad about his sibling. At the same time he may be over protective or proud of his special sibling. The emotions they experience are often mixed and confusing, so allow your child to express these emotions in whatever way works for him. Talk about it and affirm to your child it is okay to have these strong feelings. We all know that unexpressed emotions can build up and come out at unexpected moments, so it's really important to teach your children early that it's okay to let it out.

- **Acknowledge your typical child's accomplishments.** Many typical children develop resentment when they observe their special needs sibling receiving recognition for doing everyday tasks. Your typical child needs the same kind of recognition for tasks that are commensurate with his abilities. Take time to acknowledge when he does well in school or does something special at home. Remember that your special needs child is likely complimented multiple times a day, so you want to balance this with recognizing your typical child's strengths as well.

- **Appreciate the ways your typical child supports your special child.** I'm not saying your typical child should be responsible for therapies, babysitting or daily care of the special needs sibling. In the course of sibling relationships, how does your typical child help? For example, a typical sibling may be a great source of social interaction for an autistic child. Even though it may just be playing to the typical child, you can remind him how playing helps the special needs sibling. Remind your typical child that he is part of the solution. This will help him to feel important and realize the whole family helps your special needs kid, not just mom and dad.

- **Recognize when your child lets you handle issues.** Show your typical child that you recognize his contributions even if that means doing nothing. We always acknowledged when our typical son was quiet and off to the side so we could calm the situation down. We always thanked him for his cooperation and praised him for the proper response.

- **Consider if your typical child would benefit from a support group.** Connecting with siblings in similar circumstances will help your child understand that he is not the only one. Kids at school may not be able to understand the challenges, so helping your child connect with other kids who do understand can bring a huge measure of relief. There are two organizations that have online support groups.

  - SIBS, for brothers and sisters of disabled children and adults (www.sibs.org.uk)

  - Sibling Support Project (www.siblingsupport.org)

- **Make sure your typical child has his own toys and clothes.** While it may be financially difficult to manage, make an effort to ensure your typical child has things that belong to him. It helps to have a place in the home where he keeps his possessions and he does not have to share.

- **Encourage your child to excel to his capabilities.** Many typical children will want to hold themselves back as it creates a sharper contrast between themselves and their special sibling. It is important to encourage your typical child to go out for sports or clubs or classes that engage his talents and allow him to excel. It is important for him to recognize that it is okay if he is successful, even if his special sibling will never see the same achievements.

POINTS to PONDER

1. How has your typical child been affected by having a sibling with a disability?

2. What are 3 things you can do to help your typical child manage the emotions and reactions to the situation?

3. List 10 fun outings you can do with your typical child to create some special one-on-one time?

4. What activities can your typical child participate in that can utilize his strengths and boost self-esteem?

Section 4

Take Charge
of the Special
Ed Process

*In this section you learn why you need
to take charge and lead when possible,
and how to work with the school to
maintain a positive relationship.*

30

You Are the Team Captain!

"The most common way people give up their power
is by thinking they don't have any."
~ Alice Walker

One of the most challenging things about working with the school district is the feeling you are incidental to the education process. And nothing can be farther from the truth! In the development of an IEP you're supposed to be a fully participating member of the team. For a 504 plan, you are also supposed to be a contributor to the plan (although the law is not as strict about required parent involvement as it is for IEPs). Whether it is an IEP or 504, always remember that you are the captain of your child's education team.

Some of you may shudder at the thought of being a team captain. Some of you may pull back from a more assertive position. Some of you may be frightened to be any kind of leader. I am just trying to encourage you to muster all your strength to understand that you know your child best, and there is nobody else who cares about your child like you do, because you care not only about your child's learning and school experiences, but what happens to her for the rest of her life. It is your job to manage your child's K-12 education. Despite what school personnel say, you must step up and stay active! This can be extremely difficult because school administrators can be intimidating and dismissive.

Some of you have a basic personality that does not want to confront authority. For those parents whose personality is non-assertive, it is doubly hard to be the team captain.

I am taking this position because it took me years of frustration before I knew I had to rely on myself to follow through, and I am not by nature an assertive person. I always accepted "No!" readily, because I thought no meant no. I was too afraid to assert my demands to those in charge. I only became assertive because the demands were not for my personal benefit, but for my son. I found the strength to fight for the support he needed. Because it was my son's future at stake, I got the strength to turn a no into a yes. When I would readily accepted no to requests for my own benefit, I thought that perhaps that it was a trivial request, or perhaps I did not feel entitled to the request. I knew that these requests from the school were crucial life requests for my son. There was nothing trivial about them.

Districts can be manipulative.

Excuse me for calling a spade a spade; districts may manipulate to get the results they want. That is to get you to sign off on the bottom line. They will not follow proper procedures, misquote the law, skew assessments, and even deliberately misrepresent the truth. They change tactics in midstream causing more confusion and frustration. Learn to play chess with them by strategizing and responding with productive actions.

The best way for you to take charge is to become educated in the laws and procedures for specific situations. When you arm yourself with knowledge of the law, you can no longer can be manipulated by statements like, "We don't think your child needs this service anymore, so we removed it." On an IEP they cannot remove services without using data to demonstrate the service is no longer needed. If the law is not specific about your child's situation, check with other parents and see how they reached a resolution. Do research or consult an advocate or attorney to help you strategize. You need to be proactive and assertive! You are the one constant in your child's education from preschool to college, and you have the ultimate responsibility for your child's educational success.

Get help to be assertive.

If you have issues dealing with difficult people, find a way to resolve them. Some ideas for helping yourself:

- Have a mock meeting before the real special education meeting.
- Watch mock meetings on YouTube and practice the techniques.
- Talk to other moms to find out how they dealt with overbearing special education teams; especially in your district.
- Consult a therapist to decrease your fears.

It's crucial that you step up and take the reins; do whatever it takes. It is not an easy transformation to grab the reins. Especially if you have never done it before. It does not come naturally for everyone. If it is particularly difficult for you, give yourself permission to recognize that you need help and allow yourself to get it. You can find an advocate, or even a fellow Special Ed Mom, who is willing to come to meetings with you. That person should act as a coach so that eventually you can take charge yourself.

This process is especially difficult if you have a frustrating and withholding district. I personally am conflict avoidant, and in our previous district every IEP was a battle royale. They were rude and condescending. They denied most of my requests, and they offered the most convoluted reasons why they would refuse services.

At one meeting I was fighting for social skills classes for my son. They denied him the social skills classes claiming it was his fault that he was missing out on social interaction with other kids because it took him so long to eat his snack! Can you imagine? They totally ignored the fact that the most social part of recess was when the kids ate snacks. And my son would just sit there silently not knowing how to interact. Yet they claimed because he was so slow in eating his snacks that it was his fault, and therefore he was not entitled to social skills training. I don't know if this is circular reasoning or just an obvious lack of any reasoning.

The IEP meetings at that district were super frustrating and caused a feeling of defeat. Most parents are in the same situation, where they feel very intimidated by the schools. The school personnel are professionals and have their own lingo. If you don't know the basics, it is easy to feel intimidated. Some school staff are experts at manipulating you to make you feel like you have no right to ask for what your child needs; or worse yet, that you don't know what your child needs.

After hiring an attorney, I finally understood how to fight back. Within months we got the services we requested. The district was not happy about it, but who cares, because our child got the support he needed.

13 Ways to Demonstrate You Are In Charge at Meetings.

1. **Be the first to arrive at the meeting.** If possible, sit at the head of the table.

2. **Participate in meetings.** Do not just listen and sign off on what they recommend. Ask questions and discuss solutions. Plan ahead on ways you can contribute or questions you can ask.

3. **Come with ideas for solutions.** The school will offer only what they already have. By finding or suggesting other solutions, it shows that you are leading the charge to find the best options for your child.

4. **Bring your IEP/504 binder to meetings, and know it inside and out.** Every time you receive a document from the school, put it in the binder; especially IEP reports and notes you take. Include report cards, examples of your child's work (in-class, homework and home activities). It should include anything that pertains to his education, including any record of contact with the teacher and special education staff. When you show up at a meeting with a notebook, you look organized. You may not feel organized but appearances count. The person who looks like she is prepared is seen as valuable and proactive.

5. **Spread your documents out to take a bit more space than usual.** A lot of documents makes the school aware that they are dealing with someone who has done their homework and who truly understands the situation.

6. **Educate the team on your child's disability.** Despite their 'expertise,' degrees and titles, they are not experts on your child. Prepare examples of where your child struggles in school and at home. Your observations may be different than what the staff has seen. Your educating them demonstrates that you have the most knowledge about your child's challenges.

7. **Bring somebody to take notes.** Might sound silly, but if you have an 'assistant,' it gives you an air of authority.

8. **Provide positive feedback and validation.** When somebody on the team has a good idea, or effectively helped your child, tell them so during the meeting. The person complimenting others takes on the aura of a boss. Why is that? Part of a boss' job is to encourage others. Also, when you give a compliment, you display confidence that you have the status to compliment somebody.

9. **Refer to your knowledge of the law regarding the process.** If there are challenges you are trying to overcome, find references to recent cases. Quote the IDEA (Individuals with Disabilities Education Act), Section 504 of the Rehabilitation Act or your state's special education laws. Print out pertinent sections. If they disagree, ask for a copy of the law they are following. Get the book *Special Education Law* by Pamela and Peter Wright, and bring it as a reference. It is an excellent book to own and become familiar with. If it's all tabbed up and highlighted, that's even better. Again, when you show you are prepared and committed, it will be easier.

10. **Bring research to support your requests for special services.** The schools will often refuse services saying there is no evidence that particular service can help. Being prepared to counter their position with research will show that you know what you are talking about.

11. **Be neutral with your emotions.** Unfortunately society views emotional outbursts as weak. Staying unemotional during meetings and other interactions helps you appear more in control. If this is difficult for you, practice ahead of time, or develop strategies for calming yourself in the moment. You can cry or get mad when it's over, but during the meeting, act like an executive in charge.

12. **Thank the team.** Like compliments, the one who thanks the team is seen as the person in charge.

13. **Be the first to send a follow up email after meetings.** Thank everybody for their time and provide a copy of your notes. Ask if anybody has changes to the notes (a great way to validate your notes).

Step up! Be the captain of the team!

POINTS TO PONDER

1. How do you feel about being in charge? Do you need to do some work to help you take charge?

2. What are 3 things you can do at the next special education meeting to demonstrate your being in charge?

3. Do you feel the rest of the team undermines your authority? If so, which particular team members and how do they do it? Are they undermining because they don't like you, it's their way of showing their authority, or is it because they don't want to give you what you want?

31

Discover Your District's Special Ed Profile

"All truths are easy to understand once they are discovered; the point is to discover them."
~ Galileo Galilei

Your strategy must be based on your district's history and methods. To do that you must uncover your district's special education profile. By getting to know how and why the district makes decisions, you are better able to strategize getting what your child needs.

To discover your district's profile, do the research! It will be well worth the effort. The following resources can help.

Special Education Policy Manual

Most districts have a formal manual that outlines how the district approaches special education. While the manual is meant for employees, parents are entitled to a copy of it. You can search on Google to try and find it. If you cannot locate it, then request a copy from the school district.

Due Process Complaints

Due process (a legal term) is when a parent or a district chooses a formal legal hearing to work through disagreements about services. Your state should have a database where you can look up all the due process complaints that have been filed in your district. In California this database is called Special Education Decisions and Orders and is managed by the Office of Administrative Hearings. In your state is may be called something different, but you can start with these terms when you go to search for it. The results should provide complete documents on the complaints. You can learn the nature of the complaint and how it was decided. This helps in understanding the issues (or details) that could not be easily resolved.

Lawsuits

Go to your county courthouse and search for lawsuits that were filed against your district. If you have access to LexisNexis (a case law database) you can do this from your computer at home.

School Accountability System

Each state has a system to measure the progress, or lack of progress, of each district and school. The system will include a school report card showing the demographics of the school, general budget information, etc. Using this you can calculate the percentage of students receiving special education support. If a school has a high number of special education students, you can assume the district is generous with services (the national average is 13% of students). If the percentage is low, then you can assume they are stingy with services. Just this fact alone gives you a clue about the size of the battle you will be up against.

School District Budget

Follow the money. We know that money is always an issue for districts, so examining the budget helps you see how funds are spent. Do they spend a lot on legal fees and not as much on special education? Look at the expenditure per student versus expenditure for special education student.

In 2015, the national average of expenditure per student was $11,356 (National Education Association, 2016). They have not looked at average spending for students with disabilities since 2000, when it was $12,474 per student. That is 90% more than what they spent on student without disabilities in 2000. Think of it this way: in 2015 the average spending for a student with a disability should have been $21,576. If your district is spending significantly less than this for special education students, and their legal expenses are high, that is a hint that they have a habit of refusing services.

Parent Stories

Document conversations with other parents that reveal how different special education situations were handled. If you can, join a local support group and attend meetings so you can talk to parents one-on-one and gather as much information as possible.

Parent Training & Information Centers

These centers are federally funded. They offer education and support for parents and children with disabilities. Even though each center covers a large region of a state, it will offer insight about your specific school district. Most have a free advocacy consulting service. It is worth contacting them about creating a strategy for your district. You can find your center here: www.parentcenterhub.org/find-your-center

School Personnel

Most school personnel are not going to share information with you. Some are willing to do so behind the scenes. It may not be somebody on your child's team, but rather a well-meaning teacher or administrator who genuinely wants to help. Ask questions in a gentle, non-pushy way. Do not press if people seem tight lipped. If you volunteer at school, and often help the teachers, you may find staff that will reciprocate by shedding some light on how to convince the school to help you.

Search Google

Search for your district and relevant terms to find more information on your district. For example, search for 'district name' + 'special education' or 'district name' + 'your child's disability.' Don't just look at the first of Google. Go through several pages and see what you are able to find.

Talk to a local advocate

Offer to pay an advocate to get answers about the district. Find out what she believes are the biggest challenges and ask for examples of cases she has found success with. Not all advocates will be willing to share their insights, but some might. That information could be very worthwhile.

Keep a notebook to track the profile

It helps to have a notebook where you record all the information so you can add to the district profile each time you learn something new. It may take you several months, or even a year, to create a clear picture of how they handle special education. Even if your child is already getting help, continue to gather information. Unless you move, you will be dealing with this district for a very long time, so all the research will be helpful at one point or another.

POINTS TO PONDER

1. What do you know about how your district handles special education?

2. Who do you know to assist you in finding out this information?

3. Are there any school personnel who seem sympathetic to your cause and would be willing to help you?

32

Question Everybody!

"By doubting we are led to question,
by questioning we arrive at the truth."
~ Peter Abelard

You are your child's biggest advocate! While the school and outside professionals are suppose to help your child, you are still the best authority on what he needs. You should research, ask questions, and introduce new ideas. Do not rely solely on the experts to tell you how things are or what should be done. **If it doesn't feel right, question it!**

Many years back I was working with a business coach, and I had to fire an employee. I was having the hardest time doing it, and my coach said, "This is not personal, it's business." Keep the same mindset when advocating for your child. Don't worry if your questions have upset somebody or insulted their sense of professional expertise. You can't just sign the IEP so everybody is happy with you and treats you nicely when you are at school. Now is the time to be logical and assertive; speak up when things do not seem right. Of course you want to do this in a diplomatic and non-aggressive way. You're not here to show how strong you are or how much you can push. You are here to help your child!

You are your child's voice in these meetings, so speak up! Let the team know if you agree, disagree or want another opinion. If you are too emotional about the whole situation, find somebody else who can be at the meetings and assist with making decisions and pressing for answers. Find a way to work through the emotions so you can focus on the task at hand — helping your child.

If it doesn't feel right, speak up!

Unfortunately, I have had to learn to question medical authorities. I almost died in 2006 because a team of six doctors made the wrong call, and my husband almost died twice because of similar mistakes. Misdiagnoses is rampant in the medical world, and it is not entirely the doctors' fault. They are pushed to see patients in an assembly line fashion. They tend to focus on their own specialty because that is what they know, and that is what they see all the time.

In a perfect world, you must become an expert in education and health concerns for your child as well as your entire family. This sounds so overwhelming, so remember that I am talking about in a perfect world. As much as you can, gather medical information so you can talk to the doctors about specifics, so you can ask informed questions and make informed decisions. If your intuition makes you hesitant about what a doctor is recommending, trust your gut. Do your homework and make sure the decision feels right before you follow along.

It is important to seek out second opinions when the first opinion does not feel right. A second opinion can alleviate your anxiety and reassure you that you are making the best decision. This is the whole basis of the independent education evaluation (IEE), one of the procedural safeguards provided to parents who disagree with the school's assessment. A parent can request an IEE at public expense if they do not feel the school's evaluation provides a true picture of the child's challenges (see chapter 50, *Requesting an Independent Educational Evaluation*). Do not feel guilty for wanting a second opinion. Good doctors and ethical professionals will always agree that more than one opinion is always helpful.

This doesn't mean you are disrespecting your doctor or bucking his authority. You are just assuming the responsibility of co-deciding what is best for your child. Your doctor has a medical degree and spent years acquiring knowledge, but he is not the expert on your child. He diagnoses what he commonly sees, and can miss what he comes across infrequently. Many doctors do not keep up with the latest discoveries.

I learned early to question doctors.

When my older son was 8 months old he had the Roto virus. He was extremely ill, requiring an emergency room visit. He slowly began to improve, and his pediatrician recommended we feed him yogurt to replenish the gut flora he had lost. Even with all our care and efforts, he did not get better. He cried often, and his stomach would tighten. He was gassy and in pain.

For two months we made several visits to the pediatrician. She said we had to give it time. On the fourth visit I requested a referral to a pediatric gastroenterologist. She said it wasn't necessary and refused to provide it. My mother's intuition said she was wrong, and I paid out of pocket for my son to see the specialist. When we went to see the GI doctor, I told him that my son had Roto virus, and the pediatrician had recommended yogurt, but he wasn't improving. Within 2 minutes of talking to this new doctor he diagnosed the problem. He explained that any virus that causes excessive diarrhea is going to strip the gut of bacteria, including lactobacilli. As a result, he became lactose intolerant, and the yogurt was causing all his stomach pain. Sure enough, we took him off the yogurt and he got better within a few days. I returned to the pediatrician and told her what the GI doctor said. She brushed it off with no apology. We immediately switched pediatricians.

Pediatrician #2 came highly recommended. When my older son was a toddler he had 11 ear infections in a row, (5 of them were in both ears at the same time). The pediatrician did not seem concerned about it. In retrospect I realize my son should have been referred to an ear nose and throat doctor (ENT) to be evaluated for tubes. He was speech delayed, likely caused by lack of clear hearing from the ear infections. Pediatrician #2 said my son would "just grow out of it."

Once again, the doctor was wrong. My son never did 'grow out of it' and ended up requiring speech therapy until he was eight. The doctor's lack of awareness cost nearly two years of early intervention, and according to the audiologist, probably also caused my son's auditory processing disorder. I know it wasn't intentional, but the effects it had on me and my son's life were monumental. It is an understatement to say that I wish I had known the significance of those ear infections much sooner.

When I discovered the long-term consequences of the ear infections, I became angry at the pediatrician. I trusted him to take care of my son, and he failed me. In my advocacy work for auditory processing disorder, I have learned that the majority of pediatricians don't even know what APD is, let alone the fact that ear infections can cause it. Even so, I had to do work to let go of the anger I felt towards the doctor who overlooked something that could have contributed to making things worse.

Do not feel bad about questioning authority.

I'm not saying that all doctors are bad. What I'm saying is that some pediatricians may lack knowledge in some areas, and it is your job to make sure all bases are covered. Just because everything is going well, and you feel the pediatrician's care has always been good, that doesn't mean he will always know what to do when unusual problems come up. Even the best doctors can have holes in their knowledge.

Do your research and arm yourself with facts and questions. When the school refuses services, or worse yet they say you are wrong about your child's problems, do your research to back up your point of view. If your MD cannot answer your questions, find another one. If your mother's intuition tells you that something isn't right here, listen to it!

You are not beholden to these professionals just because they are trained specialists or have MD after their name. They have a specific expertise, but you are the parent, which makes you the expert on your child! Speak up when you don't agree!

Track Everything and Stay Organized!

"Organizing is what you do before you do something,
so that when you do it, it is not all mixed up."
~ A. A. Milne

We are busy moms. It is super tedious to record things. However, I promise you that keeping track of each interaction with the school is one of your most valuable assets in this journey. So often I have talked to parents who complain the school refused to help, but they have no documentation to show the many times they have contacted the school.

In my own experience, I have used these records many times. There have been many occasions where 6 or 8 months after an event I am able to cite specific emails or phone calls. You can bet the school is shocked when I not only cite what was said, but the date, time and everybody who participated in the communication.

Document EVERYTHING

The key here is to be a maven about documenting every single event or record. You never know when this will be valuable, and it is very difficult to recreate in retrospect. Document as you go along, and it will be much easier when you really need it.

1. Make a list of team members.

Who is involved in your child's education this year? Make a list of each person, their title, role, IEP goals they help with, email and phone number. This is not only for easy reference, but helps you understand who has what responsibility. Keep this list from previous school years to know which providers worked with your child. Maybe even add some notes about their adequacy or attitudes

2. Document all conversations.

It's very important to log the day, time, person and reason for the communication. It does not have to be a fancy computer file. A simple spiral notebook where you log each event is sufficient.

In a separate section of the notebook, put a written copy of each communication with the school. This is particularly important regarding a verbal conversation. You must follow up with an email! It should not just be, "Thanks for talking to me today." You need to reiterate what the conversation was about, when it took place, who was involved, and what the conclusion was. Make sure you CC the case manager, principal, your spouse, your advocate or anybody supporting your child, so the team knows the conversation took place. Copy yourself as well, and when you receive the copy, print the email to put into your files. You want to keep a notebook with all these conversations organized in chronological order so it is easy for you to reference.

3. Organize all special education paperwork.

Get super organized with the mounds of paperwork involved in your child's special education experience. IEP or 504 paperwork should be organized chronologically. Be sure to include meeting requests, the final draft of IEP or 504 plan, amendments, assessment reports, progress reports or any documents related to the special education process. If you are not good at organizing these things, I have created an IEP organizer system which you can download in the printables section of my website: www.specialmomadvocate.com

4. Organize assessments separately.

Organize assessment reports by type and then by date. If you feel the assessments show a picture over time, create a table that shows the data for each time it was used for your child. This can show an interesting picture of your child's progress (or lack of progress), and could be a valuable tool for convincing the school your child needs help. This is especially true for reading, writing and math measures, which are usually done twice a year by the teacher. It is excellent evidence to show a lack of progress so the team will consider other options.

5. Take your own meeting notes.

Make sure you take notes at all meetings. While legally there should be a district representative who notates the entire meeting, there is no guarantee you will get an intact copy of those notes, or that specifics are included. The meetings can go quickly. Things are easily forgotten. Taking your own notes gives you a reference to make sure the school is doing what they promised. If you have trouble participating and taking notes at the same time, bring a family member or friend whose sole purpose is to take notes for you.

You could also record meetings, but the school may discourage or disallow it. If the school really opposes it, you can offer to send them a copy of the audio file for their records. If you want to do a recording, check with your district ahead of time to make sure you follow their protocol for advanced notice to record. You can find somebody to transcribe the meeting so you can have a written copy of everything that was said.

6. Keep a log of your child's experiences.

While IEP and 504 meetings are not held in a courtroom, it still feels like you need to defend your position. Evidence is your best asset in proving that your child needs help. Documenting your child's daily challenges can help you show the school where your child is having difficulties and why you are fighting so hard to get services. Just like your communication log, document all memorable incidents related to school.

Write down the problems your child is having in the classroom and on the playground. Document when your child receives services at school. Document what the teacher or special education professionals say about how your child is doing.

Document what happens at home. Sometimes kids hold it together really well at school, but the signs show up at home: fatigue, irritability, meltdowns, etc. Another key indicator is how she behaves while getting homework done. Are certain subjects harder than others? It may be helpful to include some videotaped examples of how your child behaves at home. When meeting with school personnel, make sure you have a way to play the video without internet so you can show them that you are not exaggerating the problems at home.

This log of your child's experience should give a complete picture of her daily struggles. A lot of this information is unknown to the IEP team. Demonstrating it may open their eyes and help them reconsider the refusal of services. If they still refuse services, then your log becomes valuable evidence during mediation or due process when a third party may take a different view of things.

7. Ask teachers for copies of assignments.

Oftentimes teachers do not send home assignments until they complete a term and report cards come out. Sometimes they don't send assignments home until the end of the year when they send the child's entire work folder. As a result you have no way of gauging how your child is doing. To know what's happening with your child's progress, about once a month ask the teacher for copies of tests, major assignments or writing samples.

Keep all the assignments chronologically in a notebook so you have a way to show progress (or lack of progress). Make sure to write the date on each assignment if your child has not already done so. When the team comes to the IEP, they are going to bring samples of your child's work. Usually they bring the best examples. That is where your notebook of assignments becomes important because it shows the true picture of her performance.

8. Keep all report cards and standardized test results.

Grades and test results can give a picture of your child's progress and success over time. Keep them in a separate tab in your notebook, organized chronologically.

9. Include all medical records.

Even if the doctor's visit was not directly related to your child's disability, it is a good idea to keep medical records together. The school may question when you last took your child to the doctor, or what the doctor said about a specific issue. Having those records on hand enables you to answer those questions on the spot.

10. Document all private assessments and therapies.

Keep a log of times your child has to seek help outside of the school. This includes tutors, outside therapies or even extra materials to work on at home. Keep all reports and any receipts showing payments made. If you end up in due process, there is a chance you could be reimbursed for these expenses. At the very least, showing it to the school demonstrates your effort and determination to help your child succeed.

While the documenting process is a pain, you will be grateful you did it. I usually put all documents in a pile in one spot and then once a month, add them to my files. I have had to reference conversations and assessments several times. It is wonderful that I can find what I need without a big hassle. If you do end up having to go to due process, well-organized exhibits will be critical to your success.

34

The School is Not Your Enemy

"Misdirected focus on paperwork, on procedures, and on bureaucracy frustrates teachers and fails to give children the education they need."
~ Christopher Bond

I know that it feels like you are in a terrible battle with the school when you are having a hard time getting help for your child. The truth is, the challenge is not due to the staff of the particular school. It's the special education bureaucracy that makes it hard for everybody.

The personnel must follow the rules of the district, laws of the state, as well as federal laws. They are boxed in from many sides, and this stifles their ability to make positive decisions and move forward. Generally it's the district that is put in the position of enforcing the blanket rules. People want to keep their jobs, so they must comply with these rules.

A story about Texas special education.

In 2016, the Houston Chronicle did an exposé on the denial of special education in the state of Texas. In 2004 the Texas State Legislature passed a bill that put a 'recommended' cap of 8.5% on the number of special education students in all state schools. The national average is

13.3% of the student population. In effect they were telling schools they had to reduce their special education services by nearly 5%. While it was written as a recommendation, it was enforced like a law. The Houston Chronicle did extensive research and interviewed teachers and administrators who revealed the lengths they went through in order to meet this unrealistic goal.

Some Texas districts required teachers to try some alternative teaching approaches to help children improve before initiating the evaluation process for special education. As a result students went years without proper support while the teachers had to prove the students continued to struggle in their classes.

Some districts actually lied to parents, telling them they had to pay for evaluations or that there was a waiting list. One district moved all the evaluation request forms to the district office, making it more difficult for teachers to start the special education process. Some teachers admitted to talking parents into removing their children from public school and choosing homeschooling or private school instead.

The districts and schools became experts at manipulating the law, and parents who did not know better were unable to get services for their children. It is estimated over 250,000 students were under served because of this 8.5% 'recommendation.' The schools were complying with what they were told to do. While they seemed like they were the enemy, they were following the rules in order to keep their jobs. They behaved as if they were the enemy, but it was not because they *wanted* to be the enemy.

Most districts and schools find themselves fighting a similar predicament. Teachers and special ed professionals choose this profession to help children. It is hard when they are put into positions where they are asked to deny services, particularly when they know or suspect that denying services will actually harm the students. Can you imagine the distress that the professional experiences?

Who holds the purse strings on the team?

When you are in a special education meeting, pay attention to the person who is citing the law. It may be the principal. Most of the time it's someone from the district. This is the person who actually makes the decision as to whether or not the district will spend the money. The other people on the team are not making that final decision, but they have to go along with it.

In our former district, a school staffer gave us the low down on why the district was so reluctant to help our child. While not a wealthy area, many families in that district were well off. When their child needed special education services, the parents would show up to the very first meeting with a lawyer. They did not try to work with the system on their own, but instead left the gate fighting like an angry bear. As a result, the district had to bring their own lawyer. Consequently, correspondence had to be handled through the lawyers. This all cost a lot of money. The more that was spent on legal fees, the less the district had for special education.

Knowing that made us realize we were fighting an uphill battle. We did hire a lawyer and we got our son support. We did not have unlimited resources to keep a lawyer on retainer for years on end, so we decided to move to a different district. This experience made me understand that I had been angry at the wrong group of people. The school was not against us. They were just doing their jobs of preserving the district's money.

The school is not your enemy; it's the bureaucracy.

Understand that the school is just as trapped as you are. That helps you have some empathy for their position. If you come to the table with that awareness and understanding, it helps to create a better relationship between you and the school. You can acknowledge it by saying, "I know that you guys have rules that you have to follow. I know that this is really hard because you have only so much money you can spend." It helps them to see that you are willing to work with them. It avoids setting up an adversarial tone from the beginning, and instead enables you to work together to solve the problem.

I strongly encourage you to reframe your view of the district. I know they feel like an enemy. I know you feel like you're in some sort of a battle with them. Remember that their decision-making is a result of their own self-preservation. Can you really expect a person to put his job over and above your needs when he has his own family to worry about? You and your child are just one of many who are victims of this process, but the school is not aiming their arrows just at you.

Not all districts will respond to empathy.

Of course, there are districts that are deliberately adversarial. A hostile posture may be their way to get you to back down. It's harder to have empathy for people who are being outright nasty, and empathy may not get what your child needs. You need to use your judgment on how far empathy and negotiation will get you.

POINTS TO PONDER

1. What are the reasons your district says no?

2. What have other parents said about this?

3. How can you let the people at school know that you understand their position?

Letter Writing Tips

Never write a letter while you are angry.
~ Chinese Proverb

Communication with anybody in the school or district should be tracked thoroughly. This is a crucial point. If you do not have proof in writing, the school can deny the interaction or claim a different version. Letters are the preferred method of communicating, but emails are okay too.

Important components to include in your letter.

Just like a business letter, you should include general information so the letter looks professional. In order to serve as a good record of the communication, your letter should include the following:

- Date
- Your child's full name
- Your child's grade, classroom placement and teacher(s)'s name
- A specific statement about your concerns
- A specific statement about what you want to happen (focus on what you want, not what you don't want)
- Your address, phone and email where you can be contacted
- A courteous closing that includes some form of 'thank you.'

Formulating your concerns and requests.

This is the meat of the letter so spend some time putting it together. Remember to describe your concerns in an objective way. You do not want to be accusatory or judgmental. Simply state the facts as you see them. Succinctly explain your concerns and request how you want those concerns addressed. Never demand a specific outcome. Diplomacy is important when writing letters to the school.

Refining the first draft.

- Write it and leave it for a couple days, then come back and review it again. This is especially important if you were emotional when you wrote the letter. It is crucial to keep the letter as neutral as possible and not show how upset you are.

- Read the letter out loud to check for grammar and how it flows. Make sure it does not ramble on too long and the sentences are clear and concise.

- Ask someone else to provide feedback. Writing the letter is a big step, and often an emotional one. It is a good idea to ask a fellow special education mom or a friend to review the letter.

- If the letter is a critical juncture in your negotiation with the school, you may want to ask an advocate or even an attorney to review it.

- Consider all changes carefully if it comes from individuals who are not well versed in the special education process.

Templates for letter wording and format.

There are many great resources for special education letter templates, so I will not provide templates here in the book. The best resource I have found to help with letter writing is *Wrightslaw: From Emotions to Advocacy* by Pam Wright & Pete Wright.

36

How to Foster a Positive
Special Ed Meeting

"Always go into meetings or negotiations with a positive attitude.
Tell yourself you're going to make this the best deal for all parties."
~ Natalie Massenet

I know that tight feeling in your stomach just before you walk into a special education meeting. I feel it too. It is especially true if your school district is difficult. I still get it with our current school that is generally cooperative. It is important to go in and do your best to make the most of the meeting. The other participants may not always set a positive tone, so it's up to you to make the meeting work for your child.

20 tips for creating a
positive meeting environment

I know this is a long list, and you may not remember them all at your first meeting. You will have many more meetings along this journey. Do your best and incorporate more tips with each subsequent opportunity.

1. Visualize a positive outcome.

In chapter 8, I talk about visualizing healing. You can use these same techniques for the meeting. Envision a positive outcome, ease of negotiation, and walking away with the best plan for your child.

2. Practice ahead of time.

Before the meeting, practice what you are going to say and run different scenarios on their responses. This will boost your confidence and also help you brainstorm about different approaches.

3. Prepare ahead of time.

Write down your child's needs in order of importance. Organize your paperwork and find out who will be at the meeting. If there are changes planned, try to learn what they are considering. If they have done assessments, ask for copies ahead of time so you can review and prepare your questions and concerns.

If they already have a draft of the IEP or 504, ask for a copy of that as well. If you have questions for one of the specialists, email the questions ahead of time so that person has the answers. You want to do everything possible to see what they are considering, and to know how they reached their decisions. The more preparation you do, the more likely the meeting will not last forever.

4. Dress professionally.

First impressions are everything. If you arrive in cutoffs and a t-shirt, you are giving the impression that this is not serious. Everybody else will be dressed for work, so you do the same.

5. Bring a recent photo of your child.

If your child will not be at the meeting, bring a photo and leave it on the table. This reminds everybody that you are talking about a specific individual, not just any student. It's even better if the photo shows the child doing something he could not do the year before. This reminds everybody that they are all there to support the child in progressing.

6. Stay calm and avoid strong emotions.

If there is one thing that will make a big difference, it is remaining calm. Treat this like a business meeting. Save your tears and anger for home. Your relationship with the school is very important and staying calm and unemotional shows you are serious about working with them. Crying will not elicit sympathy. It rarely gets them to change their mind. If you get angry, you alienate team members. It is difficult to repair those rifts.

If you have issues with emotional outbursts, practice strategies to help maintain a logical, business-like approach. This includes facial expressions. While you may not say anything, your face can reveal your feelings. Practice having a poker face so nobody knows what is on your mind as you listen to the discussion.

7. Be diplomatic and avoid blaming.

I strongly urge you to resist calling the school out and saying they are not doing enough. Blaming does nothing except hurt feelings. That causes teams members to want to step back from the process.

8. Don't interrupt.

Allow each person to complete their thought before you jump in to reply. This is common courtesy, but hard to do when emotions run high and you strongly disagree with what somebody is saying. Exercise patience and respect everybody's right to have their say.

9. Bring well-organized paperwork.

If you have a well-organized binder with all your paperwork, it is easier to look up historical information. I review how to organize your paperwork in Chapter 33.

10. Take notes.

Make sure you are writing down who was there, what was discussed and decisions that were made. This shows them you take the meeting seriously, and it gives you a permanent record.

11. Bring a friend or advocate.

These meetings can be intimidating. It is helpful to have somebody who is in your court. Another special education mom, a spouse or even an advocate can make a huge difference in helping you stay calm and gain clarity. This is especially important if your emotions are intense and you may just bubble over. In that case an advocate is your best choice.

12. Be willing to negotiate.

While you definitely want the best for your child, the goal here is to establish a plan that allows your child to make meaningful progress. Remember that while you might want a five star education, the district does not have the resources to provide it. Furthermore, they are not required by law to provide it. So you must be willing to negotiate and get what you can. Examine your child's needs and consider the long-term goals, and press for the services that are going to move your child towards those goals.

13. Be open-minded.

You may have a clear picture of what services your child needs, but be open to hearing other options. The school personnel do have a lot of knowledge and resources, and they may possibly suggest an alternative that is a better than your original plan. This will demonstrate flexibility on your part, and facilitate more brainstorming

14. Actively participate in brainstorming.

You are an equal partner so do not remain quiet when they are deciding on goals, accommodations, services and modifications. Even if you cannot add ideas, at least acknowledge the ideas they are considering. Give your opinion on which options you think would be best.

15. Ask questions.

The team does not expect you to know everything, so feel free to ask as many questions as needed. Do not apologize for asking questions, and do not feel embarrassed if you do not understand. It is a lot to digest and by asking questions you are showing them your desire to understand.

16. Share how you support your child at home.

Over the years I have found this to be a valuable part of special education meetings. By sharing what we are doing at home to help our son progress, the school then realizes I am just as involved in his education as they are. If you are doing therapies or extra learning programs or employing behavioral supports, take a few minutes and tell them about it. It is very important that they know you do not expect them to do everything, or to carry the burden alone.

17. Keep your child's long-term goals in mind.

It is easy to get off track, so you want to make sure you are focused on what you are trying to accomplish. With each decision you want to ask yourself if it is moving your child towards the long-range plans you have laid out. Have a written list of those plans and reference them if necessary. Make sure the goals, services and accommodations are working towards those long-range plans. If the team is selecting ideas because it worked for other kids, or because that service is what they always offer, make sure it fits what your child really needs.

18. Have some empathy for their position.

If you read chapter 34, *The School is Not Your Enemy*, you will realize that they are in a difficult position. They did not get into education to harm kids but to help kids. It is difficult for them to have to refuse services when there appears to be a need to support the child. Empathy helps you soften your approach. Be more understanding and willing to hear their point of view. I'm not suggesting you give in because you feel sorry for them. It just helps you demonstrate a level of understanding that they do not usually get from parents.

19. Schedule a follow up.

Ask for a 60-day review of the plan so the entire team can assess how it is working.

20. Send a summary email.

After the meeting send an email thanking all the members and providing a written summary of the meeting from your perspective. Invite them to reply if they feel you have recorded anything incorrectly. Make sure you include any To Do items for team members so it is clear who is responsible for what.

37

Recognize and Report
School Retaliation

"Let me embrace thee, sour adversity,
for wise men say it is the wisest course."
~ William Shakespeare

Feathers get ruffled when we assert our rights. That is to be expected when people disagree. However if the school has made threats, or in any way made you feel like you or your child is not welcome at school, this is illegal. It's not only illegal, it is considered discrimination based on disabilities.

In our previous district this happened to us, and I had no idea the school personnel were breaking the law. Once we hired a lawyer, nobody would talk to us anymore. The teacher even said she wasn't allowed to talk to us about everyday issues. The people working the office were cold and rude, and the principal would walk the other way if she saw us coming. IEP meetings were contentious, angry and very unproductive.

Section 504 of the Americans with Disabilities Act (ADA) has federal laws, which prevent discrimination based on an individual's disability. This protects students with IEP or 504 plans. These laws also prohibit retaliation against anybody for exercising their right to obtain FAPE (free appropriate public education). Section 504 prohibits schools or districts from retaliating against parents or students for complaining, filing due process, testifying or in any way advocating for the rights of the child. Section 504 requires the school district to respond to and investigate any reports of parents or students being harassed in this context.

Types of retaliation you may see in special education.

Delay tactics

A common tactic used by schools is to respond slowly. They may delay meetings, not respond to emails or phone calls or provide complex explanations to avoid implementing services. It is often subtle and hard for a parent to ascertain if it is retaliation or just sloppy organization.

Control tactics

Sometimes school personnel will refuse to talk to the parents except for a very narrow time frame. They are also betting the parent is not knowledgeable on special education law and they will misquote the law to make the parents back down. Learning the law can help you spot non-compliance, which can get the district back in line or be a basis for a retaliation complaint.

Punishment tactics

The school may openly threaten parents or employ drawn-out due process tactics to delay providing FAPE to the child. Teachers may suddenly give your child failing grades or the district will suddenly lose all of your child's records. Some administrators have been caught filing false child protective services reports in retaliation. At this point it would be prudent to hire an attorney to protect both the parents and the child from further harassment.

Filing a complaint with Office of Civil Rights.

It's very important to remember these actions are serious. They not only effect your ability to advocate in the future, but they can affect your child's experience in school. While we always hope things will get better, if the situation has made it impossible for you to advocate for your child, the best way to handle this is to consult with an attorney about filing a discrimination complaint with the Office of Civil Rights.

Look online at: http://tinyurl.com/ycq4m6j6 for information on how to file. Any agency that receives federal funding must abide by the civil rights laws, so you are well within your rights to report the school and have the incidents investigated. This includes public colleges or private institutions that receive federal funds.

In order for the Office of Civil Rights (OCR) to find a complaint to be retaliatory, it must demonstrate an adverse action on the person filing the complaint. OCR has provided a 5-part test to help determine if an action is retaliatory:

1. Has the student or parent engaged in an activity protected by the Americans with Disabilities Act (i.e. advocacy)?

2. Is the district aware that the student or parent has engaged in this activity?

3. Can the parent show that the school district participated in an adverse reaction after the parent engaged in the protected activity?

4. Will a neutral, third party determine that there is a cause and effect relationship between the protected activity and the adverse action?

5. Can the district offer a valid reason for the action that would otherwise explain why it was taken?

Sometimes it can be difficult to prove that the action is retaliatory, but that should not keep you from filing a complaint. It may be wise to talk to an attorney because schools who engage in retaliation are the most difficult to work with on all levels.

It's Not Your Job
to Work at School

"Good teachers know how to bring out the best in students."
~ Charles Kuralt

One of my clients got an email from her child's teacher saying he cannot go on the upcoming field trip unless a parent goes with him. The teacher said they do not have somebody who can watch him. Since he often gets over stimulated or upset, the school said that a parent must come to keep him calm. This was the teacher transferring a school-related responsibility to the parents. It discriminated against the child based on his disability. The school is not allowed to make parent attendance a requirement for field trips or any participation in school.

Subpart D, section 104.34 of Section 504 requires the school to provide equal access in academic and nonacademic settings. This law covers students with IEPs and 504s. It is against the law for a school to exclude a child from school-related activities because the behavior due to his disability makes it difficult for the teacher to manage.

This means the school must provide equal access to field trips. Schools are not allowed to ask the parent to provide the oversight in order to facilitate this equal access. Unless the activity on the field trip is a risk to the child's safety, the school must provide equal access to the activity. If the school says the trip is unsafe, they must justify their position. Unless all students are required to have an adult attend, this request is illegal.

In 2015, a civil rights group called Public Advocates, uncovered a pattern in California that showed public charter schools violated state law by requiring all parents to volunteer a minimum number of hours per year. This was not just special education parents but parents of all the children. In some cases the students were not allowed to participate in school activities because the parent had not met the volunteer requirement. In response the California Department of Education issued a memo reiterating that public schools cannot require donations, volunteer hours or any specific contribution from the parents. In addition, students cannot be barred from school admission, activities or privileges if the parents do not meet specific volunteer requests.

The teacher cannot ask you to provide special help for your child.

Nancy is a third grade student who is in general education classes most of the day, but she gets pulled out for specialized math instruction. She has sensory issues, particularly with textures, and has a lot of difficulty with general education art projects. The general education teacher told the mom that she was going to send her daughter to the resource room during art unless the mom volunteered to help during art instruction. This teacher is requiring the mom to do the teacher's job, and it is illegal for the teacher to deny the child her education unless the parent is present.

Unfortunately teachers are overwhelmed with larger class sizes and often do not have time to provide individualized support. In these cases the teacher and parent should call a team meeting and discuss options for supporting the student during art instruction.

It's really wonderful if you want to volunteer at school and provide extra support for the teacher. There is no better opportunity to see first-hand what is going on at school. It becomes a problem if the teacher or administrator requires you to volunteer as a condition of your child receiving instruction or special services. Then you need to inform them (in writing) that they are violating the law by requiring you to work at school in order to provide **your** child her education.

Understand the Special Ed Process

In this section you will get a high-level overview of what is involved in special education, as well as some details of the more critical steps.

39

A Roadmap of the
Special Ed Process

"I always wish I had a road map for how to navigate my life as a parent and a producer, but in truth, it's a lot of trial and error."
~ Raney Aronson-Rath

So how do you get the school to help? This is the $1 billion dollar question. Unfortunately there is no simple answer. How you get help depends on how the particular school district responds to requests for special education and how effectively you can fight if they say no.

Your best option is to find out everything you can about how the district handles special education. Try and connect with parents, talk to staff, and compile a special education profile of the district. You can hire an advocate familiar with the district since she would help you wind your way through the bureaucracy. While it will be a challenge, this chapter provides an overview of the special education process so you have an idea of how the system works.

There is no single best response when the school beats around the bush or outright refuses services. Strategize like you're playing chess. Consider your opponent, your options and choose the best way to move forward. Sometimes it works out great and sometimes just so so. Along the way you will learn a lot and hopefully your child will get the support for optimum success.

If I had the perfect answer, I would be happy to give it to you. It will take time, effort, research and learning to come up with an approach that will be successful. Just remember to keep moving towards the goals. The journey is not straight forward; but you will make progress if you persist.

The following chart is a general overview of the special education process. It provides a roadmap to help you understand how the process works. In Section 5, I explain each of these steps and what you can do to achieve success working with the school.

The Special Education Process

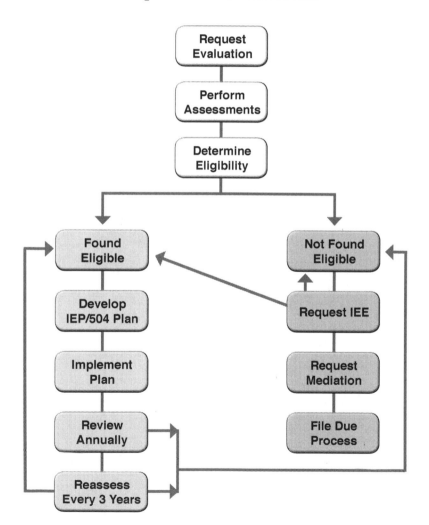

40

Know Your Rights
and the Law

"Good people do not need laws to tell them to act responsibly,
while bad people will find a way around the laws."
~ Plato

It is critical that you are thoroughly prepared before meeting with the school. Because they don't expect parents to be knowledgeable about special education law, you have a leg up in meetings when you are armed with this knowledge. Also, by knowing your rights and the correct procedures, you become an equal contributor in your child's education plan. There are three levels of law you need to understand:

- **Federal law:** Consists of IDEA and section 504 of ADA.

- **State Law:** Each state has its own way of interpreting and implementing federal law.

- **District Policies:** Each district has its own policies for implementing special education.

This book is not intended to teach you about the specifics of the law. Several books would be required for that. Instead I provide a high level overview of special education law. If you are looking for more in-depth knowledge, I highly recommend *From Emotions to Advocacy* and *Special Education Law*, both by Pam and Pete Wright.

Federal Law

There are two Federal laws that affect students with disabilities:

- IDEA (Individuals with Disabilities Education Act)
- Section 504 of the ADA (Americans with Disabilities Act)

The IDEA is a set of laws created to define the process for identifying children with learning challenges as well as guidelines for implementing special education in the schools. The IDEA provides the laws that govern individual education programs (IEPs).

The Americans with Disabilities Act protects the civil rights of individuals with disabilities. Section 504 of the ADA specifically addresses the rights of students with disabilities in the school environment. All students with IEPs are protected under ADA, but students with 504 plans are not protected under IDEA. The reason why is the IDEA only applies to students who qualify for an IEP (individualized education program). Section 504 applies to all students with any kind of disability regardless of whether they qualify for special education support.

IDEA (Individuals with Disabilities Education Act)

The IDEA (Individuals with Disabilities Education Act) is a federal law that assures each child with qualifying disabilities will receive a Free and Appropriate Public Education (FAPE) in their local public school. The law further ensures that this education will be individualized to meet the specific needs of each student.

An IEP is created for a student who needs specialized instruction or services based on the guidelines established in the IDEA. Chapter 43 (*The Mystery Behind Qualification for Special Education Services*) explains the specifics on qualifying for an IEP.

Generally speaking, a child with an IEP has a disability that significantly impacts his ability to access his education. For such a student, simple accommodations are not sufficient to keep the child on a par with his peers. Usually he needs extra services, like speech therapy or occupational therapy, to help him access his education. Some students with IEPs can do grade level work in some subjects but not in others. Some have pervasive delays that make it impossible to do grade level work in any subject.

With IEPs, the curriculum can be modified. Modifications mean the student is not expected to perform at grade level in one or more subjects. For example, the child may go to a resource room to work only on math, not other subjects, because grade-level math is too hard for him.

An IEP plan should include all of the following:

- Present levels of performance (PLOP)
- Annual goals
- How progress towards goals will be measured
- Description of specialized equipment the child may use
- Modifications to curriculum
- Accommodations that are made in the classroom (such as sitting closer to the front or going to a quiet room for tests)
- Accommodations for state-mandated testing
- Additional special education services to be received
- Percentage of special education versus general education instruction
- Transition plan for post-high school education (for students 16 and older)

IEPs are planned and written by the IEP team, which includes the parents. Creating an IEP includes assessments by school therapists, academic evaluations and input from all team members. The plan should be a joint effort by all involved, and not the school telling the parent how it will be. The IEP is reviewed annually. The child is reassessed every 3 years to determine if he still qualifies for services. IEP plans usually cost the school money because additional support services are required.

IDEA is not a static law. As parents sue districts and new case law is established, changes are made in implementing IDEA. Hence it is important to understand recent rulings before making your case to the district. If you have a particularly difficult situation, hiring an attorney may be warranted. That attorney should specialize in special education so that he can best utilize all legal resources.

Section 504 of ADA (Americans with Disabilities)

A 504 Plan is used for children who have some form of disability that makes it difficult for the student to access his education. It's generally a disability that is not as pervasive as a child with an IEP. A child with a 504 Plan would not receive any services outside the classroom. Instead the student would be accommodated in the classroom to help equalize the playing field so his disability does not put him behind his peers.

With a 504, the student completes the same curriculum as non-disabled students, but the student may be given accommodations to make it easier to complete the work. For example, a child with dyslexia may be given additional time on tests; or may be given written class notes. A student with ADHD may be given movement breaks to help with hyperactivity. A student with a visual processing disorder may be given preferential seating at the front of the room. A 504 can also be set up for a child with medical or mental disabilities, such cancer or bipolar disorder.

By law a parent's input is not required for the 504, but the school does have to notify the parents if a plan has been created. This means the plan can be implemented without the parent's approval. Although the school usually does an assessment to determine if a child qualifies for support in school. The school does need permission from the parent to do the assessment. If the parent provides a diagnosis from a specialist outside the school, this can be used to qualify the student for a 504 plan.

After qualification is decided on, a meeting is held to determine what the child needs to achieve his potential. In this meeting specific classroom accommodations are established. The 504 Plan should be reviewed annually, but there is no law requiring this. A 504 plan does not include extra services, so it usually does not incur any additional cost to the school.

Key differences between a 504 and IEP

Guidelines	504 Plan	IEP Plan
Governing Law	Section 504 of the Rehabilitation Act of 1973	Individuals with Disabilities Education Act amended 2004
Overseeing Agency	U.S. Department of Education: Office of Civil Rights	U.S. Department of Education: Office of Special Education and Rehabilitation Services
Ages covered	Entire life	Birth through age 21
Eligibility	Student must have a disability AND the disability affects the student's ability to access the curriculum.	Student must qualify in one of 13 categories of disability, AND disability affects the child's ability to access curriculum or affects ability to perform tasks necessary to engage in curriculum.
Written Plan	Does not require written plan.	Does require a written plan.
Evaluation	Law does not specify evaluation procedures. Simply states "periodic" evaluation.	IEP must be reviewed annually and student must be reevaluated every three years.
Parent involvement	School must get permission from parent to do the evaluation. Parents must be notified that a plan has been created. School can create a plan without parent participation. School is not required to invite parent to meetings. School does not have to provide progress reports to parents.	Parents are required to be part of the IEP team. Parents must be given 10 days notice of any change in placement. School is required to invite parents to all meetings. School must provide regular reports to indicate progress on goals.
Customized curriculum	Curriculum is not customized for the student. The student completes the same curriculum as students without disabilities.	The IEP must be an individualized plan that meets the needs of the student. This may require different curriculum, change of classroom, different teacher, additional services etc.

Review	No requirement to review annually.	Must review the plan annually. Student must be reassessed and requalified every 3 years.
Goals	No goals or progress monitoring.	Goals must be written, measurable and reviewed annually.
Accommodations	Student may be given accommodations to 'equal the playing field' so they are able to access curriculum.	Students may be given accommodations to make it easier to access their education.
Modifications	The student can have modified assignments of the regular grade-level curriculum, such as doing fewer problems on a math test or not have to complete homework. The student cannot have a completely different curriculum.	The student can have modified assignments, such as doing fewer problems on a math test or not have to complete homework. The student can have a modified curriculum where they do a completely different curriculum than non-disabled students.
Services	The student is not eligible to receive extra services.	The student is eligible to receive services such as speech therapy, occupational therapy, a 1-on-1 aide, etc.
College	Section 504 protects the student in colleges that receive federal funding. The student may receive the same accommodations as they had in high school, but it is up to the individual college to decide what accommodations will be provided.	IDEA does not protect the child in college. The child would receive protection under Section 504 instead. The student would only receive accommodations in college, no modification to curriculum and no services.
Procedural Safeguards	Section 504 does not have specific guidelines to protect the rights of the parent and child.	IDEA has a clearly defined set of procedural safeguards that must be followed to ensure the rights of the parent and child.
Recourse	The parent has a right to file a complaint with the Office of Civil Rights.	There is a specific due process procedure that can be followed by parents and the school to register and resolve complaints.

States have their own laws too.

The IDEA and Section 504 are the laws regulating special education, but each state has its own set of special education laws as well. The states must abide by the federal laws, but the federal laws are vague about what determines eligibility and how special education is implemented. For example, the federal laws list the categories for qualification, but they do not provide a definition of what each category means. So "other health impaired" in one state could be different in another state.

State laws often clarify or supplement federal laws to provide guidelines for the school districts. Each state must provide the minimum of the federal statutes, but some states improve on the statutes adding stricter guidelines. For example, the IDEA gives a 60-day time limit to complete evaluations, while some states shorten this to 45 days. Check the website for your state department of education to find the specific laws for your state.

Districts have their own policies.

Districts create policy manuals used by all personnel to implement special education. These policies will often outline the process used to identify students with disabilities and the timeline to do so. These policies will also specify forms to be used and guidelines for parent procedures. For example, if meetings are to be recorded, the district policies should outline how much notice is needed and who should be notified of the intent to record.

Reading the district policies may help you identify some of the specific personality traits of your district. While they will not reveal the reasons they say no, it may enlighten you as to some of the more difficult hoops personnel and parents need to go through in order to put special education in place.

To find the policies for your district, try searching for policies + "special education" + "district name" in Google. If you cannot find it there, request a copy from your district.

Parent Rights

When an IEP meeting starts, the first thing the facilitator does is hand you a copy of your parent rights and asks you to sign a document saying you received them. This process is required by law to ensure that you are informed of your rights in your child's special education. The rights listed are simply a summary of the IDEA and state laws that govern your role in the special education process. It is a good outline to help you know what topics you need to learn more about.

How can you learn about special education law?

The process of understanding special education law is long and intense. There are many resources to learn about the law. The following resources are the best I have found:

- **Wrights Law.** Started by an attorney who won a Supreme Court case in special education, Wrights Law is a cornerstone for understanding special ed. Their website alone is a wealth of information, but they also have books, digital classes and in-person classes. You can find out more at www.WrightsLaw.com.

- **Council for Parent Attorneys and Advocates.** A non-profit started by parents dealing with the special education, COPAA has become an invaluable resource for parents and professionals. You must become a member, but it is only $50 per year for parents. They have online message boards as well as classes on special education. Find out more at www.copaa.org.

- **Parent Centers.** Each state has federally funded Parent Centers that provide support and information at no cost to the parent. They offer classes, workshops, support groups, informal advocacy and lending libraries. Find your Parent Center at www.parentcenterhub.org.

41

Learn the Lingo!

"The limits of my language mean the limits of my world."
~ Ludwig Wittgenstein

It is critical that you learn the more common terms used in special education. Many terms are stated in acronyms, so it is not easy to surmise their meaning from conversation. This chapter covers acronyms and definitions that are most commonly used throughout the special education process. You aren't going to learn them all at once, but this provides a great resource when you come across a term you don't understand.

Special Education Acronyms

504	Provides accommodations to students with disabilities under Section 504 of the Americans with Disabilities Act.
ABA	Applied Behavioral Analysis
ADA	Americans with Disabilities Act
ADD	Attention Deficit Disorder (now called ADHD)
ADHD	Attention Deficit Hyperactivity Disorder
ADL	Acts of Daily Living

ADR	Alternative Dispute Resolution
AIM	Accessible Instructional Materials
APE	Adaptive Physical Education
APD	Auditory Processing Disorder *(formerly Central Auditory Processing Disorder)*
ASD	Autism Spectrum Disorder
AT	Assistive Technology
AYP	Adequate Yearly Progress
BD	Behavioral Disorder
BIP	Behavioral Intervention Plan
BOE	Board of Education
CBA	Curriculum Based Assessment
CCSS	Common Core State Standards
CEC	Council for Exceptional Children
CP	Cerebral Palsy
CST	Child Study Team
DD	Developmental Delay
DOE	U.S. Department of Education
DS	Down Syndrome
DSM	*Diagnostic and Statistical Manual of Mental Disorders* by the American Psychiatric Association
ECE	Early Childhood Education
ED	Emotional Disturbance
EI	Early Intervention
ELL	English Language Learner

ESD	Extended School Day
ESY	Extended School Year
FAPE	Free and Appropriate Education
FAS	Fetal Alcohol Syndrome
FASD	Fetal Alcohol Spectrum Disorder
FBA	Functional Behavioral Assessment
FERPA	Family Educational Rights and Privacy Act
GE	General Education
HI	Hearing Impaired
HO	Hearing Officer
IA	Instructional Assistant
ID	Intellectual Disabilities
IDEA	Individuals with Disabilities Education Act
IEE	Independent Educational Evaluation
IEP	Individualized Education Program
ITP	Individualized Transition Plan
LEA	Local Education Agency (e.g. school district)
LRE	Least Restrictive Environment
NCLB	No Child Left Behind Act
OAH	Office of Administrative Hearings
OCD	Obsessive Compulsive Disorder
ODD	Oppositional Defiant Disorder
OCR	U.S. Office of Civil Rights
OHI	Other Health Impaired

OSEP	U.S. Office of Special Education Programs
OSERS	U.S. Office of Special Education and Rehabilitation Programs
OT	Occupational Therapy
PBS	Positive Behavioral Supports
PCL	Parent Concerns Letter
PLA	Parent Letter of Attachment
PLOP	Present Levels of Performance
PT	Physical Therapy
PTI	Parent Training and Information Center
PWN	Prior Written Notice
RTI	Response to Intervention
SDC	Special Day Class
SEA	State Education Agency
SED	Severe Emotional Disturbance
SID	Sensory Integration Disorder
SLD	Specific Learning Disability
SLI	Speech/Language Impairment
SLP	Speech Language Pathologist
SPED	Special Education
TBI	Traumatic Brain Injury
TS	Tourette Syndrome
VI	Visual Impairment
VocEd	Vocational Education
VR	Vocational Rehabilitation

Glossary of Terms

I put together the following terms that are most commonly used in special education. It is important to know what they mean so you can speak about them during special education meetings.

504 Plan	A 504 Plan is used for children who have some form of disability that makes it difficult for the student to access his/her education. It's generally a disability that is not as pervasive as a child with an IEP. A child with a 504 would not receive any services outside the classroom. Instead the student would receive accommodations in the classroom to help equalize the playing field so the disability does not put him/her behind peers.
Applied Behavioral Analysis (ABA)	A research-based therapy that is used to change behaviors in a child. Most commonly used for children with autism spectrum disorder (ASD).
Accommodation	A change in the way a student completes assignments or receives instruction in order to accommodate for a disability. The change does not modify the content of the curriculum.
Achievement Gap	The difference in academic performance between students from different groups. For example, the difference between a student with a disability and same-age peers without the disability. It could also be the difference between English language learners and native English learners.
Adaptive Physical Education (APE)	A modified physical education curriculum that accommodates students with disabilities.
Adult Student	A child is considered an adult student if the student is over 18 years of age, or an emancipated minor, and continuing to attend high school.
Advocate	A professional who is knowledgeable about the special education process and special education law, but is not a lawyer. An advocate is hired by a parent to help manage the interactions with the special education team and school district.

Alternative Assessments	Alternative ways to measure student performance. It is not a standardized assessment, but usually assignments the student has completed. Could include projects, demonstrations, oral reports, essays, etc. Alternative assessments are sometimes used when a student is unable to participate in standardized assessments.
Alternative Dispute Resolution	Alternative methods for resolving disagreements without going through litigation. Mediation is an example of an alternative dispute resolution.
Annual Goals	Measurable goals that are required in an IEP. They should be written specifically for the student and should be measurable and something the student is working on improving.
Assessment	Any standardized method that is used to measure performance of a student. IQ tests and reading level assessments are examples. Usually used to measure what a student knows or is capable of and where the student needs to improve. Assessments are used to determine if a student qualifies for special education.
Assistive Technology Device	Any equipment that is employed to assist a student in accessing curriculum. For example, a computer that enlarges text for a visually impaired student or an iPad used to type notes for a student who struggles with writing.
Behavior Intervention Plan (BIP)	A plan that is put in place to assist in monitoring and improving the behavior of a student with disabilities. A BIP is created based on the data from a functional behavioral assessment (FBA).
Child Find	The law that requires schools to identify, evaluate and provide services to students with disabilities.
Compliance Complaint	When a school has failed to abide by Section 504 of the ADA or IDEA, parents can file a compliance complaint with the state board of education.
Cumulative File (Cume File)	A file maintained by the school district that has all educational records of a student. Includes attendance, report cards, behavioral reports and notes from teachers. Does not usually include special education information, but some school districts include it. FERPA gives parents the right to inspect and have copies of the cume file.

Developmental Delay	A delay in the physical, cognitive or functional development of a child.
Disability	A physical, cognitive, functional, social or emotional impairment that affects day to day life. If it affects the student's ability to access their education, they would be entitled to special education services.
Due Process Complaint	When parents feel the school is not meeting the needs of their child with disabilities, the parents can file a Due Process Complaint to request a Due Process Hearing. If a parent requests an IEE and the school feels they have done an adequate job in evaluating and providing services, they also can file a Due Process Complaint against the parent.
Due Process Hearing	A formal hearing, similar to a court, intended to resolve disagreements between parents and school districts regarding services for special education.
Early Intervention	A system of evaluations and therapies used to assist babies and toddlers with developmental delays or health conditions. Early intervention is usually provided by state-funded regional centers up until age 3. From 3 onward, it is provided by school districts.
Extended School Day	A provision for a special education student to receive school-funded instruction for a period longer than the standard school day.
Extended School Year	A provision for a special education student to receive academic instruction beyond the end of school year (usually during summer). The goal of ESY is to provide continued instruction to prevent the child from regressing during the vacation period.
Free Appropriate Public Education (FAPE)	FAPE is a public education for children with disabilities that is provided in the least restrictive environment. This education is provided at no cost to the parents and should ensure the student makes meaningful progress each year. It could include supplemental services such as writing therapy, one-on-one aide or specialized physical education.

Functional Behavioral Assessment (FBA)	An FBA is a formal assessment of a student's behavior that includes observation, written assessments and interviews. The goal of the FBA is to understand the motivation behind a student's behavior so remedies can be employed to change it. An FBA is used to develop a behavioral intervention plan (BIP) to support the student during the school day.
Functional Curriculum	A school curriculum focused on skills of daily living as a means of teaching students self-care and how to interact with others.
Gifted	A child is considered gifted if formal assessments show that they have significantly higher than average ability in one or more areas. Usually two standard deviations above the norm on an IQ test. It is common for gifted children to develop asynchronously or to have learning disabilities. Students who are gifted with learning disabilities are called twice ex-ceptional.
Higher Education	Education provided by universities and other institutions that award academic degrees, such as community colleges, and vocational schools.
IEP Team	The group of individuals who are required by IDEA to col-laborate and create an IEP. IDEA requires the following members on the team: parent(s), general education teacher, special education teacher, service providers, school district representative, person knowledgeable about evaluating the child's disability. In addition, the student can join in as well as other professionals invited by the parents or the school.
Inclusion	For a student with disabilities, inclusion means providing all, or most, of academic instruction in a general education classroom.
Independent Educational Evaluation (IEE)	Formal assessments done for the student by a qualified professional who does not work for the school district. Par-ents have a right to ask for an IEE at public expense if they disagree with the school's evaluations or decision, but the school is not always required to pay for it.
Individuals with Disabilities Education Act (IDEA):	The Federal law that entitles some students with disabilities to special education services. Students who do not qualify under IDEA may be eligible under Section 504 of the ADA.

Individualized Education Program (IEP)	The document created by the IEP team that describes what services, modifications and accommodations a student will receive as part of their special education. The document also includes annual goals.
Individualized Instruction	When instruction and curriculum are modified to meet the pace and abilities of an individual learner.
Learning Style	The preferred method a person uses to learn new information. Visual, auditory, and kinesthetic are the three most common learning styles.
Least Restrictive Environment (LRE)	A federal mandate in the IDEA that requires a school, whenever possible, to place students with disabilities in a learning environment with the least amount of educational and environmental restrictions. For example, placing the student with disabilities in a general education setting rather than a self-contained special education class.
Mind Map	A visual diagram that is used to assist in diagramming written information in preparation for writing a paragraph or essay. It can also be used to assist with visualizing or structuring information as a means to organize or learn the information.
Modifications	A modification is a change to the curriculum that alters the requirements for achievement by a student with disabilities. For example, only having to do one page of homework instead of three.
Occupational Therapy	A special service provided by an occupational therapist that focuses on the development of functional activities. It could include therapy ot help things such as gross and fine motor skills, writing, activities of daily living, swallowing or sensory diet.
Office for Civil Rights (OCR)	A Federal agency within the Department of Education that is in charge of ensuring civil rights for citizens of the USA.
Office of Special Education Programs (OSEP)	A Federal agency in charge of making sure that states comply with IDEA.

Paraprofessional (Para)	A para works in the school providing individualized support to students with disabilities. The para is not a teacher and must work under the supervision of a teacher or other trained professional. A para is sometimes called an aide.
Parent Training & Information Center (PTI)	Parent Training & Information Centers are federally funded agencies that provide information, training and support to parents and children with disabilities.
Placement	The school setting(s) that a student is assigned to receive general education and/or special education instruction or services as specified in the IEP.
Post-secondary Education	Education provided after high school such as college or vocational schools.
Prior Written Notice	A document created by the IEP team that is given to the parent when the team proposes a change or has refused to make a change. The PWN provides an explanation for the choice the school has made. If the school does not provide a PWN, the parent can request it and the school must provide it.
Procedural Safeguards	Processes that are defined by Federal law that protect the rights of parents and school districts throughout the special education process.
Proficiency	The ability to do school work at grade level.
Prior Written Notice	A notice supplied by the school to the parent that includes an explanation of why the school has refused a specific request for special education services or placement.
Regression	When a student loses skills they had previously mastered.
Resource Room	A classroom managed by a special education teacher where students with specific learning challenges come to for part of their day to received individualized instruction. Usually students in resource are in a general education setting for the rest of the day.

Response to Intervention (RTI)	A process of providing specialized support to students who are having difficulty with specific subjects in school. The students are monitored for improvement. If no improvement is seen, the student is sometimes referred for a special education evaluation to see if they qualify for special education services. There is no timeline defined for how long a school can use RTI to help a student who is struggling.
Retention	To hold a student back and have them repeat a grade instead of promoting them to the next grade.
School Psychologist	A professional who is trained to use educational assessments to determine challenges and eligibility for children who are having difficulty in school.
Screening	Like a mini assessment, a screening is a brief test or observation that gives an idea if a child has challenges that warrant a more formal assessment.
Secondary Education	High school education (usually grades 9-12)
Section 504	Section 504 is a civil rights statute in the Americans With Disabilities Act (ADA) that requires schools to provide supports for students with disabilities so they have equal access to their education.
Self-contained Placement	A classroom in a school that is separate from the general education setting where a child with more significant disabilities may spend all or most of their day. The class is usually taught by a special education teacher and includes several instructional aides.
Transition Plan	The transition plan shows the path a student is expected to take for after high school. It could include preparation for a job and independent living, or it could include planning for college. Starting in 9th grade, transition goals should be established and reviewed each year to help the student move towards a successful transition.
Vocational Education	Education focused on learning a specific profession.

42

Request an Evaluation

"Everything that can be counted does not necessarily count;
everything that counts cannot necessarily be counted."
~ Albert Einstein

Under the IDEA, the Child Find laws require every district to identify and evaluate children who exhibit signs of disabilities. We would hope under the Child Find laws that the school would notify you of their concerns so they could to evaluate your child. Unfortunately, this does not always happen. Therefore you must start the ball rolling! Maybe you have been concerned for awhile and have tried to work with the teacher. Maybe your child is already receiving services, but another area of concern has come up and you want the school to assess for the new problem. Whatever the reason, it is important for you to know how to request an evaluation and follow through on it.

How to request an evaluation.

You start by writing a letter asking that a formal evaluation be done to see if your child qualifies for special education services. The request should be sent to the principal, with a copy to the head of special education for your district. The request should include:

• Child's name, grade and teacher(s) names.

- Specific request for a comprehensive educational evaluation.

- Include specific reasons you are making the request, including your belief that the child has a learning disability. Do not state the specific disability, just provide examples of instances that show areas of concern that indicate a possible disability.

- Any formal diagnosis from a doctor or educational professional.

- Include a request for a response to the letter within the state's timeline (in California it is 15 days).

- Indicate in how many days you will follow up on the letter (usually 5 school days)

- A thank you for their anticipated help and cooperation.

See chapter 35, *Letter Writing Tips*, for more detailed information on how to write a letter to the school.

What happens if the school approves the evaluation?

First jump up and down, get really excited that they approved, and you can move to the next step!

Then provide consent for evaluation. Under both IDEA and Section 504 the parent must give permission for evaluation. The school provides a permission form for you to sign. Once this approval is received, the school must follow a timeline to insure assessments are completed within a reasonable time frame. IDEA specifies a 60-day timeline from time of permission to evaluate to completion of the evaluations. Some states modified this timeline, so check with your own state to verify the time allowed.

Once the evaluations are completed, all the results are compiled into an evaluation summary report, and a special education meeting is called to review the results. The team will discuss the assessment reports and decide if the student qualifies for special education services. At that point, they will decide if a plan is necessary, and whether an IEP or 504 plan is the most appropriate course of action. You should be invited to this meeting and it is important to be fully involved in these discussions. They will probably not write the plan at this meeting, but will instead schedule another meeting to create an IEP or 504 plan.

What if the school denies the request for evaluation?

Schools are not required to do the evaluation if they do not agree that there is evidence of a disability. If they refuse, they must provide a formal refusal that states the reasons for denying the evaluation. If they do not provide you with a formal refusal, ask them for a Prior Written Notice, which must contain all the reasons for the refusal (See chapter 49, *Your Right to Prior Written Notice* for details on this document). If you disagree with their reasons, you can try other approaches:

1. Request a meeting with the school and try to change their mind. Bring an advocate or experienced special education parent with you. Keep in mind if you strong arm the school into evaluating, their evaluation may not have the results you desire. They can easily do a minimal evaluation or skew results to demonstrate our child does not need special education services.

2. Request an Independent Educational Evaluation (IEE).

3. Pay for your own private evaluation.

4. Request mediation at public expense.

5. File a complaint with your state board of education

6. File a due process complaint. This should only be used as a last resort. Definitely use an attorney if you go this route.

Evaluations are the only method that can be used to qualify your child for special education support in school. IDEA requires the school to evaluate, but only if the school suspects a disability exists. It is important to understand how to ask for them, and get help from an advocate or attorney if the school makes it difficult to get an evaluation.

$\backsim$

43

The Mystery Behind Qualification for Special Education Services

"How dreadful...to be caught up in a game and have no idea of the rules."
~ Caroline Stevermer

Many parents are surprised when they obtain a diagnosis from a doctor, and then the school tells them the diagnosis does not qualify their child for special education. Qualification can be a complex process, and it is fraught with subjective interpretation.

The basis for qualification.

Remember, as I've said earlier, it is important to understand that the school does not diagnose children with disabilities. They are only concerned with looking for an impairment that affects the child's ability to perform in school. A doctor or other professional may diagnose a disability, but it is up to the special education team at school to decide if that disability affects the child at school.

IDEA and Section 504 do not provide specific procedures for determining how a child qualifies for special education support. Consequently, districts can manipulate their process to make it appear as if a child does not qualify when in fact the child really should qualify. Not all districts do this, but it is common enough that results can vary district to district, even if the assessments used are the same.

Understanding the common practices used to qualify helps. While you may not know the exact process your school uses, it gives you a starting point to ask questions to obtain more clarity on how decisions are made.

Qualifying for an IEP

For a child to qualify for an IEP, the student must meet three criteria:

1. The student must have difficulty accessing the curriculum.

2. The student must qualify under one of 13 categories of disability.

3. The student requires specialized instruction and related services.

What does "accessing the curriculum" mean? It means the student has difficulty performing grade level work at a similar speed, competency and method as his peers. Difficulties can be identified through poor grades, incomplete work, achievement tests and assessments that show areas of difficulty. Students with these challenges often need extra assistance in school.

Examples of extra assistance include pull-out classes with a specially trained teacher, occupational therapy to help with handwriting, or a different curriculum to help with learning. Usually this extra assistance costs the schools money because it requires purchasing additional materials and often paying a specialized teacher. This is why schools are so reluctant to provide the services.

In addition to difficulties accessing curriculum, to qualify for an IEP, a student's disability must also fall into one of the qualifying categories of disability as described by IDEA:

1. Autism

2. Blindness

3. Deafness

4. Emotional Disturbance

5. Hearing Impairment

6. Intellectual Disability

7. Multiple Disabilities

8. Orthopedic Impairment

9. Other Health Impaired

10. Specific Learning Disability

11. Speech or Language Impairment

12. Traumatic Brain Injury

13. Visual Impairment

IDEA does not define #9 "Other Health Impaired" or #10 "Specific Learning Disability." These terms are often used as catch buckets for disabilities that do not fit elsewhere.

The Discrepancy Model

Unfortunately, IDEA does not specify the process for qualifying for a disability, so this is left up to the school. Prior to 2004 IDEA required schools to use the discrepancy model, which looks at IQ tests and compares them to the 'norm.' If a student scores significantly lower on one area of the IQ test, while the rest of the IQ test came up average or above, the child is considered to have a learning disability. For example, if Sally scores an average of 108 on most sections of the IQ test, but she scores 84 in reading, that significant discrepancy indicates the presence of a learning disability in reading.

Unfortunately the 'norm' is not specified in IDEA. Some schools use 100 as the norm, which is the number of an average IQ. To be most effective the norm should be compared to the student's own IQ. If they make the comparison to an IQ of 100, it means a student who has a high IQ but performance in the average range would be disqualified. For example, if Billy has an IQ of 121, and he scores 94 in the math section of the IQ test, he would not qualify for special education if the school uses 100 as the norm. Clearly though his math abilities are significantly lower than the rest of his abilities.

This approach will often exclude gifted students from receiving special education services. It also means a student may qualify in one school district and not in another.

While the IDEA originally required this model, they did not specify how large a gap from the 'norm' was needed to qualify. As a result, states were able to decide this. The general rule of thumb is school performance that is at least two standard deviations below the 'norm' would qualify the student for special education. In California it is 1.5 standard deviations below, which is usually 21 IQ points. So there should be a 21 point or larger gap between the overall score on the student's IQ test and the lowest score in order to qualify.

Going back to Sally, if we compare her overall average of 108, and reading at 84, she would qualify under California law because her reading is 24 IQ points lower than other sections. BUT, if the 'norm' of average IQ (100) is used, she would only be 16 points below and would therefore not qualify. If your school uses the discrepancy model, it is important to know what norm is being used.

Critics of the discrepancy model have said it does not reveal the full picture of a student's abilities, and therefore excludes a lot of children from getting help. Since 2006 two other methods of identification have been used to qualify students.

Response to Intervention (RTI)

The first alternative is response to intervention (RTI). Special teaching methods are utilized for students struggling in the classroom. If after a period of time those methods do not help a student improve, the student may be referred for special education testing. There are some problems with this model.

- The law does not specify how long RTI should be used, so schools can implement it for years. This allows schools to postpone assessing the students for an indefinite period of time. Consequently the student does not receive the help he needs.

- Even if a student receives RTI, there is no way to identify the disability. As a result, there is no way to know if the intervention is appropriate. Often they give the same exact intervention to every student, so it is hit or miss as to whether it will help.

Processing Deficit Model

Another approach for identifying students is the processing deficit model. It requires assessing specific areas of processing that are known to impact learning. This could include auditory processing, visual processing, working memory, phonological processing, and fluid intelligence. The processing abilities that are measured are tied to specific learning skills. For example, phonological processing is necessary to learn how to read phonetically. If a student exhibits weaknesses in specific processing abilities, the student is deemed to have a learning disability.

The benefits of the processing deficit model, is that it pinpoints the exact skills the student is lacking, and permits identification of appropriate interventions. The problems with this model are:

- It takes more time to assess for specific processing deficits.

- There is no guideline as to how poorly a student must perform in order to be considered to have a processing deficit.

A student with an IEP will also need specialized instruction and/or services in order to make progress on the curriculum. Often students with IEPs spend most of their day in general education but are pulled into the resource room for specific subjects where they need help from a special education teacher. The processing deficit model does not identify the curriculum or specialized instruction that are needed. Students with IEPs can also receive specialized services, such as speech and occupational therapy, to help with the deficits that cause their learning problems. The processing deficit model can identify the need for these specific services.

By now you can see why it is so hard to qualify in some districts. The schools set the parameters for qualification. In effect, they can limit access to special education services. This is where your documentation of your child's performance can help. If you can show patterns of difficulty, need for assistance and reduced academic performance, you can demonstrate to the school that your child is struggling to access curriculum and needs more assistance in school.

Qualifying for a 504

When a student has a disability that does fall into one of the 13 categories of the IDEA, but the student does not require specialized instruction or services, he still may be eligible for a 504 plan. With a 504 the student is offered accommodations in the classroom to make it easier for him to complete his schoolwork. So a child with dyslexia may be able to do all his schoolwork, but he may need extra time or frequent breaks in order to complete it with the same competence as a student without dyslexia. A 504 plan does not cost the school money because they are not providing specialized instruction or services to the student. Instead the burden goes to the general education teacher whose job it is to make sure the student gets the accommodations specified. In elementary school this is not a huge effort because the student has one teacher. However, in middle school and high school they have six teachers a day, and it can be very difficult to ensure enforcement of the accommodations.

A 504 plan is covered by section 504 of the Americans with Disabilities Act. Unfortunately it does not list specific disabilities, and this is where the schools can manipulate the information to avoid providing a 504 plan. Section 504 defines disability as:

- Has a physical or mental impairment that "substantially" limits one or more major life activity (such as reading or concentrating).

- Has a record of the impairment (i.e. a diagnosis from a doctor or school assessments demonstrate a disability).

- Is regarded as having an impairment, or a significant difficulty, that isn't temporary. For example, a broken leg is a temporary impairment. A chronic condition like hearing loss would be considered an impairment.

A student with a disability does not automatically qualify for a 504 Plan. He must be evaluated by the school and determine if the disability has a significant impact on the child's ability to learn and participate in school. As with an IEP, several methods are used to determine if a child has a discrepancy between ability and performance. Of course interpretation is up to the school, so while it's easier to get a 504, you still may get push back.

With a 504 Plan, the student is offered accommodations in the classroom to make it easier for him to complete his schoolwork. Accommodations level the playing field by providing support for the disability.

Accommodations are usually implemented by the teacher, playground supervisors or sometimes they are given for homework. They may include assistive technology such as a computer, iPad or FM system (frequency modulation system). They do not include any kind of services or specialized instruction outside of the general education classroom. The student must complete the same schoolwork as other students. They just get support to do it.

Ask about qualification methods.

If you are unclear about how your school determines qualification, then ask. They should have a specific and clear process they utilize to make these decisions. If they are vague or they refuse to explain how these decisions are made, it is an indication that they may manipulate results to help skew decisions.

If your child has an IEP, IDEA clearly states that parents are entitled to all evaluations and reports that are used in the qualification process. Obtain copies of these reports and do your own analysis of the qualification. Sometimes you will find pieces that were missed or numbers that were miscalculated, and this can open a new conversation about qualification.

44

8 Reasons Schools Say No

"Until you realize how easily it is for your mind to be manipulated,
you remain the puppet of someone else's game."
~ Evita Ochel

Unfortunately more districts seem to refuse services than there are districts that willingly provide them. The reasons are often more than just financial. There are many reasons the schools say no. Learning the 'personality' of your district gives you insight into why they say no. Understanding their approach makes you better equipped to select a successful strategy. Following are eight reasons the schools will say no to special education services.

#1 Budget Is an Issue Because Federal Monies are Scarce

The #1 reason services are denied is for financial reasons. Schools rarely admit that. Understanding the financial challenges they face will help you see why they work so hard at saying no.

While the federal government requires states to implement IDEA, it is only required to pay 40% of the bill! When IDEA was first implemented, the federal government 'estimated' that it would cost 50% more to educate a student with disabilities than the average student. Based on this estimate, the federal government determined that it would pay

40%, leaving the states to fund just 10% additional educational costs per student. There are two problems with this across-the-board decision:

1. IDEA has never been fully funded.

2. The cost of special education has increased dramatically.

Because IDEA has not been fully funded, the states never get their full 40% share. Since IDEA's enactment in 1975, the federal government has never funded the full 40% it promised. In 2014 states only received an average of 16% of the original 40% federal commitment. The states and school districts have had to assume the burden of the remaining costs (McCann, 2016).

Between 2000 and 2014, the percentage of students requiring special education services has remained consistent at 13%. But the services needed have become more intensive and more expensive. For example, from 2000 to 2014, the number of students with autism spectrum disorders has gone up 500%! These children require more costly interventions, yet there is no increase in funding. Obviously the budget issues are real!

Clearly the system is broken. This is the stress you see when school staff attend meetings. Many really want to help your child, but they struggle to find the money for the necessary services. In the end it comes down to the funds available.

#2 The Special Ed Budget is Drained by Legal Fees

At the first school our oldest son attended, the district was horrible about providing services. Thank God one teacher really wanted to help our son. She pulled me aside quietly and advised what I could do to get the help he needed. I was amazed when she told me why they were so stingy with services. The income level was high in that city, so parents would frequently arrive at the very first IEP with a lawyer. Because the parents automatically assumed they would encounter resistance, they came out fighting right out of the gate. Naturally the district had to respond in kind, so they brought lawyers to IEPs and paid lawyers to help with paperwork between meetings. The end result? The district's legal bills were so massive it drained the money needed to provide special ed services. Think of it! More money for lawyers than for the children!

We decided that hiring a lawyer was the best way to go because that was the only way that this district would pay attention. It worked! They realized it would cost them less in services than in legal bills.

If you are lucky enough to live in a middle or upper class city, you are not guaranteed services. In fact, the opposite is often true. The residents' income level may determine whether or not the district budgets are often puttered away by this legal tango.

Several years later we had moved to a new town where I met a parent whose son had been in special education (by this time his son had already finished high school). He told me that 15 years prior, he and several other parents had sued the school district for not providing adequate services. As a result, the district realized that spending money on legal services was not helping the children. They changed their approach and now do an excellent job of providing support. They also focus on helping the children when they are younger, because they realize that will save money in the long run. They knew it would help many kids grow out of the need for services when they got older.

I am not telling you that using a lawyer is the only way to get the right help. I just want you to realize that each district has its own personality. If you understand the district personality, it will help you select an effective approach for getting help.

In 2010, in the state of California, 10% of students in public schools (686,000 students) received special education services. Of these, only 1 percent, or 6,860 parents, filed due process against the school. Of these, only 3 percent, or 205 families, ended up in a protracted legal battle. These statistics show that most cases do not often end up in court.

In 2013, NBC did an investigative journalism piece about California districts denying services to students. In their report they included a list of the number of cases each school district faced in due process from 2010 to 2013. At 4,253 cases, Los Angeles Unified School District was first on the list and had over 15 times as many due process cases as the second district on the list. San Diego Unified School District got that second spot with 243 due process cases (Nguyen, V., Villarreal, M., Paredes, D. & Nious, K., 2013). The majority of districts had less than 10 cases go to due process. Our current district had zero cases. This sort of information is extremely helpful. It clearly shows, depending on the personality of your district, how likely you are to end up in a legal battle to get help for your child.

#3 The School does not have adequate resources to help your child

Budget deficits are a real issue for many districts, but this does not excuse them from providing services. One of the basic concepts of special education law is Free Appropriate Public Education (FAPE). It dictates that the schools provide educational support for the educational needs of the student. If the student requires services that are not usually provided at their home school, the school is obligated to pay for a resource outside of the school. It is against IDEA for the school to claim they cannot provide a particular resource because they have no personnel to offer it.

Frequently the school will say a child does not need a specific resource in order to get around this law. It is up to you, as the parent, to investigate if this service is being provided to other students in the district. If so, how is it being provided? If no other students receive this assistance, or if they are getting support outside of the school, that could help you understand that there is a resource issue. This information enables you to negotiate with the school. Let them know that you are aware that the service is not available, and that you are also aware the law requires them to provide it if your child needs it. If the school continues to refuse the service, you may suggest an alternative service that may not be the same, but may be helpful in a similar way. This approach helps the school save face while getting your child the help he needs.

#4 Special Ed staffer doesn't want more work

The staff member who evaluates your child will most likely be the person determining if services are needed. It is also likely they will be the person providing those services. This presents a conflict of interest. Since most staff members are already very busy, the decision to provide services may be influenced by how overworked the person feels. While most school personnel really want to help your child, the reality is that their schedules may be tight.

A private assessment offers a neutral opinion about the needs of your child. It can reassure you whether or not your child really needs specific services. Schools are required to review private assessments, but they are not required to follow those recommendations. Even so, having them can help you make a case for providing the service in school.

#5 The school does not have the resources for a satisfactory evaluation

Budgets deficits impact both the students in need of services, as well as special education evaluators. The professionals who do the evaluations have very packed schedules. Fitting in assessments and comprehensive reports can be a huge burden. There are months in the school year in which they have 4-5 IEPs per week! That is because they have legal deadlines to meet annual IEP annual reviews. They must do their report writing in the evening or weekends, because they must schedule assessments and IEP meetings into the short school days. Consequently, they may rush through it. They cannot do as thorough a job as they might like. The end result does not reflect their knowledge or abilities. It is simply a case of too much work in too little time.

Also, the assessors themselves do not get to choose which assessment tools to use. It is the district that ultimately chooses the assessment tools. The district also dictates what can be measured with these tools and what standards or skills are in alignment with the assessment. That means that even if an assessor sees a behavior, pattern or ability, he may not be able to report it because the district limits what areas an assessor can report on for a specific tool. The district can also limit the assessor's ability to assess if he wants to use a tool outside of the chosen instruments. So even if he is trained on other tools, he is not allowed to use them unless the district approves their use.

When our oldest son was in Kindergarten, I came across an article that caused me to suspect that he had auditory processing disorder. I brought it to the attention of the IEP team. Both the school psychologist and speech therapist both told me I was wrong; that I did not have their degrees, and I did not know what I was talking about. For six months I kept pushing for at least an auditory screening, but they said it was unnecessary. I then took my son to a learning center that did the SCAN-C and TAPS auditory screenings. He was found to have significant deficits. The SCAN-C competing words test showed he only understood 9% of what he heard if competing sounds were present! The school still insisted I was wrong. They did agree to a screen him themselves. They called in a contracted audiologist. She administered the Differential Screening Test for Processing (DSTP), which showed he had a significant deficit in auditory processing.

Even with their own results showing a problem, the school still refused to do a proper auditory processing assessment. Desperate to help our son, we paid out of a pocket for a private audiologist who specialized in auditory processing to assess him. He was diagnosed with severe auditory processing disorder.

Looking back on the situation, do you think the school psychologist and speech therapist really knew what they were talking about? No, they just did not have the tools or the knowledge to do a proper assessment. When my private screenings showed a problem, the school had to pay for a specialist, on their dime, to do their own screening. The school psychologist and speech therapist never had the ability to prove or disprove what I was saying. If I had not persisted, I would have caved to their pressure. My son would not have gotten help for a major challenge.

#6 Child's disability does not qualify

In order to qualify for special education, the student must have a disability, and that disability must affect the child's ability to perform in school. Unfortunately the process for determining both these things can be subjective and hard to pin down (see chapter 43, *The Mystery*

Behind Qualification for Special Education Services). While it may be very clear that your child has a disability, just having a diagnosis does not automatically qualify the child for specific services. It is up to the school to determine if that disability affects the child's performance, and if so, what support the student should receive. Unfortunately it is easy for schools to skew assessments or interject opinions into the process, so that makes the student's eligibility far from cut and dry. It is this area that some schools have become master manipulators.

If you are concerned your child's disability should qualify him for special education, there are steps to take after the school has disqualified him. First, request a Prior Written Notice, which should include an explanation of how and why your child did not qualify. If you disagree, then request an Independent Education Evaluation (IEE). The IEE is done by a private evaluator at the school's expense. The school is required to take these results into consideration when determining qualification. If after the IEE the school still says your child is ineligible, you need to determine if the school is properly following federal and state guidelines for determining eligibility. If you feel there are inconsistencies, you may have to request mediation or take the school to due process in order to get the school to change their mind.

#7 School says your child's behavior is the problem.

In chapter 30, *You Are the Team Captain*, I shared how my son was denied social skills support in Kindergarten. The school blamed him for his lack of social skills, saying he took too long to eat snack, and so he had less time to play on the playground. They ignored the fact that eating time was the most social part of recess because that is when kids had conversations. He had less time up and running around, so it was *his fault* he lacked social skills.

This is how absurd things get when the school starts to blame your child for his difficulties. It is common when you first approach the school for them to say the problems are caused by the student's behavior or lack of motivation. The school may imply that a lack of parenting is the real source of the problem, and many parents will back down because they don't know how to respond. Parents may respond defensively, getting angry and trying to explain their position.

A very interesting study by Dr. Galen Alessi was published in Professional School Psychology journal (Alessi, 1998). It sheds an interesting light on this response by the school. Looking at 5,000 cases of students across the USA who were evaluated for special education services, the schools' psychologists in the study state the curriculum, teachers and faculty were NEVER the reason a child did not do well at school. Think about that! The school psychologists' perspective was that problems a child experienced at the school were in no way caused by anything that happened in school.

Instead, the school psychologists said that parenting was the primary contributor 10-20% of the time, and 80-90% of the time it was the children themselves who caused their own learning problems. Some school psychologists in the study informally admitted they don't agree, but if they stated openly that the school environment was a factor, they could lose their job or be made very uncomfortable.

This is really crucial for parents to understand, because when you walk into the IEP meeting you have to realize that they are already biased against you. This is not intentional, but an aspect of the way the school culture works. It is an entrenched belief that the child or parents are the source of the problem. If you point this out, it could cause friction amongst school staff. So remember this while negotiating. Understanding their position reinforces your ability to find solutions because you know where they are coming from.

If they do turn to your child's behavior as the source of the problem, ask them to provide data to show you how that behavior impacts your child at school. When in doubt, always ask for the data!

#8 School Personnel are Trained to Say No

A while back at an event I met an administrator for a middle school in California. He said his district actually sent special education employees to seminars teaching them how to say no and refuse services. Instead of spending money to enhance their knowledge and offer more services to the kids, they actively promoted denying services. This would be a critical piece of information in assessing the personality of the district, and it would help determine the strategy for the parents. Getting services out of a district like this would be like squeezing water from a rock, and I would encourage parents to hire an advocate or attorney from the start.

In chapter 34, I mentioned the investigation in Texas that uncovered another example of refusing services. The Texas Education Agency (TEA) mandated that districts reduce their special education student percentage to 8.5% even though the national average is 13.3%. While the TEA denied that it was a mandate and more of a guideline, school administrators enforced it like a law. It was potentially such a grave violation of IDEA, the federal government launched an investigation to determine if the TEA broke federal laws.

Remember if your district has a history of denying services, employees become experts in ways to say no. Getting them to say yes will require a focused strategy and knowledge of the law. This is when having an advocate or lawyer at the IEP meeting can help move things in the right direction.

POINTS to PONDER

1. List all the times your school has refused services.

2. What reasons did they give for refusing services?

3. What do you believe are the real reasons for refusing services?

4. What have other parents done to change their mind?

5. Are there any cases against your school where the parents won and received services? What were those rulings?

45

Parent Concerns:
An Invaluable Contribution
to the IEP

"Behind every young child who believes in himself
is a parent who believed first."
~ Matthew Jacobson

The IDEA requires parents to be full participating members of the IEP team. That means not only participate in the process, but they also have a right to add their voice to the official IEP document. Most parents do not realize that they can bring a written statement of their concerns and that it must be included in the IEP document. It should be added to the IEP without editing by team members. There should be a section of the IEP called Parent Concerns in which your thoughts should be added.

If you end up having to go to mediation or due process, this part of the IEP is critical because it demonstrates that you expressed your concerns to the IEP team. The IEP should be developed around the needs of the child, not the general description of their disability. Written parent concerns is one way of demonstrating what those needs are, and will be taken into consideration during mediation or due process.

Sometimes during the course of the IEP meeting, the case manager will ask you what your concerns are. By pre-writing them, you will be prepared to answer this question in detail and not leave out any information.

What should you include in your Parent Concerns?

1. **List all areas of challenge.** You should include anything about school or the school experience that you feel is a challenge for your child. It could be academic, behavioral, social/emotional, logistics, assessments or progress issues.

2. **Be succinct yet detailed.** Do not create a super lengthy and detailed essay. This is not your child's biography. Just state your concerns, and why it is a concern. Whenever possible, include data to support your concern. For example, if a child is repeatedly failing tests, this concern should be noted. Provide the dates and grades on the tests.

3. **There is no limit on length.** You do not want it to be pages and pages. You do want it long enough to express all concerns. If the school tells you there is a limit, ask for the state statute that mandates a limit on parent input.

4. **Focus on your child.** Do not include information beyond the scope of your child's challenges. For example, do not say that you feel they have the wrong speech therapist or you feel the school is not addressing certain needs. Stick to your child's experience and the challenges you are concerned about.

5. **Include all concerns, not just new concerns.** Include things that have been addressed in previous IEPs, not just new concerns. If current services or strategies are helping, then state that. If you feel more needs to be done, then state that. This should be a list of all the reasons your child has an IEP.

6. **Include concerns about services.** If you feel your child has challenges that are not being addressed by the IEP, include that in this section as well.

Samples of parent concerns to be included in the IEP:

- Billy has difficulty with reading. His academic testing shows he is 2 years, 5 months behind. Billy's challenges with reading significantly impact his ability to access the general education curriculum in all subjects. Billy needs specialized instruction to address his specific reading deficits, including decoding, fluency and comprehension.

- Ann has a diagnosis of ADHD which impacts her ability to stay focused and sit still; which in turn significantly affects her ability to complete assignments and participate in class. Her current accommodations allow her to take breaks and get extra time to complete assignments. This is working well.

- Jordan has significant executive function deficits. This impacts his ability to stay organized, plan assignments, write essays, and turn in homework. He is currently receiving no support for this challenge. We feel that additional support and/or services are necessary to ensure he is receiving FAPE.

- Joan's qualifying disability on the IEP is autism. At the IEP meeting on March 1, 2017, it was decided that she be placed in a self-contained classroom. Since that move we have seen an escalation of emotional outbursts and repetitive behaviors. We do not agree with the placement as we feel it is causing her to regress rather than improve.

How to get your Parent Concerns included in the IEP.

1. One week before the IEP, send a request to the case manager asking her to add your Parent Concerns to that section of the IEP.

2. When sending your request, include the phrase, "Please add verbatim." This makes it clear that you are aware editing is not allowed.

3. Attach an electronic copy of your Parent Concerns so it is easy for the case manager to cut and paste them.

4. When you get the draft of the IEP, verify that your concerns were added verbatim.

What if the school refuses
to add your Parent Concerns?

If the school refuses to include your parent concerns verbatim, ask them why they refuse to include it. The IDEA clearly states that parent input is required. Event though the IDEA does not require them to follow the input, they must include it. If they claim it is school policy to not include parent concerns, ask for a copy of that policy. If the case manager continues to refuse, you can reject the IEP until your concerns are added. If she still refuses, then it is within your right to file a complaint with your state department of education.

46

Write Stellar IEP Goals

"Goals are dreams with deadlines."
~ Diana Scharf

Writing IEP goals is an art unto itself. It takes time and effort to master. As a member of the IEP team, it is crucial you learn the basics of writing goals. This gives you the knowledge to know when the goals written by the team are in the best interest of your child.

I know what it's like to come into the IEP meeting and have them rattle off goals and I have no idea whether the goal is appropriate or not. The goals do need to be specifically formatted. That makes it very intimidating to provide input when the team is so experienced. The entire IEP team is supposed to write the goals together, but often the school personnel will come to the IEP team with all the goals already itemized. They skip the step of asking for your input and just assume you will accept what they have written.

This is why it is important for you to learn about how to write goals. You will not be an expert, but you will know how to determine if a goal is adequate or not. The best approach: ask for a copy of the draft IEP ahead of the meeting so you can review the goals and make changes to bring to the meeting.

The purpose of IEP goals is to ensure the child is making meaningful progress in his education. It is important that goals be individualized for your child so they meet the specific challenges your child faces.

It is common for IEP teams to recycle goals between students because it is less work in writing and measuring. It is your job as the parent to make sure the goals really address your child's challenges in a way that will help him make progress.

While the goal specifies an intended outcome for a certain task, a critical aspect of the goal is to indicate how success is measured. Without a uniform way to measure progress, it is difficult to know if the child has achieved the goal.

How to write effective goals.

SMART goals is an acronym used to describes the components that go into creating a goal that will help a child make reasonable progress. S-M-A-R-T stands for:

- SPECIFIC: They must specify what they are meant to achieve and how that achievement will be measured.

- MEASURABLE: The goal can be measured or counted in a way that demonstrates progress on the goal.

- ACTION WORDS: The goal must specify the area of need (reading, math, attention, etc.); in what way the area will change (improve, maintain, decrease, etc.); and the level that demonstrates success (independently, at grade level, etc.).

- RELEVANT: The goal is relevant to a challenge the child faces as a result of her disability.

- TIME BOUND: How long will the student have to achieve the goal? This is also an indicator of when the goal will be reviewed for progress.

The following steps are guidelines for writing IEP goals. You can also use this to check that the school's goals fit the proper framework for your child's needs.

1. Identify a specific need for your child.

Where is she struggling in school? There is an area of the IEP called Present Levels of Performance (PLOP) where these areas of concern should be described. The PLOP should include areas of strength, areas of weakness and how the student's disability impacts the student's education. The PLOP is a description of what your child is doing right now. The goals you write will describe what your child WILL BE doing one year from now. Every concern notated in the PLOP should be addressed with a goal, accommodation, modification, or a combination of these things.

2. How does this impact your child's educational progress?

What skills is your child struggling with that cause this need? Are these challenges academic or functional (skills of daily living, behavior, social skills, etc.)? The goal should be written to address these challenges.

3. Define the baseline.

How is the child performing in this skill right now? This is the baseline, and it should be measurable. It could be done with a formal assessment, academic assignments, or data collected through observation. It is important to have this measure so you know the starting point so it is clear when she has made progress.

4. Determine an attainable goal that addresses the need.

Write out the specific skill that your child will use as a way to improve this area of need. Make sure the goal is set to stretch your child to do more. If the goal is too easy, then your child will not make as much progress. It is also important because if the goals are set too low and are achieved, the team cites that as a basis for disqualifying the child from special education. I know from experience that when you say a goal is too easy, it really catches the attention of the rest of the team. It communicates that you have higher expectations for your child. It also tells the team that you are paying attention. The point is to make progress. If you feel the team is setting the bar too low, or too high, make sure you speak up.

5. Decide how the goal will be measured.

Will it be observation and data collection, formal assessment, class assignments, or curriculum-based tests? Will just one measure be used or more than one?

6. Who is responsible for measuring the goal?

It is important that the language specify who is responsible for measurement. If is just says 'the IEP team,' it does not assign the responsibility which increases the risk that nobody will be measuring progress.

7. Write the goal in positive language.

As much as possible frame the goal as an achievement. With behavior goals this is not always possible because the goal may be to reduce the behavior.

8. Make sure the goal is clear and easy to understand.

When a teacher reads IEPs, they skim. They don't read in detail. If the goal is complex and hard to understand, they may miss the point. If you have to read the goal several times to understand it, then it is too hard to understand. The language needs to be simplified.

9. Include modifications and support.

This would mean any modifications to curriculum, specific tools used (such as a computer or special paper), and any personnel who will support the child with the goal (such as the resource teacher or aide). Note that modifications and support should not include name-brand strategies on how they will help the child achieve the goal, but simply a general description of the type of support used to achieve the goal. For example, if a student is working on improving writing, the teacher may offer 1-2 prompts, and this would be part of the goal. The teacher may use a specific writing program to help the student learn to write better, but the name of this writing program would not be included in the goal.

10. Determine the time frame to achieve the goal.

Although most goals are written with an annual time frame, there is no requirement for it to be one year. The goal may be something the student is working towards in order to participate in a particular event or other milestone. The time frame should be realistic and reflect the needs of the student.

Use the IEP Goal Formula to write the goal.

There is a generally accepted template that is used to ensure that the language of the goal includes all required components. The goal formula is:

By _____ student will _____,
     (time frame)   *(goal/achievement)*

in _____, as measured by _____,
    (setting/context)   *(assessment method)*

with _____ and with _____.
     (% accuracy)   *(supports)*

- **Time frame.** When will the child show she has achieved the goal? Most often it is one year from the IEP annual review date, but sometimes it can be before then; perhaps by the end of the school year or by a specific event.

- **Goal/achievement.** This describes the actual task the student is working on mastering. You want to be very specific about what that skill is. For example, if the child is working on writing essays, you might specify that he demonstrate the ability to write a 5-paragraph essay using a graphic organizer with 2 or less prompts from the teacher.

- **Setting/context.** This refers to the environment the child is in when the skill is measured. For example, if a child is working on social interactions with other children, that goal would be measured during free time, lunch or recess, not during class instruction time.

- **Assessment method.** This indicates how progress will be measured for the goal and who is responsible for tracking this measure. So first, who is in charge of measuring the progress? Then, how will that person measure the progress? Will a specific assessment tool be used, will data be collected, will it be through observation or through written assessments?

- **% Accuracy.** This is a measure of how much progress is expected on the goal. If a student is able to pronounce a specific sound in speech 0% of the time, the goal may specify that the student needs to pronounce the sound 50% of the time or 2 out of 4 opportunities. This needs to be very specific. It will be the measure that is used to show progress.

- **Supports.** This would indicate any accommodations or support from teachers the students might receive in the context of demonstrating the goal. For example, if a student has a social skills goal, the supports may be the student will initiate a conversation with peers with no more than 1 prompt from the aide.

Perform an efficacy check for each goal.

Review each goal and check for the following to make sure it is written properly.

- Is the goal easy to understand?
- Does it address a specific need for your child?
- Is the goal attainable for your child?
- Is there a time frame specified?
- Is the goal measurable?
- Is the goal written in positive language?
- Has each area of concern in the PLOP been addressed in the IEP goals?

IEP Goal Banks

There are actually online databases that have searchable goals that you can use in your child's IEP. It is well worth the time to research the banks and find goals that cover similar territory. You may modify the goals you find, but they provide a good starting point and a lot of ideas for generating your own goals. In this way you can help the IEP team develop goals that truly meet your child's needs. To find links to each of these goal banks, visit www.specialmomadvocate.com/resources.

IEP Goals and Objectives Bank by Bridges4Kids

This resource provides goal objectives, but not fully written goals. It is organized by subject matter, then skill mastery and finally specific objectives. While it will not give you complete goals, it provides an excellent resource for determining which skills to focus on.

IEP Goals and Objectives Bank by Wamego USD 320 School District

This resource provides goals sorted by subject and then by grade level. It offers 131 pages of specific goals that are prewritten using the IEP Goal Formula.

IEP Goal Bank by Autism Educators

This resource is organized by subject and provides hundreds of goals across all skill levels. One interesting aspect of this goal bank is they recommend products to help work towards the goal. The goal information is free. Most of the products must be purchased.

IEP Goal Bank by State of Illinois

Organized by subject, this IEP goal bank identifies specific goals and how they relate to learning objectives. It provides developmentally appropriate skill levels for different grades, which provides a way of determining the next achievement level for your child. It does not give specific language for the goals, but is a unique tool to help plan progress.

Monitor those progress reports!

Most goals will be reviewed annually. Most districts send out quarterly progress reports along with report cards. Where severe behavior is involved, progress may be documented monthly. There is no federal regulation about how often reports must go out, although your state may have its own statute. Find out your district policy for progress reports.

Note the dates on your calendar. If you do not receive a progress report, check with your case manager to find out when it will be sent.

Often when you get the progress reports, nothing is written for some of the goals. There are many reasons for this, and not necessarily because support wasn't given or progress was not made. In one district I worked in the training for inputting progress reports came after the report due date. Obviously the progress on the goals I monitored was blank. Do not panic if there is no progress shown. Simply email the case manager and ask for an update on progress because it was missing from the report.

Progress reports are important because they give you a snap shot of how your child is doing. If there are two progress reports in a row that show no progress, bring this up with the IEP team right away. Do not wait six more months for the annual IEP review. Keep all the progress reports together in your IEP binder so you can easily reference them.

47

Accommodations
vs. Modifications

"Be strong, be fearless, be beautiful.
And believe that anything is possible when
you have the right people there to support you."
~ Misty Copeland

It is very important to understand accommodations and modifications. While services cost money, accommodations and modifications usually don't, so it is easier to get them. Accommodations and modifications can be provided in an IEP or 504 plan. It is crucial to know that:

• Accommodations change HOW your child is learning.

• Modifications change WHAT your child is learning.

What are accommodations?

Accommodations change the process your child uses to learn. They are physical, environmental or equipment changes that make it easier for your child to do their schoolwork or to be in school. They are generally used for students who are in a general education setting but have a disability that makes it difficult for them to fully access their education. Accommodations are provided on both 504 and IEP plans.

Accommodations do not alter the content of an assignment, but instead compensate for a child's disability so the child is able to do the assignment. Accommodations do not change how an assignment is graded, but it may change how the assignment is presented to the student. For example, a child with dysgraphia may be allowed to provide verbal answers to a test while a teacher's aide writes the answers down. Accommodations are meant to 'level the playing field,' not to create an unfair advantage for the student.

Accommodations should address the specific needs of the child based on the challenges she faces as a result of her disability. There are hundreds of accommodation options. The special education team should carefully select the best options to insure the student is able to access the curriculum.

Some accommodations can be provided on standardized testing. This should be specified in the IEP or 504 Plan. The accommodation cannot change the testing material, but it can specify changes that will make it easier for the student to participate in the testing.

Examples of accommodations include:

- Extra time in tests

- Preferential classroom seating

- Copy of class notes

- Option to have instructions repeated multiple times

- Permission to take movement breaks at regular intervals

- Permission to type instead of hand write an assignment

- Text to speech software for students with visual or writing challenges

- Extended time on homework

It is important for you to research accommodations that help with your child's disability. There are many associations and private websites that have extensive lists of accommodations. You do not have to accept the accommodations the team suggests if you feel you have one that would work better. Bring your ideas to the special education meeting and be open to discussing and brainstorming to find the best options to support your child. You can find links to several accommodation banks by visiting my website at www.specialmomadvocate.com/resources.

What are modifications?

A modification changes the academic expectation for the student. It may lower the academic standard to meet the needs of the child, or it could change the way the student is graded. It can include a reduction in assignments, changes in curriculum, alternate ways of grading, or adaptive materials. Modifications are generally used for students who are significantly behind grade level work, or whose disability impairs her ability to complete grade-level assignments. Modifications should always address a specific concern that has been described in the IEP or 504 plan.

Modifications do change how a student is graded since her grades are based on a difference in curriculum from her peers. This is important to understand because in high school it can affect the credits a student accumulates for graduation. If the student is taking classes that are classified as special education, it may not count towards a diploma, and instead the student may earn a certificate of completion. Also, if the student is expecting to attend a four-year college, some universities will not accept a student without a minimum number of credits in grade-level work. Check with your high school on whether your child's modifications will change her requirements for graduation and beyond.

Examples of modifications include:

- Special education classes for specific subjects, usually math or language arts.
- Reduction in curriculum so the student has less to complete.
- Excusal from exams or other parts of the curriculum.
- Grading on effort rather than academic achievement.
- Using alternative books or curriculum for the subject.

Modifications should be made based on the individual needs of each student. It is not appropriate to assume that modifications should be the same for two students with similar qualifications for special education. Individualized modifications should be discussed and decided on by the special education team to assure the child will meet the goals outlined in her plan.

48

When Not to Sign
at the IEP Meeting

"You must agree to disagree, a trait so rare these days!"
~ Ramana Pemmaraju

Note: This chapter does not apply if your child has a 504 plan. The school is not required to get your signature in order to implement a 504 plan. It is still wise to follow the guidelines about voicing disagreement when you are not comfortable with decisions made in the 504 meeting.

The IDEA does not require a parent signature for implementation of the IEP. However, some states *do* require that a parent sign before the school can move forward. Even if it is not a requirement, schools will encourage you to sign that piece of paper at the end of the IEP. There are three reasons they want this done there and then.

1. The convenience of your being there and knowing for sure it is done.

2. While IDEA does not require signature, you live in a state that does require parent signature before it can be implemented.

3. They know most parents believe once it's signed, it's done. They count on your not knowing that you have a right to ask for a continued IEP to continue discussing services for your child.

Before signing that paper, you really want to think about whether or not you are comfortable with all decisions. Even if implementation does not depend on your signature, you may not want to sign. If you think you may need to show disagreement down the line, you may not want to sign. Make sure you have no questions in your mind. Talk happens quickly in IEP meetings, and they fly through assessments and goals that are hard to understand. Are you certain the services offered are exactly what your child needs? Did they remove services that you think your child still needs? Did you understand everything discussed or do you want more time to review it?

If you have any questions, even just a niggling doubt, then do not sign that paper. You have every right to tell them you want to review it more before signing. As a general rule, I would definitely not sign if any changes are made during the meeting. Let them know that you will sign when you get the final copy.

Not signing may not prevent them from implementing the IEP. In some states your signature is just a formality. Educate yourself ahead of time on the laws in your state. That way you will know if not signing really helps postpone implementation of the IEP.

Review the IEP for completeness.

If you do not sign because you want to review the IEP in more detail, here is a checklist of things to verify:

1. Is your child's personal information correct (name, birthdate, grade, etc.)

2. Is your contact information correct?

3. Review qualification. Do you agree with the category(ies) that your child qualifies under?

4. Review general education versus special education classroom time percentages. Do you agree with what was discussed in the IEP meeting?

5. Review present level of performance (PLOP). Does it provide a fair snapshot of your child's present levels? Does it include information from teachers, therapists and parents?

6. Review parent concerns. Were all your notes included exactly as you wrote them?

7. Review each goal. Do you feel the goals cover the needs of your child? Are all the goals measurable? Does it state how they will be measured? Do you feel there should be more goals?

8. Review modifications and accommodations. Do you feel they are appropriate for your child? Does it include all school situations where your child has difficulty (classroom, standardized testing, lunch/recess, assemblies, field trips, etc.)?

9. Review supports and services offered. Do the services seem appropriate? Is enough time allotted? Does your child need more services?

10. Have your submitted changes been included in the final draft?

11. Review the signature page. Were all members that were required to be present actually at the IEP meeting?

What if you do not want to sign the IEP?

You can return the IEP unsigned and provide a list of reasons you disagree with the document. You can approve implementation of the parts you do agree with, but not approve the parts you do not agree with. Attach a separate document outlining your perspective and which parts you agree to have implemented.

Send the school a letter that lets them knows what parts of the IEP you disagree with, and request another IEP meeting to continue discussing the services and accommodations offered in the IEP. If your signature is a requirement for implementation, your child's previous IEP will continue to be provided until the new IEP has been agreed upon.

Even if you do not sign and have additional meetings, the school can still refuse to add services. If you cannot come to an agreement on what the school is willing to offer, in some states the district representative then has the authority to implement the IEP, but must document their reasons in a Prior Written Notice (PWN). In the PWN the school has to justify their reasons for refusing additional support. If they refuse further IEP meetings, you then have the option to move to mediation or due process as a means of working out the disagreement.

49

Your Right to
Prior Written Notice

"I think sometimes you need a little more explanation
than the characters that you're allowed on Twitter."
~ Tomi Lahren

Prior Written Notice (PWN) is one of the procedural safe guards put in place to protect the rights of all parties, including parents, child and the district. The purpose of the notice is to inform parents that the school would like to take action (or refuses to take action) on evaluation, services or placement for your child. It gives the parents an opportunity to respond before the action takes place. It is also used to provide an explanation when the school refuses a parent's request. Unfortunately schools often neglect to send a PWN, and most parents do not realize they can request it. Done correctly, the PWN also protects the district and shows they have done their due diligence in providing FAPE to the child.

What should they include in the PWN?

- A description of the change in services to be made or a statement that a change requested by a parent will not be implemented.

- An explanation of why they are making this change or refusing this request.

- A description of each evaluation, assessment or report that was used in making this decision. They must use data to back up their decision. They cannot just say they disagree. They have to offer proof that validates their decision.

- A description of other choices that the IEP team reviewed and considered and why they did not choose those options.

- Any other reasons that were considered when making this decision.

- Advocacy resources the parent can contact for help in understanding special education laws and rights.

- Where the parent can obtain a copy of procedural safeguards (parent's rights).

- It must be written in your native language.

When should you request a PWN?

It is against the law for the school to fail to send a PWN, so keep a record of the process it took to obtain it. The notice should be sent in writing. A phone call or conversation is not adequate for a PWN. They should send one automatically, but often do not. There are four instances when you should request a PWN:

- The school has proposed to change the qualification or placement for your child.

- The school proposes a change the services provided in your child's FAPE (free appropriate public education).

- The school refuses your request to change the qualification or placement for your child.

- The school refuses your request to change the services provided in your child's FAPE (free appropriate public education).

Failure to provide you with a PWN is grounds for a compliance complaint with your state department of education. While it is important to maintain a positive relationship with the school, filing a complaint is sometimes necessary to get them to follow proper procedure.

50

Requesting an Independent Educational Evaluation

*"The fact that an opinion has been widely held is
no evidence whatever that it is not utterly absurd."*
~ Bertrand Russell

If you disagree with the findings of the school evaluation, it may be time to request an Independent Educational Evaluation (IEE). The IEE is done by an agency, or individual, that is not employed by the school district. They are an independent set of eyes assessing the child. It does not have to be focused on academic or learning skills, but can include any challenge the student is having in the school setting.

The school is required to review and consider an IEE, but they are not required to follow its recommendations. It can be very beneficial in helping the parent make a case for the student, or in some cases, it may show that the school's evaluation reached the appropriate conclusion.

There are several reasons to request an IEE.

- You feel the results of the school's evaluation were inaccurate or insufficient.

- You feel the evaluation did not accommodate for the child's disability (e.g. they did not use enlarged type for a child with a visual impairment).

- The person administrating the evaluation was not qualified or properly trained to do so.

- The district denied your request for an evaluation.

- The evaluator used inappropriate or outdated assessment tools.

If the parents disagree with the school's assessment, and request an IEE at public expense, the school has two options:

1. The school agrees to pay for the IEE. They can suggest a list of providers that the parent can choose from. The school is not allowed to require parents to use that list. Be sure to research any agency you choose, asking them how often their evaluations have helped gain services for students. Ask them for parent references so you can talk to parents who actually used them. This will ensure the agency is not biased in favor of the school district.

2. The school can file a due process complaint and request a hearing. The purpose of the hearing would be to demonstrate that the evaluations done by the school thus far were appropriate and an IEE is not necessary. If the hearing officer deems the IEE necessary, it will be done at public expense.

If an IEE is requested, the school cannot just ignore it or refuse the request. They must follow one of the above options to be in compliance with the law. First, they can provide an IEE at public expense. If they feel confident their evaluation was sufficient, they can file a due process complaint so they can present their case to an impartial hearing officer.

Requesting an IEE can ruffle feathers with the school, so if you are trying to maintain a positive relationship, you may discuss the option with your team before you request it in writing. It will help them realize how serious you are about advocating for your child.

How to request an IEE.

1. **Send a written request for IEE.** Write a letter to the case manager or school administrator stating that you disagree with the school's

assessments therefore you are requesting an IEE at public expense. Each time an evaluation is done by the school you can request an IEE if you disagree with it. You are not required to explain why you disagree, although the school may try to elicit an explanation as a way to delay the IEE process.

2. **Wait for the school to respond.** Unfortunately neither federal nor state laws have outlined a reasonable timeline for schools to respond to an IEE request. The law simply says the schools must respond without unnecessary delay. Your state may have a specified number of days, so it is good to verify that so you can hold the school to it. 15 days is usually a reasonable time to wait before checking on the approval for the IEE.

3. **Take action on the response.** If the school approves the IEE, then schedule the appointment so you can get the evaluation completed. If the district files for due process, then hire an attorney to help you defend your case. If the school denies the IEE without filing due process, or does not respond to your request, write a letter to the head of special education at the district. Let him know that the district has violated your rights. It would be prudent to consult an advocate or attorney to help you decide whether you will continue to try to get the IEE, get the IEE at your own expense, or file a complaint.

If necessary, file a compliance complaint.

If your district has not approved the IEE without filing for due process, or they have not responded to your request, you may have to resort to filing a compliance complaint. Contact your state department of education to ascertain the process for filing the complaint. Make sure to include all documents, including the initial request, and any follow up attempts you made to get the school to comply.

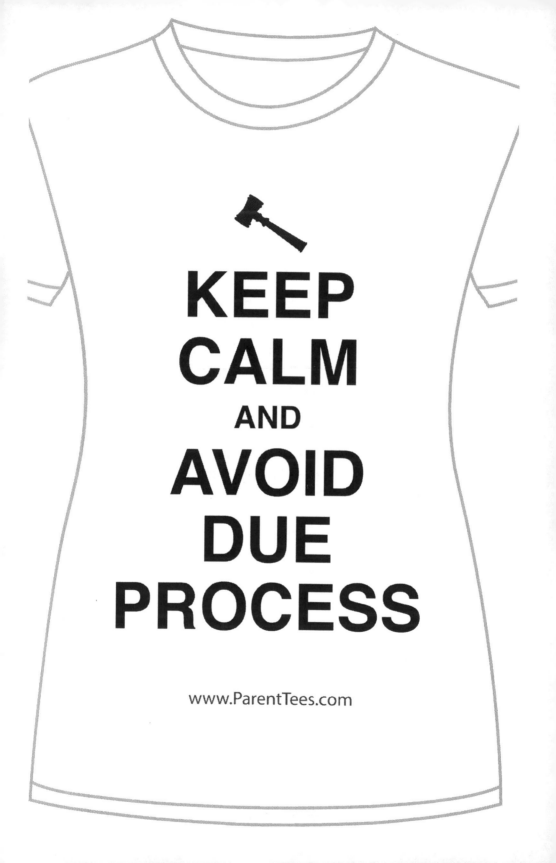

51

Mediation or Due Process

*"There is a higher court than courts of justice and
that is the court of conscience. It supersedes all other courts."*
~ Mahatma Gandhi

Unfortunately sometimes parents and the school may spend a lot of time discussing and negotiating options, but never actually reach a consensus on what the child needs. It is always better to find common ground informally. If that cannot be done, the law does provide alternative paths to resolution. In special education law, these two courses are mediation and due process.

What is mediation?

If you find yourself really struggling to reach a consensus with the school, you can request mediation to help resolve the differences. A mediator is a neutral party who sits with parents and the school and works to help them reach an agreement. If you are trying to establish or modify an IEP for your child, you have the right to request a mediator who is paid for by the state. If you have a dispute over a 504 plan, there is no requirement that the state provide state funded mediation. If you file a complaint with the Office of Civil Rights for non-compliance, they may provide a mediator to assist in resolving the complaint.

Mediation allows the parents and the school to present their information and thoughts on what the child requires, and then the mediator helps the two sides reach an agreement on what should be done. This is not a legal proceeding; it's like having a business negotiator who can help you reach a compromise. You may not end up with everything you had hoped for, but it's a step in the right direction to help your child without the costly expense of a due process hearing. If the mediation process fails, then your next option is to request a due process hearing.

We brought in a 'neutral' mediator in our previous district when our former district refused to give our son the services we felt he required. The state assigned us a mediator. He met with the whole team at the school. Shortly after the meeting began it was very clear that the mediator sided with the school district. He was not thinking about our son at all. He made our job as parents more difficult, and the meeting became even more contentious.

Shortly thereafter we hired a special education lawyer. Only then did we get results. So just be aware that mediation is a less threatening step that you might choose, but keep your eyes open. It's not always the neutral process it is portrayed to be.

Moving to Due Process

Sometimes no matter how hard you push, the school will not budge. Then it may be time to utilize your right to due process. This is not a lawsuit, but a hearing process that allows both sides to present their case for and against providing services. An independent hearing officer (IHO) oversees the process and will decide if the child is eligible for services and which services should be received. Due process begins when the parent (or school) files a due process complaint. Once the complaint is filed, a due process hearing is held.

The hearing is run like a court proceeding, with rules for submitting evidence, providing testimony and questioning of witnesses. The final decision is based on facts of law, not emotional pleas. The process is laid out in a 45-day timeline, but it usually lasts longer because of the need for additional assessments or scheduling of all parties. If the IHO decides in your favor, the school may be required to cover some of your legal costs. If they decided in the school's favor, you would be responsible for all your legal fees. The school has to cover all their own costs no matter what the decision is.

Moving to due process is a serious choice and I would recommend you consult with a special education attorney who has experience with these hearings in your school district. You do not have to try mediation before going to due process, but it is often best to give mediation a chance and let due process be your last resort.

Summing Up and
How to Reach Me

"If you get, give. If you learn, teach."
~ Maya Angelou

So how do you get the school to help?

This is the $20 billion dollar question, and there is no straightforward answer. The truth is, how you get them to help is very dependent on the school district you are in.

Your best option is to find out all you can about how your district handles special education. You need to try and connect with parents, talk to staff and be an investigator in compiling a special education profile of the district. Alternatively, you can hire an advocate familiar with the district, so they have a good chance of helping you wind your way through the bureaucracy. While it will be a challenge, there are some really key elements that you can pay attention to in order to optimize your chance of getting your child the support needed in school.

Impossible is not a word I use. I find a way, even if the way is slow. Start seeing what you CAN do and find ways to work through the things you can't do. Find ways to help your child outside of school while you go through the process of getting help within the school. This is a big journey you are taking, and just by reading this book you are showing your tremendous love and willingness to do what it takes to see your child through this.

I'll never forget the first IEP we had in our current district. Friends whose kids were in special ed in the district assured me that the team would be awesome, but I was so nervous after our experience in our former district. Boy was I completely agog as I watched the team around the table brainstorming on how best to help our son. Right on the spot they were adding services and accommodations and proactively creating a plan to give him full support.

I started crying right there because I never imagined an IEP could be like this. I never dreamed school personnel would care as much about my son as I did. This is the experience I hope you can have so you can focus on loving and nurturing your child rather than fighting the schools.

How to Reach Me

If you feel overwhelmed by the process, or just want a friendly ear, feel free to call me. I do offer a free 30-minute consultation, and in that time I can let you know how I can help you.

To connect:

email: hello@specialmomadvocate.com

website: www.SpecialMomAdvocate.com

Acknowledgments

I want to start by thanking my husband, Steve, who for all these years has put up with my investigative pursuits that led to the truth. Steve, you amaze me with your ability to trust my intuition even when it seemed I was walking into a fog. I know sometimes my ideas cost us a lot (in money and time), but when things began improving, you trusted me to lead the way. You are amazing in wholeheartedly supporting the therapies, biomed and listening to me talk about it all! These kids are so lucky you are their dad, and I am so lucky you are my partner in crime – I mean life. Love you!

I want to thank my older son who has been a trooper on this crazy journey, always willing to try one more thing. Eventually you became your own caretaker as you are vigilant about making sure you do everything to take care of your body and mind. I am so proud of all the work you have done and all the progress you have made. I feel blessed to be your mom!

And of course heaps of gratitude to my younger son whose joyful spirit and enduring optimism have carried me through some challenging days. You are a treasure who lights up our home, and you too have been awesome about therapies and biomed to make sure your body is working optimally. I am doubly blessed to be your mom too!

And so much gratitude to my mother whose patience and persistence helped me get this book edited and into excellent shape. Thank you for all the time, advice and coaching when it was so hard for me to endure. I love you more than I can say, and I am so grateful you are my mom. Some of my best character traits come from you, and I know I could not have recovered my boy without all you taught me about persistence, resilience and the pursuit of solutions. You are the ultimate problem solver, and that was the knowledge I needed to find results for my kids. Thank you, mom!

And so much gratitude to my dad who taught me to be curious, to never stop learning and to pursue subjects deeply so I gained depth of understanding. Your way of seeing the world shaped my way of exploring it, and I know it made me a great researcher and gatherer of facts. You taught me what I needed to find the truth so I could find solutions. I love you so much dad, and I am so grateful to be your daughter.

To my friend Vickie Bockenkamp (www.toolsforlearning.com), the best accountability partner and friend for a huge project like this. Thank you for sticking with me and listening to me go on and on about this project. I so appreciate your feedback and helping me hone in on some of the more important pieces to highlight. You and I need to try doing one of these together!

I have so much gratitude for Nadia, David Garcia, Dr. Barbara Blume, Sonia Story, and Linda Garcia for helping me believe my son was brilliant and had the potential to overcome his challenges. It takes a lot of courage to have hope for what seems like the impossible, but all of your encouragement and therapies made it a reality. You were the angels that kept me moving forward. When times were tough, I would hear your words, and they renewed my hope. Words can hardly express how grateful I am for that!

I want to say thank you to all the Special Ed Moms who shared their stories and struggles with me. We know how hard this journey is, and my hope is that I can bring some measure of comfort and wisdom to make your journey easier. You inspired me to write this book because I know more of us are coming, and we need the strength to trudge on through. I am proud to be a part of this tribe.

With many blessings and lots of light,
In gratitude,
Bonnie

About the Author

Bonnie has spent the better part of 25 years as a graphic designer and artist. Always a lover of psychology and the forces that influence behavior, it was a natural transition for her to begin working to resolve her oldest son's challenges. When he was six, a neuropsychologist said he was beyond help, and to plan for his group home care as an adult. Bonnie could not accept that nothing could be done, and she set on a path to find solutions to help her son. He is now an honor student and destined to live a typical life.

Having been through the special ed system as a mom, and now as a counselor, she saw the need for support for the parents who carry this challenging burden. She has helped parents who struggle with districts who refused services, and she has coached parents in finding ways help their child succeed against the odds. Bonnie knows the fear a mother feels when her child's future is uncertain, and that is why she chose to shift her life focus into educational consulting. She has a thriving practice as an educational consultant and advocate for parents who find themselves struggling with the special education journey.

She is the author of Special Ed Mom Survival Guide: How to prevail in the special ed process while discovering life-long strategies for both you and your child. She is also the creator of Grounded for Life: 52 Exercises for Daily Grounding, and co-author of Same Journey, Different Paths: Stories of Auditory Processing Disorder. She has a masters in educational counseling and another in spiritual psychology. Her bachelors degree is in architecture. She lives in Ventura County, California with her husband, two boys and their two furry felines.

Find out more:
www.SpecialMomAdvocate.com
www.LandauDigital.com

References

Alessi, G. (1988). *Diagnosis diagnosed: A systemic reaction.* Professional School Psychology, 3(2), 145-151. http://dx.doi.org/10.1037/h0090554

Bender, M. L. (1976) *The Bender–Purdue Reflex Test.* San Rafael, CA, Academic Therapy Publication.

Borges, L.R., Paschoa, J.R., & Colella-Santos, M.F. *(Central) Auditory Processing: the impact of otitis media.* Clinics. 2013; 68(7):954–959.

Curtin, S.C., Warner, M., & Hedegaard, H. *Increase in suicide in the United States, 1999–2014.* NCHS data brief, no 241. Hyattsville, MD: National Center for Health Statistics. 2016.

McCann, C. *IDEA Funding.* http://www.edcentral.org/edcyclopedia/individuals-with-disabilities-education-act-funding-distribution.

National Education Association. *Rankings & Estimates: Ranking of the States 2015 and Estimate of School Statistics 2016.* 2016.

National Scientific Council on the Developing Child. (2015). *Supportive Relationships and Active Skill-Building Strengthen the Foundations of Resilience:* Working Paper 13. http://www.developingchild.harvard.edu Los Angeles USD 2016 Annual Report (https://achieve.lausd.net/cms/lib/CA01000043/Centricity/Domain/317/iSTAR%20Annual%20Report_15.16_FINAL_20160830.pdf)

Nguyen, V., Villarreal, M., Paredes, D. & Nious, K. *Schools Delay or Deny Services for Vulnerable Students.* www.nbcbayarea.com/news/local/Public-Schools-Delay-Deny-Special-Education-Services-231960511.html. 2013.

74762085R00214

Made in the USA
San Bernardino, CA
20 April 2018